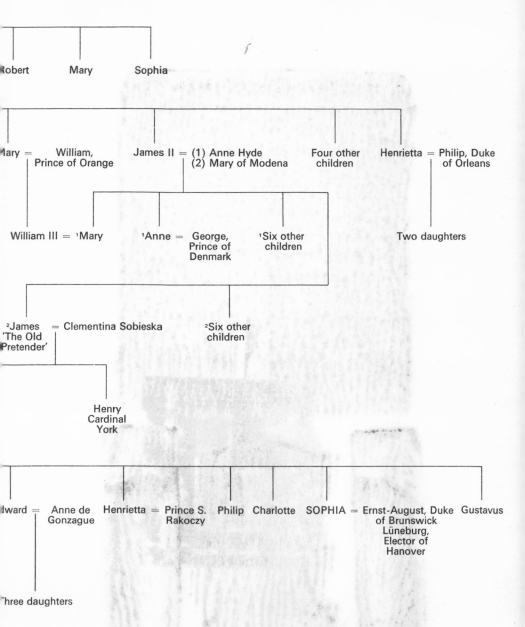

Robert Mary Sophia

Mary = William, James II = (1) Anne Hyde Four other Henrietta = Philip, Duke
  Prince of Orange   (2) Mary of Modena children   of Orleans

William III = [1]Mary [1]Anne = George, [1]Six other Two daughters
      Prince of children
      Denmark

[2]James = Clementina Sobieska [2]Six other
'The Old   children
Pretender'

Henry
Cardinal
York

dward = Anne de Henrietta = Prince S. Philip Charlotte SOPHIA = Ernst-August, Duke Gustavus
  Gonzague   Rakoczy   of Brunswick
                         Lüneburg,
                         Elector of
                         Hanover

Three daughters

PRIVILEGED PERSONS

HESTER W. CHAPMAN

PRIVILEGED PERSONS

FOUR SEVENTEENTH-CENTURY STUDIES

REYNAL & COMPANY
in association with
WILLIAM MORROW & COMPANY
New York

FIRST PUBLISHED 1966

© 1966 BY HESTER W. CHAPMAN

LIBRARY OF CONGRESS CATALOG CARD NUMBER 66–24558

PRINTED IN GREAT BRITAIN

CONTENTS

ILLUSTRATIONS

ACKNOWLEDGMENTS

I have great pleasure in recording my gratitude to Their Royal Highnesses Prince and Princess Ernst-August of Hanover, who enabled me to solve the mystery of Königsmarck's murder, while throwing a new light on the Electress Sophia's relationship with her daughter-in-law, the uncrowned Queen of George I. Their hospitality and interest made this part of my research a memorable adventure. I am equally indebted to the Marquess of Ailesbury for his generosity in allowing me to use his *Life and Loyalties of Thomas Bruce* (see p. 312 under Cardigan, Earl of). This definitive and accomplished biography is an indispensable guide to the maze of the original Memoirs, of which the manuscript is in his possession, together with a number of Ailesbury's letters.

Special thanks are due to Miss Rosamond Lehmann for her intuitive and meticulous criticism, as also to Mrs Cyril Jenkins for sound advice and much enjoyable discussion. I am very grateful to Mr Timothy Cape for his aid in translation of German sources, to Mrs Fabienne Hilliard for her suggestions as to the meaning of certain passages in Héroard's *Journal* and to Mr George Rylands for reading my proofs. I wish to thank the Curator of the National Portrait Gallery for his help over the illustrations, and Messrs Frisby of Dorchester for their excellent photograph of the Mazarin portrait at Mapperton House.

I acknowledge with thanks the gracious permission of Her Majesty Queen Elizabeth II for the reproduction of Louis XIII's portrait in maturity, and am obliged to the Marquess of Ailesbury for leave to present that of his ancestor. The portrait of the Electress Sophia as a girl has been reproduced through the kindness of the Earl of Craven; that of her in old age is the property of Lady Lenanton (Miss Carola Oman), and that of Hortense Mazarin belongs to the Honourable Victor Montagu, to all of whom I am deeply indebted. The pictures of Louis XIII when young appears by kind permission of Mrs T. A. Tritton, of Parham Park.

FOREWORD

THE lives of these four personages—a French king, a German princess, an Italian duchess and an English nobleman — cover a hundred and forty years of European history. In their own day, all such people had power and fame; but the parts of these particular individuals in the dramatic pageant of the seventeenth and early eighteenth centuries were minor and their influence was slight. Yet their names are to be found in the indices of innumerable histories and biographies; and every now and then their lives are rewritten, in spite of the fact that they are thought of as background figures.

This anomalous treatment has partially veiled both their characters and their careers. A re-assessment might be brought about by placing them, as if they were the dramatis personae of a morality play, under symbolic headings. Thus Louis XIII represents tragedy; the Electress Sophia, success—against considerable odds; Hortense Mancini, adventure bordering on farce; and Thomas Ailesbury, chivalry and honour. These rather arbitrary labels are inadequate, but in perspective they may prove helpful, in that their function is more that of sign-posting than of pigeonholing.

These men and women do not, at first glance, resemble one another. Indeed, their temperaments so vary that the only gift they share—that of vivid self-expression—is not apparent until the results begin to light up their vicissitudes and adventures. All were what we now call privileged persons; all presumed that they would receive not only consideration and respect, but also homage, from their less highly placed associates. It is the purpose of this book to attempt the re-creation of such tributes in a succinct and pleasurable manner.

To
NOEL WILLMAN

LOUIS XIII

(SEPTEMBER 1606 – MAY 1643)

He hath a tear for pity and a hand
Open as day for melting charity;
Yet, notwithstanding, being incens'd, he's flint;
As humorous as winter, and as sudden
As flaws congealed in the spring of day.

HENRY IV, PART II

ONE

I

ON August 2nd, 1589, Henry III, the last of the Valois kings, was stabbed by a fanatic monk and lay dying in the palace of the Louvre. He was childless: his younger brother, Francis of Anjou, had predeceased him; he therefore named his Protestant cousin and brother-in-law, Henry of Navarre, as his successor.

When the Béarnais monarch entered into his inheritance he was thirty-six. Marguerite de Valois, to whom he had been married for seventeen years, had borne him no children. Within a few months of his accession he divorced her; in 1593 he became a Catholic; and in February 1600 he married Marie de Medici, daughter of the Grand Duke of Tuscany and Joan of Austria. On September 27th, 1601, their son Louis—the first Dauphin of France for fifty-eight years—was born at the palace of Fontainebleau.

The birth of this child crowned the extraordinary, the almost miraculously triumphant progress of his father, who within twelve years of his coronation had restored prosperity, some degree of internal order and her former European status to the impoverished, chaotic and rebellious kingdom of his predecessor. Henry IV's administrative gifts, his tireless energy and his protean abilities amounted to genius. With his grandson Louis XIV and their fifteenth-century forbear Louis XI, he has been given pride of place over all the kings of France; and indeed they make a formidable trio. But although Henry's fame is lit up by a personal appeal which the other two never possessed, his pre-eminence rested on a shifting mass of contradictions. His character was even odder and more startling than his career.

That kaleidoscopic mingling of cruelty and kindness, of brutal indifference and imaginative sensibility, of wild spirits and embittered gloom, bewildered while it fascinated those he mocked, bullied, manœuvred, flattered and indulged. He was alluring and repellent, crude and subtle, fastidious and gross; his moods were

15

incalculable, varying with a speed which defeated enemies and allies: so that those nearest him were in thrall to a perpetual uncertainty, moving in a turmoil of conflict and surprise—and none more strenuously than his second wife, who would have been pitiable if she had shown one redeeming quality, one spark of intuition or common sense.

Marie de Medici was a lonely, neglected, inward-looking young woman of twenty-seven when she left the Pitti for the Louvre. Some weeks before she reached Paris her marriage with Henry had been consummated. She may not have known that his people called him the *Vert Galant*, that his mistresses and their bastards had long been installed in his palaces, and that his first wife continued to frequent and entertain him. It then dawned on the stout, slow-witted Florentine princess that she could not hope to outshine such enchantresses as the ex-Queen Margot, Henriette d'Entragues and Jacqueline de Bueil. But she could and did make scenes about them, scenes which her bridegroom so resisted that screams, curses, slaps and the thud of colliding bodies resounded through the private apartments to ante-rooms and presence chambers until jealousy and resentment had worn themselves away. Then the resplendent pair would emerge to receive homage and distribute favours. In that last long twilight of the Renaissance the shrew and the lecher, the scold and the warrior became symbols of France's glory, in a setting which combined splendour, squalor, luxury, elegance, great art and atrocious taste.

For in these vast and magnificent pleasure-domes the genius of Rubens, Claude, de Champaigne, Le Sueur and Le Nain combated but did not always conquer heavy walnut furniture, intricate tapestries, over-decorated ceilings and a subsidiary conglomeration of armour, marble, ivory, gilding and porcelain. Everything, everywhere, was carved, painted, twisted, bulging, gleaming. Yet it seems that this robust and vivacious King and Queen dominated their surroundings. His stocky, muscular figure, long head, thick red lips and pepper-and-salt beard contrasted, not unpleasantly, with her changeless solidity and high-coloured curves. Both faces had the healthy glow of well-fed animals; and his jocund alertness was set off by her bovine self-assurance.

There was every hope that such a couple would produce a brood of strong and lively children. When Marie de Medici's labour began, at eleven o'clock on the evening of September 26th, the King, who had talked of 'my son the Dauphin' throughout her pregnancy, lost all his optimism. He drove the midwife into a frenzy of impatience by repeated inquiries of 'How soon will it be born? Will it be a boy?' until she curtly told him that she would see to his wishes, if he let her alone to care for the Queen. Twenty-four hours later the heir was produced in the presence of four doctors, a number of other officials and three princes of the blood, all of whom stood facing the delivery chair at the moment of birth.

For some time Henry refused to believe in his good fortune. He kept on saying that the child must be a daughter, and would not answer the Queen's inquiries. When at last he received ocular proof of its sex, he burst into tears and rushed to tell his wife, who swooned away. But the baby's struggle to emerge had enfeebled it to the point of death. The midwife sent for wine, took a spoonful and conveyed the contents from her own mouth into his; he at once recovered. Ignoring her protests, Henry snatched him from her and called for the doors to be opened. As some two hundred courtiers surged into the bedchamber he held out his son, exclaiming, 'This child belongs to you all,' while the tears poured down his face. He then publicly handed over the Dauphin to the two persons who were to mould his character and watch over every moment of his formative years: Madame de Montglat and Dr Jean Héroard.

Madame de Montglat was a gaunt, harsh-featured, middle-aged lady, whose husband was Master of the Household to the King. She gave herself up entirely to her charge, spending her whole day with him and his wet-nurses; he slept in her room throughout his babyhood. Her devotion was unselfish and her methods were disciplinary. While Héroard, trying not to be over-indulgent, was nevertheless inclined to spoil the Dauphin, he unconsciously combined with the Lady Governess in evolving a nursery routine which would have killed most children. His journals of Louis's progress are unique in European history.

Héroard was fifty when Henry IV installed him as his son's physician. Before attending Henry III he had studied veterinary surgery; his *Hippistologie*, a book on the structure of the horse, made him famous. Within half an hour of the Dauphin's birth Héroard had written a long description of his physique. Thereafter, for twenty-seven years, he recorded every detail of Louis's days and nights, no matter how trivial or intimate. Each mouthful of food, each drop of drink, all his functions and most of his talk—even the inarticulate gurglings and yells of infancy—were meticulously set down. This vast memorial to an unparalleled and adoring conscientiousness runs into several million words. One aspect can be summed up by the list of medicaments prescribed in a single year, when Louis was taking the waters at Les Forges. During those months he had been bled forty-seven times and had taken two hundred and twelve purges and two hundred and fifteen clysters. That he remained active and vigorous, though often unwell, till he died of tuberculosis at the age of forty-two, shows a phenomenal resistance.

Surgical treatment began when he was two days old. As he seemed to have difficulty in taking his food, a membrane beneath his tongue was cut—three times—by the King's surgeon. He then so gorged himself that a second wet-nurse was called in and the milk of both women was reinforced by broth, which he swallowed as greedily. He was now constantly on view and visited by a number of highly placed personages. When he was a month old his public life began with a state entry into Paris, where he received the city fathers; he then held two more receptions, one at the Tuileries and one at the Louvre. On the same day he was established with his household at the old palace of St-Germain-en-Laye, the reconstruction of which is still to be seen.

Here he remained until his fourth year, a healthy, good-tempered and fittingly precocious child. He was eighteen months old when Héroard told him, 'You must always be good and just, Monseigneur. God put you into the world to be a good king, and if you become so, He will love you.' Louis smiled and seemed to understand; at the same age, when his wet-nurse inquired, 'Well, Sir, when I am old and must walk with a stick, will you cease to love me?' he replied 'No'—'quite seriously', according to the doctor.

He appeared to respond in the same manner to the advances of all his visitors, of whatever degree. Foreign envoys, market-women, huntsmen, sentries and ministers had almost as frequent access to him as did his parents, whose contrasting approach emphasized their discordant relationship. The Queen never fondled or kissed him, never even picked him up; his father would play with him by the hour, give him sips of wine, share his broth, let him tug at his great beard and carry him out to see the torch-lit ceremonial of the *curée* in the palace courtyard. He was not a year old when he was shown to the people, many of whom had come from the provinces to see him; as he appeared at a window in the arms of Madame de Montglat, all knelt and a number were in tears.

So one of his earliest recollections was that of being hailed as a divinity, the future father of his subjects, a soldier and a leader. This impression was enhanced, before he could walk, by gifts of a miniature suit of armour, a sword, muskets, cannon and a bow and arrows; by the time he was four he had learnt how to use, clean and repair these possessions, which he preferred to all his other toys.

The glories surrounding him contrasted, bewilderingly, with the coarsest and most unsavoury aspects of human existence. His father's habits were such that he stank abominably — at their first meeting Marie de Medici had shuddered away from his embrace — and both parents would send for him while enthroned on their close-stools. Their courtiers' bawdry sometimes became a game in which Louis played the principal part, a favourite gambit being his marriage with a Spanish princess. Asked 'Who is Papa's darling?' he would tap his stomach. 'And who is the Infanta's?' Héroard then pursued, upon which the child would point to his penis. That his future bride was not yet weaned gave this dialogue an added piquancy.

The resultant awareness was sharpened by the presence of his bastard brothers and sisters — 'the St-Germain herd' — whom he learned to tease and relegate. Henry, Catherine, Louise, Gabrielle, Alexander and Caesar might be stronger and bigger than himself: but they were, he said, only 'pretending' princes, 'made of filth', privileged to hand him his shirt and forced to submit to his jealous slaps and pushes. And yet, they were rivals and enemies; for his father loved their mothers as he did not love the Queen; why was she always discontented and aloof? Very soon Louis realized that the father he adored was, somehow, at fault; so his confusion turned to furious animosity when Madame de Montglat, his dear 'Mamanga', or the King himself whipped him for disobedience and caprice. He was three when Henry, producing the birch-rod, asked 'Who is that for?' 'For you,' Louis angrily replied. 'We shall see,' remarked the King, and beat him for three-quarters of an hour, pausing every now and then to moralize and explain, while Héroard stood by, watch in hand. Mamanga's methods were more direct. 'Come, Sir, lift up that arse!' was the prelude to the punishment which in no way affected his loyalty to her or to his father. Already he could feel and value their devotion, although his helplessness under their hands so enraged him that he would scream, 'I will kill you—kill the whole world! I'll kill God!' and then run away to sulk and brood: but never for long. 'You do not beat him enough,' was the King's only criticism of the Lady Governess. 'I profited by constant beating, and he must do likewise.'

Louis's calm was best restored by his visits to Héroard's study: those piles of books and papers fascinated him; but when he was shown the volume dedicated to his most intimate functions, he turned away in disgust, only returning as the doctor added, 'It also contains the history of all your weapons.' Then, guiding his hand, Héroard would help him to write to his parents; his first letter, composed at the age of two, ran, 'Papa, God give you and Mamma good day, I would see you to make you laugh. Goodbye, good day, I am, Papa, your very humble and obedient son and servant. Dauphin.'

I I

Apart from the reverential treatment due to his position, Louis's upbringing followed the pattern of the time; that combination of barbarity and culture, of high accomplishment, brutal discipline and crude horseplay helped to form the background of all upper-class children. His inability, or rather refusal, to follow some of the accepted standards sprang from a sensitivity which seems to have been innate; certainly it was not inherited. From the moment he began to take in what was going on round him—according to Héroard, before he was two—he shrank from obscenity and loose behaviour. (As soon as he grasped the implications of the Infanta dialogue, he refused to repeat it.) In this respect he was cut off from, and misunderstood by, those nearest him. The love and care of his father, Madame de Montglat and Héroard did not greatly affect this isolation. He was not an unhappy child: but he was morally lonely, and thus too often at odds with his contemporaries to achieve serenity or contentment.

So he grew up restless, what is now called highly strung, and in constant need of violent and strenuous diversion. Fortunately, this was satisfied by all forms of sport and, later, active service in the field; by the time he was nineteen he had become a skilled professional soldier.

Meanwhile, his affectionate and rather clinging temperament was strengthened by high spirits, a natural wit and, less agreeably, an increasing belligerence about his own status. He knew that, after his father, he was the most important person in the kingdom; and here arose another discrepancy, a further puzzle. The hierarchy in which he had second place was disrupted by a number of persons thrusting themselves into positions to which they had no claim, not even the left-handed claim of his half-brothers and sisters. Among the most formidable were his mother's protégés, the Concini. Louis's private war with this couple—and thus with the Queen—lasted for fourteen years.

When Marie de Medici left Italy she brought with her a suite of several hundred persons; among these were her dwarf foster-sister, Leonora Galigäi, and a handsome, flashy, quick-witted adventurer, Concino Concini. Both were bent on making their fortunes, and Concini's first step was to ally himself with the only person for whom the Queen had any affection. From their earliest years together Marie had been dominated by Leonora; when Concini asked for her hand, jealousy halted the Queen's consent. Between them, this unpleasant pair managed to overcome her objections, and soon after her arrival in Paris they were married, enriched and established in greater splendour than any of the French nobility. Their influence over their mistress was paramount, and they were hated accordingly; but from the point of view of Henry IV they were useful, because they stood between him and Marie's tedious outbursts over his infidelities, When he deserted her for some new beauty she would fling herself, sobbing, into Leonora's arms, while Concini administered soothing flatteries and vows of deathless loyalty.

A number of the more far-sighted courtiers, envisaging the King's death before his son's majority, made a pro-Concini group. This party so increased during Louis's infancy that both Leonora and her husband had free access to his nursery. It did not take him very long to perceive their machinations; and he became increasingly resentful of their power over his mother. He was

playing with a toy chariot in which he had placed several miniature royalties when Concini came upon him and said jovially,
'Where is my place, Monseigneur?' 'There!' Louis replied,
indicating the footboard, and the smiling Italian withdrew,
unabashed.

Having tried, unsuccessfully, to relegate the bastards and the
Concini, Louis found himself at odds with his father's mistresses
and, more daunting still, with Queen Marguerite, once the most
beautiful and brilliant woman in France, a poetess, a musician
and a patron of the arts, whose memoirs are now better remembered than her many lovers. That this plump, gay, middle-aged
siren should be on friendly terms with his father was horribly
bewildering—how could she be a Queen while his mother lived?
Louis was naturally pious; and he knew that only heretics (his
father had been one, but that was long ago) divorced their wives
in order to marry again. The euphemism of annulment was beyond
his grasp; so he rejected the blandishments of Queen Margot as
sternly as he did those of the Concini; in this he was assiduously
encouraged by Madame de Montglat, Héroard and those of his
attendants who were busy thrusting their irons into the flickering
blaze of palace intrigue. But the alluring lady persisted, Louis
succumbed and they were friends. She became 'little Mamma',
and he looked on her as an ally, the more especially because, after
the births of his sisters Élisabeth and Christine, his own mother
treated him more coldly than ever. She often hit him, whether he
had been naughty or not; no doubt she resented his companionship with his father.

For the power so carelessly exercised by Henry IV sprang from
his ability to adapt himself to any company; he was as much at
ease with artists, merchants and soldiers as with his courtiers or his
Condé relatives. He had no use for protocol and ceremony,
detested dressing up—he generally wore a torn shirt and grubby
cloth hose—and rather mingled with than appeared to his subjects, who repeated and handed down his tropes till they became
part of his legend. (The authenticity of his remarks about Paris
and a Mass, and every peasant's chicken stew, is doubtful.)

Naturally Louis copied his father, although he did not, in these
early years, reproduce his aesthetic tastes. What he most enjoyed
was to watch, his hands clasped behind him, while the King
inspected the additions to his palaces. Henry would swing him up

while he himself sat astride a parapet, interchanging jokes and technical information with the workmen, turning every now and then to snatch off the child's hat or pretending to let him fall. In the same way he sometimes received foreign envoys and high officials while Louis stood between his knees, and although he would interrupt these conferences to play with him, his son seems to have taken in enough to grasp the nature, if not the range, of his inheritance.

By the time he was five Louis had shed most of his babyish ways, his tastes were formed and his attitude towards kingship was responsible and serious. Already he perceived that playing at soldiers was a waste of time; he must learn to become one: so he attempted drill, the words of command and the oath of allegiance. His passion for all kinds of music turned to marching songs and the composition of little rhymes, to which he danced; then these delights paled before the prospect of his first hunting expedition. Which of his dogs should he take—Cavalon, Pataut, Barbichet or Grisette? 'Take mine—take Amadis,' urged the three-year-old Madame Élisabeth. Louis shook his head. 'She might be kicked,' he replied. In accordance with etiquette, Henry IV sent him the stag's hoof, some hours after their return. Louis knew the correct answer; he cut off the claw of a toy partridge, and told the envoy to take it to Papa.

So his manners improved and his rages became less frequent. When the King began to tease him about his marriage—'I wish you to give the Infanta a baby'—he replied, 'No, Papa.' 'A little Dauphin, like yourself,' Henry pursued. Louis took off his hat, bowed and repeated, 'No, so please you.' He knew what must take place for children to be made, Héroard had seen to that: and the picture did not attract him. 'I run away from love,' he told the doctor. 'Sir! From the Infanta?' Louis hesitated. 'No—' he began, then added, 'Yes, I do, I do!' These interchanges, so amusing for the grown-ups, were to have European repercussions.

With the prolonged and gorgeous ceremony of his public baptism on his sixth birthday, the clouds began to gather. His father's departure to put down a rebellion in Sedan made him very anxious. Silently he saw him off, trying to keep back his tears. When the King said, 'What, my son? You say nothing—shall you not kiss me farewell?' the sobs would come, and the Court watched while father and son wept together. 'What did His

Majesty say to you, Sir?' asked Héroard as Louis, his head bent, walked past him to his bedroom — and received a muttered answer. As soon as he was alone he cried bitterly; he could not forget the attempt to murder Henry in the previous year, on the bridge which still bears his statue. Some hours later he woke up crying, 'Papa, Papa — don't leave me!' Next day he told his nurse that in his dream two great wolves had attacked himself and the King — 'and I drew my sword and killed them both.'

He now had to face the end of his sheltered days, with the substitution of that stern, elderly statesman and Marshal of France, the Marquis de Souvré, for Madame de Montglat and her posse of nurses. 'You will cry when I leave,' she told him. 'We'll not speak of it,' said Louis. Some days later he crept into her bed, murmuring, 'It smells so good — of violet powder. I wish I might always sleep with you.' Presently, as she was combing his hair, he pointed out that he had dressed himself, 'to save you that trouble.' He returned to his own rooms to find that the new regime had begun with the departure of 'Doundoun', his favourite nursemaid. It was very hard: and rather frightening. At dinner, when Héroard forbade him red wine, he broke out furiously, 'You are a snow-man' — pointing to the doctor's grey locks — 'you're ugly!' Seizing a knife, he made a rush at his old friend. 'Very well, Sir,' said Héroard, 'I will go away for always' — and departed to his study. Louis endured this deprivation for some hours; then there were tears, apologies and promises to be good.

In 1609 Monsieur de Souvré took over; but he failed to eliminate his predecessor. He and Madame de Montglat had forgotten Louis, who was playing on the floor, when she burst out, 'The Dauphin still belongs to me, the King gave him to me at birth.' 'He was yours for a time, now he is mine,' replied the Marshal. As they glared at one another they heard Louis say, 'One day, I hope that I shall belong to myself.' That day, the most tragic of his life, was a year away — a long time by a child's reckoning.

The birth of Gaston (later Duc d'Orléans and father of La Grande Mademoiselle) in 1608 was followed a year afterwards by that of the Queen's last child, Henrietta Maria, who was to become the wife of Charles I. Two more bastards appeared almost simultaneously, and were at once rejected by Louis. 'They did not come from Mamma's stomach,' he said. He was delighted by Gaston's arrival, and made a pet of his youngest sister from the moment of her birth. 'Laugh, then, baby, laugh,' he exclaimed, bending over the cradle. 'See how she holds on to my hand!'

At about this time the stammer he had suffered from since his fifth year became worse; naturally no one connected this disability with the operation on his tongue or with the increasing pressure of his education and his public appearances. He now received envoys and attended Council meetings in the intervals of studying with his principal tutor, the Sieur des Yvesteaux, a fashionable minor poet, celebrated for his roistering ways. This dried-up little man, who had an inflated reputation as a wit, was a dull teacher, and Louis made no attempt to conceal his boredom during lesson hours; yet he was making progress in Latin, theology, mathematics, Italian and Spanish. He much preferred his shooting instructor, and took a great fancy to Monsieur de Paistry, who taught him to swim; his favourite tutor was the Court painter, with whom he exchanged sketches of birds, flowers and men-at-arms.

Then a highly controversial public event disrupted his routine. The Queen was to be crowned, an honour given to none of her predecessors. She had forced her husband's hand, and bullied him into a concession he felt to be dangerous. It was almost certain that she would outlive him, and this badge of power would ensure her carrying out the policy he had rejected. For Henry's greatest ambition was to curb the power of the Habsburg empires. So he made allies of the German Protestant states, the Dutch and the English, while continuing outwardly to approve the marriages of Louis and the Infanta and of Madame Élisabeth with the Prince of the Asturias. But although Henry was beloved by his subjects—his reforms had brought them peace for ten years and increasing prosperity for nearly twice that time—the religious of both sects could not forget that he had escaped the massacre of Saint Bartholomew by a feigned conversion to Catholicism and then, reverting to the reformed faith, abandoned it for ever on his accession. The Queen, a staunch ally of Spain and herself a Habsburg on her mother's side, shared this mistrust and, through the Concini, was working against her husband's policy. She was determined on the Spanish marriages, and also on an anti-Protestant campaign. Her regency, however short—for Louis was now in his ninth year—would seal this bargain; but her status must be established by her coronation.

It seems that Henry yielded to her because he was ageing and tired; and he may have thought that in the event of his death her policy would be influenced by Sully, a firm Protestant, who was working against the Concini. Also, he himself was in good health, and might well survive till Louis's thirteenth birthday. The real danger, as he knew (for he had received many warnings), lay in the possibility of his being murdered. He had faced death in battle and from the hand of more than one religious fanatic too often to fear it; what alarmed him was the thought of leaving the kingdom to be ruled by an indolent, stupid and bigoted woman. Therefore the powers to which she was bound must be assailed.

In 1609 he so far abandoned his principles as to prepare for war against Austria. As the victor of Cahors, Coutras, Ivry and Arques, he had his people behind him; and his armies were in good shape; so he decided to risk his wife's coronation.

This took place on May 13th, 1610. The morning of the ceremony found the King in black depression. He was now living with Sully in that minister's great new palace of the Arsenal. 'This cursed crowning will be my death!' he exclaimed. Tapping his spectacle-case on the table, he fell into a silence which Sully broke by saying, 'If I were you, Sire, I would not hesitate to postpone it. Shall I give the order, and send to Notre Dame?' 'I would have it so indeed,' replied Henry. 'But what would my wife say? She is set upon this coronation.' So nothing was done, and by the time the triumphant Queen re-entered the great courtyard of the Louvre Henry had sufficiently recovered his usual spirits to splash her with water from the window where he and the Dauphin were standing. He then drew the child forward, announcing, 'Gentlemen, here is your King!'

In fact, Henry's toleration of the Huguenots and his moves against the Austro-Spanish despots had so antagonized a small group of his Catholic subjects, that they were only waiting for the Queen's coronation to strike him down. Yet no general rising was planned, or even considered; the forebodings and visions recounted after his death either failed to reach him or were ignored. While he and Sully were working out their campaign he had broken off to say that he would never be able to leave Paris. 'They will kill me first,' he added. Then his mood changed and he continued his preparations.

There was no change, either in the mood or the plans, of Jean-

François Ravaillac, a tall, red-haired ex-lawyer and schoolmaster from Angoulême, who, hearing that Henry was about to be excommunicated, had convinced himself that he intended to make war on the Pope. He had already failed to intercept him on several occasions. On the morning of May 14th he made his confession, sharpened his dagger and prepared to be hailed as the saviour of Catholic Europe. Towards four o'clock he watched the royal coach leave the Louvre on its way to the cemetery of the Holy Innocents, and waited for it at the corner of the Rue St Honoré.

Meanwhile, the Dauphin had got up early, visited his parents after hearing Mass, dined, done his lessons and driven out to see the decorations. He returned to the Tuileries to find a summons from the Queen and went to the Louvre, running up the stairs through a confusion of voices and footsteps, to his father's cabinet. A figure covered with blood lay on the bed. His mother surged out of the shouting, weeping group and rushed towards him. 'The King is dead! The King is dead!'

A hand fell on Louis's shoulder. A man's voice, solemn and harsh, rose above the tumult. 'Your Majesty will forgive me — kings of France do not die. Here is the living King!'

TWO

I

At the age of eight and a half Louis XIII inherited a far smaller kingdom than that bequeathed by his son to Louis XV. In 1610 the frontiers of France were bounded, roughly, by the Somme, the Meuse and the Saône. Lorraine was a semi-independent principality, Avignon belonged to the Pope and Orange to the Nassaus. The proximity of Paris to the Spanish Netherlands enhanced the danger of an invasion which might be facilitated by exposure; for the fortifications of the ancient city had long since crumbled away. The river reflected the splendours of the Louvre and the Tuileries. The setting of both palaces was medieval, as is shown by a contemporary print of Henry IV's assassination.

Against a background of tall, narrow gables, cobbled pavements and crowding carts the King's coach — which, but for its canopied roof and four horses, differs very little from the nearest farm waggon — has drawn up, partly, it would seem, to avoid a collision, and partly to enable Ravaillac to spring upon the rear wheel, his dagger poised. Two seated courtiers, their backs to the horses, look the other way; the Duc d'Épernon, who was in fact the King's sole companion, leans out of the coach, not between his master and the assassin, but rather to one side, so that Henry, his hand raised as if in blessing, is in the best possible position for the attack, which is being momentarily halted by the mild intervention of a bystander. A few pedestrians are interchanging glances of surprise, and one or two lookers-on contemplate the scene from upper windows. A prancing mongrel occupies the left foreground. The general effect, one of some charm, gives the impression that there is a slight hold-up. The King's expression is deprecatory, d'Épernon's detached. The coachman appears to be having an argument about right of way with the nearest waggoner: and the horses are preparing to stand indefinitely.

Soon after this print was circulated Louis was constantly forced back into the grief and shock of his loss. Although he eventually rose above that horror, he never recovered from it; his character began to change from the moment that, standing by his father's body, he gasped, 'That wicked man—if I had been there with my sword—' breaking off to cry out, 'Am I going to be killed too? I would rather my brother were King—' while the Chancellor, his hand still on the child's shoulder, deplored 'these useless tears'. 'There are many who weep,' he added, 'for you, as for themselves. It is now for Your Majesty to work—for them, as for yourself.'

These directions were instantly obeyed. While his father's body was still warm—before the blood-stained garments had been removed—Louis received his courtiers' condolences. This ordeal lasted for two and a half hours. At seven o'clock he supped, alone, in the Queen's ante-chamber. At nine he was escorted to his own apartments by de Souvré. When he had undressed and said his prayers he asked the Governor if they could share a bed—'because I might have bad dreams'—and so slept until eleven thirty. He was then sent for by the Queen and put to bed in her room with one of his half-brothers. A quarter of an hour later he was again awake, listening to his mother's sobs and groans and to the murmur, rising to wails and shouts, of the Parisians, who now converged on the palace to mourn 'our Henry', their father, their good and gracious master.

Few such persons knew, or knowing, would have found much comfort in the fact that the new King had been born under the Sign of the Scales, and was henceforth called the Just. Louis assumed the title in faith and resolution. His duty towards his people became the mainspring of his life. So his personal tragedy began.

The structure of the nation headed by an apparently absolute monarchy was feudal. The King stood alone; then came his heir, if he had one, then the higher clergy, whose status was greater than that of his other relatives, or of the chief nobles, some of whom, such as the Dukes of Bouillon and Nevers, governed their vast estates as petty kings, married into royal houses, paid a nominal tribute of vassalage to the sovereign and led his armies. Neither group had any connection with the lesser nobility and gentry, some of them very poor, who in their turn were completely cut off from the wealthy merchants. The lowest order, whether urban or rustic, had few rights, was locally governed and seldom lacked employment; some peasants owned enough land to support themselves and their families, but in bad years they perished from famine and its resultant diseases. The professional class—lawyers, physicians, schoolmasters and priests—did not exist as such. When these persons achieved distinction, as Héroard did, they were ennobled—he became the Sieur de Vaugrigneuse—bought estates and so were absorbed into the section above theirs. Throughout the kingdom these segregations were rigidly sustained; only the most remarkable could rise from one class to another.

Thus the King's principal ministers were patrician soldiers and those cardinals and bishops who had had legal training. Officially, the army and the Church administered the country in obedience to the monarch's decrees; in fact, he had to consult three bodies—the States-General, or Cabinet, the Royal Council and the Parlement of Paris, in that order—about all major decisions. He could ignore their recommendations, but seldom did so unless he was sure of military and financial support from some outside source.

This simple hierarchy had long been rotten with territorial and religious dispute, bribery and intrigue. Henry IV's reforms halted some corruptions, which broke out afresh with his wife's regency. She had the lust of power, but no inclination, nor indeed the slightest capacity, for work. It was therefore an easy matter for Concini, now on very bad terms with his wife, to seize what gradually amounted to the dictatorship of the country. While Leonora, between bouts of hysterics, took refuge in hypochondria and invalidism, her husband became Marquis d'Ancre, Marshal of France, and, some said, the lover of the Queen Regent. He advised her to confirm the Edict of Nantes; in all else the late King's plans were abandoned. War against Austria was called off, Sully dismissed, and the Spanish marriages placed at the head of the agenda. One obstacle to the continued authority of the favourite and his mistress remained: the boy King, now within a few years of his majority, when, it was believed, he would turn away Concini and relegate his mother.

There was only one way in which the Queen and her partner could prevail: the Italian way, that of so degrading and weakening Louis's character that when he came to rule he would be unfit to do so, as the sons of Catherine de Medici had been. Within a few weeks of his father's death the tempo and style of his education began to change. He was whipped—more often than in his father's lifetime—for the slightest fault; that would bewilder him and break his spirit. He was encouraged to hunt, play childish games and develop such hobbies as cookery, sculpture and drawing; that would distract him from both lessons and duties. He was forced to resort to the companionship of valets and falconers; that would lower his standards and deprive him of social aplomb. Madame de Montglat's supervision would have been preferable; but she was soon to retire to a small house near the Louvre, where she lived in some state till her death in 1633.

Within two years of his accession Louis became aware of his mother's intentions, and resolved to outwit her by appearing to fall in with her schemes. He continued to behave like the child he had ceased to be, and was soon thought of as backward and negligible. So he acquired secretiveness before he was eleven years old. No one, not even Héroard, observed the change; but the double role increased the strain of his daily life. He never gave in to the resultant fatigue.

The first day of his reign set the pattern and the pace of those to come. For the next thirty-three years his routine remained as strenuous as on May 15th, 1610.

He was woken at six thirty to be confronted by de Souvré, who brought him the speech he was to make to the Parlement of Paris. Formerly the Governor, a large, heavy man, had merely bowed on entering; now he knelt, and his difficulty in doing so provoked a laugh, immediately stifled. Louis then rehearsed his speech and got up. After dressing, washing and prayers he sat down to breakfast, but could eat nothing. Héroard prescribed tisane (a form of purgative) and Louis went to Mass in his private chapel. At nine thirty he dined in his own apartments, interrupting the meal to visit the Queen. Then, robed in the violet velvet of mourning, he mounted a white mule and, accompanied by his Guards and a vast cortège, rode to open Parlement and receive public homage. Enthroned, his mother at his side, he looked down from the dais over the assembly of nobles, princes of the blood, marshals, cardinals and bishops, all on their knees. He signed to them to rise. The Queen also rose, and began, 'Gentlemen, it having pleased God, through an evil chance, to take to Himself our good King—' and broke down. A few moments later she was able to resume with the presentation of the new King, concluding, 'I beg you always to advise him according to your consciences.'

Murmurs of compassion and loyalty rose to greet the pale, slight, curly-headed child who stood up and, having once more announced his father's death, went on, 'I remain your King, as being his son, by the laws of the realm. I hope that God will give me—' and was no longer heard. The noise of his subjects drowned his voice.

The Chancellor, Nicholas Brulart de Sillery, now announced the regency of the Queen, which was acknowledged by the chief Councillors. The King heard Mass in public, returning to the Louvre at two o'clock. There he dined in state and received a number of officials. At six he supped, and then interviewed a delegation of Jesuit fathers, to whom Henry IV had bequeathed his heart, to be enshrined in their College of the Arrow. Permission given, they left—with the heart, as the embalming of the dead King was already accomplished. At eight fifteen Louis said, 'I'm tired,' was undressed, said his prayers and climbed into bed. A little after nine he woke and asked his sub-Governor, de Préaux, to read him a story. Half an hour later, watched by the faithful Héroard, he was asleep. All that day, sustaining a regal grace and dignity, he had not wept. Next morning, seeing Madame de Montglat for the first time since his accession, he said, 'Mamanga, I do not want to be King so soon—I wish that the King my father were still alive!' and burst into tears.

During the next few weeks he wept often, but always when alone, or with Madame de Montglat or Héroard. Their devotion was unfailing, and almost disinterested; yet his isolation had much increased, for his father's death had deprived him of the only person who loved him for himself; everyone else, his mother above all, was scheming to relegate or make use of him. If he became friendly with a page or a courtier, that person at once took on the airs of a privileged character, and so Louis realized that he was being exploited. Such an atmosphere would not have affected an arrogant or stupid child. Louis was neither; his more perspicacious contemporaries observed that he was extremely sensitive—particularly about his stammer—and that he longed for the support his father had supplied. Soon after he passed his tenth year Héroard perceived that he was not taken in by flattery—indeed, he disliked it—and remained contemptuously indifferent to the semi-facetious, semi-cringing approach of those attempting to impress him. He had one ally in Queen Margot, who would

LOUIS XIII WHEN YOUNG

sometimes intercede for him with de Souvré; she died four years after his accession.

Louis was also aware of his own danger; the thought of assassination gave him frequent nightmares, and his public appearances were sometimes a torment, for he was too proud to allow his guards to ride between him and the crowds. Neither his people's tearful adoration nor his instinctively graceful response could disguise the fact that a number of persons wanted him out of the way—and that one of these might be his mother.

Marie de Medici was innocent of any sinister design; but the clique working against her and the Concini made it their business to spread the rumour that she had been privy to her husband's murder and intended to remove Louis in favour of the infant Gaston, in order to prolong her regency. Louis may not have believed these stories; yet they haunted him: and the Queen's harshness—she was always telling de Souvré to beat him—contrasted disagreeably with her doting attitude towards his little brother. He feared her; he still hoped for her love.

There remained, then, his sisters, to whom, as to Gaston, he was devoted. He had also become attached to his eldest half-brother, the eighteen-year-old Duc de Vendôme, who had just been appointed Governor of Brittany. When the young man came to take leave, Louis cried; he may have thought that Vendôme would defend him against his enemies.

Meanwhile he determined to model himself on his father. He longed for the coronation which would enable him to carry out his most sacred duties. In October 1610 he went to Rheims, where the ceremonies began at five in the morning and lasted till two-fifteen. Halfway through, it seemed that the sceptre was too heavy for him to hold, but he would not relinquish it. ('No, no, I want to carry it myself, I wish no one to help me.') Returning to Paris, he stopped at the monastery of Saint-Marcoul, where he touched nine hundred sufferers for the King's Evil. On the forehead of each he made the sign of the Cross, repeating, 'The King toucheth thee, may God cure thee,' and put his fingers inside the sore.

A short time after his tenth birthday Louis began the struggle against his mother's domination. He was supposed to attend the Council meetings, but was never informed of them. At last, aware that something of importance was to be discussed, he appeared. All rose. Marie de Medici marched up to him, took his arm and ordered him out of the room. No comment was made, either by or to Louis, on this supreme humiliation. He and the Queen were superficially reconciled when his betrothal to the Infanta, Anne of Austria, was publicly celebrated, with that of Madame Élisabeth to Don Philip, in his father's most superb creation, the exquisite Place Royale, later the neglected and decaying Place des Vosges.

Yet all the time Louis knew that his father's plans had been discarded. To him, the Spanish royalties were 'Papa's enemies', and this mistrust was obscurely connected with the bawdy allusions to marriage which had distressed him when he was a baby. He submitted to the Queen's opening gambit correctly and with dignity. 'My son,' she began, 'I wish you to be married, are you willing?' 'Very willing, Madame.' 'But you do not know how to make a child,' Marie pursued. 'Pardon me, Madame, I do,' Louis replied. 'Who has taught you?' 'Monsieur de Souvré,' was the answer, given in a tone of finality. That this test was not to take place for nearly two years—an immense time in the thoughts of an eleven-year-old—helped Louis to enjoy the betrothal celebrations, during which he appeared as gay and debonair as his father.

Now his routine became easier. There were fewer whippings, his lessons were curtailed to two hours in the morning and two in the afternoon, he was given a miniature forge, and allowed to hawk and hunt without too much supervision. Then his whole life changed—was illuminated, joyful, exciting. He discovered Charles de Luynes.

I I

For three and a half centuries a number of people have assumed that Louis XIII was consistently homosexual. This seems a somewhat arbitrary judgment in view of the fact that his wife conceived five times and that after their marriage he fell in love with three other women. In 1947 his most distinguished and meticulous biographer* went into battle with an equally arbitrary defence, on the grounds that, in the nineteenth-century edition of Héroard's journal for 1618–19, some excerpts had been so compressed as to give the impression that de Luynes and Louis were lovers, and that the full text of these passages proved the contrary.

* L. Vaunois, *Vie de Louis XIII*, pp. 249–57.

Louis was twelve and de Luynes, an agreeable and lively Provençal gentleman who had charge of his hawks, was thirty-five when their friendship began. They had known one another before, for de Luynes had been the late King's falconer; his skill and knowledge ensured his retaining the post on Louis's accession. He was neither strikingly handsome, nor outstandingly clever; his natural gaiety and easy, pleasant manners earned him general popularity until Louis's favour made him an object of jealousy and spite.

Now that the labels of 'heterosexual' and 'homosexual' are no longer considered definitive in professional circles—for it seems that most human beings are, or can be, both—any analysis of Louis's character at this period of his life invalidates past judgment and present denial. Neither is relevant in the case of a person whose circumstances led him to seek disinterested affection from both sexes, and who, apparently finding it first in de Luynes, became emotionally dependent on his support. In fact, to describe Louis as 'falling in love' with de Luynes would be as absurd as to deny that he was obsessed by him. The important aspect of their relationship —which lasted eight years and was equally beneficial to both—is shown in the contrast between de Luynes's attitude towards the King and that of his contemporaries. When this hitherto obscure young man realized the extent of his power, he used it, but not too unscrupulously; and Louis responded ardently to the compassion and care for himself which he had been looking for since his father's death. The difference in their ages and de Luynes's genial temperament made him into what is now known as a father-figure: one capable of calling forth a varying range of emotions.

At this time Louis was surrounded, for the most part, by gross, dull, elderly men; their humour was coarse, their manners were rough and they despised the arts—music, painting and sculpture— in which he was beginning to show considerable skill. De Luynes's gentle and sympathetic approach helped him, as theirs could not, to face the first serious crisis of his reign: a revolt led by his cousin-german, the Prince de Condé, against his mother's regency.

Condé's proclamations were convincing enough; his condemnation of economic muddles, general injustice and danger from the Spanish marriages made an excellent springboard for an attack which was intended to split the country. He would then suggest that Henry IV's divorce had invalidated his sons' legitimacy, so that he himself might claim the throne on the grounds of his descent from Louis IX. He was joined in this rebellion by a number of great nobles, among whom were the Comte de Retz and the Duc de Vendôme. They now placed Brittany in a state of defence; this might lead to an invasion of the capital.

Negotiations began, a truce was signed and the Queen consented to postpone the Spanish marriages. In return, it was agreed that Vendôme should disarm and destroy the fortresses of Lamballe and Quimper. He failed to do so and, with de Retz, proceeded to arm and occupy Vannes.

For once, Marie de Medici rejected Concini's counsels of appeasement and, guided by de Villeroy, one of the late King's most trusted ministers, decided to send Louis on progress through Brittany and Touraine. In the summer of 1614 they set off together and, avoiding the fortresses occupied by Condé's supporters, were rapturously acclaimed. Very soon it was seen that the boy King's charm and dignity had ensured a bloodless conquest, with the result that as he rode out of Poitiers, he received a promise of loyalty and obedience from Vendôme. 'Obedience! He has not yet disarmed,' said Louis, and went on to the Loire, proceeding by water for the next three days, while the people waded and swam out to greet him.

By the time he reached Nantes, de Retz and Vendôme had accepted defeat and were on their way to the castle, where Louis, having touched six hundred persons for the King's Evil, was watching folk-dances and listening to the local musicians. De Retz arrived first, begged forgiveness and received no reply. Silence fell on the assembled courtiers as he assured the King of his love and loyalty. At last Louis said, 'When your deeds bear out your words, then I shall return your love.'

Vendôme's reception was even colder. The King acknowledged his obeisance with a nod, and turned away. Vendôme knelt and said, 'Sire, I come at Your Majesty's command to assure you that I have no will but to be your most humble and obedient servant, desiring only to prove my loyalty to the death.' White and shaking with anger, Louis replied, 'Serve me better in the future than in the past—and know that your greatest honour in the world is that you are my brother.' 'I do know it,' murmured

Vendôme and retired, reappearing two evenings later to ask for an audience. 'Who is it? Vendôme? Tell him I am asleep,' was the answer.

So Louis returned to Paris in triumph, the central figure of a magnificent procession, to hear a Te Deum at Notre Dame. He was now within a month of his fourteenth year. In October 1614 he celebrated his majority by appearing in Council, holding a bed of justice and riding through Paris in state. Clearly, and without once stammering, he assured the Parlement of his good-will, and went on, 'I expect from all my subjects the respect and obedience due to the royal power and authority bestowed on me by Almighty God.' Then he turned to the Queen. 'Madame,' he began, 'I thank you for all the trouble you have been put to for my sake. I beg that you will continue to govern and command as heretofore. I believe and intend that you shall be obeyed in all things and that, after me, and in my absence, you will be the head of my Council.'

This declaration was a disappointment to those who had hoped for the fall of the Concini. But Louis's advisers had made the right decision. With his mother, he had just subdued a rebellion, and they must therefore remain allies, outwardly at least. This was also the opinion of the newly appointed Bishop of Luçon, Armand du Plessis de Richelieu, principal speaker for the clergy at the last meeting of the States-General in February 1615, when it was agreed that the power to restore order and prosperity belonged to the King alone. Louis replied, 'Gentlemen, I thank you for the trust you have placed in me. With God's will, I shall justify it by my actions, by relieving my people, by doing justice to all and by conducting myself to your satisfaction.' So, at the age of four-teen, he acquired the absolute authority held by the kings of France for the next hundred and seventy-four years. The States-General did not meet again till 1789.

Now he and his mother seemed on the best of terms. She listened sympathetically when Louis complained of de Souvré's attempts to prevent de Luynes entering his apartments, and refused to support the Governor. In March of this year de Luynes was made Captain of the Palace of the Louvre and Governor of Amboise, where he received the King during his second progress. Once more, Condé tried to stir up trouble by appealing to the Huguenots to join with him against the Spanish marriages, and collected an army in Champagne, which was defeated by the Royalist troops in August 1615. Preparations for the marriages then began. Together the King and Madame Élisabeth journeyed south to meet the Infanta and Don Philip's representatives at Bordeaux.

THREE

I

THE next eighteen months—from November 1615 to April 1617—were perhaps the most critical and in some ways the most taxing of Louis's life. Faced with two tests, the consummation of his marriage and the establishment of his personal power, he passed both successfully, from the point of view of his contemporaries; but the after-effects destroyed his private happiness and his European reputation, although his people and his few intimates remained devoted and loyal. Before he was seventeen, he knew, although he could not admit, that his marriage was a failure, and that the duties and cares of absolute monarchy were and always would be an intolerable burden. He bore this knowledge with little complaint and increasing depression. He was less well behaved in his relations with his wife.

Before Louis and Madame Élisabeth reached Bordeaux they had already been married to their respective proxies. On October 21st they drove out of the city, and half a mile beyond it were met by de Cardeñas, the Spanish ambassador, and his suite. Knowing that they would never meet again, they were in tears; sobbing, clinging to one another, they stood in the road, while the ambassador contemplated them coldly. At last he advanced and, forcing them apart, said to Élisabeth, 'Come, come—you are now a Princess of Spain!' and half dragged, half carried her into the coach which was to take her to the frontier. Still weeping, the fourteen-year-old bridegroom drove back to Bordeaux, to await the arrival of the new Queen.

On November 9th she reached St Jean de Luz, to be met, among other officials, by de Luynes, who presented her with his master's letter of welcome. When he heard that she was at Castres, five miles from Bordeaux, Louis, determined to reproduce his father's gallantry, drove out to intercept her coach. As they faced one another, each enclosed in a gilded shell, eagerly watched by attendants and footmen, Louis saw a golden-haired, delicately

39

complexioned child (she was exactly his own age) dressed in green-and-silver brocade. She had exquisite hands; her nose was aquiline and rather too long; but she was pretty enough, and seemed more at ease than he did, perhaps because she had only to smile and blush and look charmingly surprised. Louis lost his nerve; he called out—in Spanish—that he was incognito, and drove back, reaching Bordeaux an hour before his bride. Their official meeting and her reception by the Queen Mother then took place.

Next day, accompanied by Héroard and de Souvré, Louis called on Anne while she was dressing. The visit was supposed to be short and formal; he prolonged it far beyond the required time. When she called for a scarlet plume for her hat, he took off his. 'Take which you like,' he said, adding, 'You must give me one of your ribbons.' She did so, he pinned the knot in his hat and they parted, apparently delighted with one another.

Four days later they were married in the Cathedral of Saint André by the Bishop of Bordeaux, returning at five thirty to the episcopal palace. Louis conducted his wife to her apartments and retired to his own, where he took off his robes of state, supped and went to bed to await the summons for the consummation of his marriage.

A few minutes later he was visited by a number of courtiers much older than himself, some married, all men of the world and experienced lovers. In order, Héroard noted, 'to give him confidence', they proceeded to tell him stories of sexual adventure; some may have been amusing, to themselves at least; all were indecent, and thus set a standard both alarming and repellent to a sensitive boy of fourteen, whose chief concern was his dynastic duty. So two hours went by.

The Queen Mother then came in, and as the company bowed and made way for her, began, 'My son, a wedding is not the whole matter; you must now come to the Queen your wife, who awaits you.' 'Madame,' Louis replied, 'I but awaited your command. I will, if you please, go to her with you.'

After this formal interchange Louis got up and put on his dressing-gown and slippers. Attended by de Souvré, Héroard, one of his former nurses (who was joined by his wife's Spanish waiting-woman), the Master of the Wardrobe, and the First Gentleman of the Bedchamber carrying a candelabra, the King and his mother proceeded to the state apartments. Anne was standing in the middle of the room. The Queen Mother said, 'Daughter, I bring you your husband. I pray you, love and welcome him.' 'I have but one wish,' replied Anne in Spanish, 'to obey and please Your Majesties.'

The King got into bed first, followed by his wife, who entered it from the other side. Marie de Medici mounted the dais and, leaning over them, said something unrecorded in a low voice. The curtains were drawn together. She then turned to the attendants and said, 'Come, let us go—' pausing to tell Héroard and the nurses to remain. She added that the young couple were not to be disturbed for two hours. At this point Héroard seems to have got out his notebook.

The gold and silver tapestries, displaying the triumphs of Artemis, that virgin goddess, encircled the huge state bed in dimly lit splendour. Beyond it, ante-chambers and galleries were crowded with courtiers. And beyond them the Queen Mother waited, with her ladies, for her son's report.

After rather less than two hours Louis drew aside the curtains and called for his gown and slippers. Before he set off for his mother's apartments he was questioned by Héroard. 'I did it twice,' he said. A short inspection of his charge proved to the doctor that Anne of Austria was no longer a virgin. It occurred to him that Louis, although now in truth a husband, might have exaggerated his prowess; yet it seemed, he added, that this was not so; and in the morning the French and Spanish nurses confirmed this belief when they brought the wedding sheets to the Queen Mother.

In all this evidence there remains, naturally, a certain element of doubt, enhanced by the fact that for the next four years Anne of Austria slept alone. Thus Héroard's statement, with that of the nurses, has been dismissed as the result of loyalty and wishful thinking.

In view of the doctor's final and conclusive phrase—*le guillery rouge**—this doubt may be disposed of; why should such a man as Héroard lie, in a report made for himself alone? It was his business, if the marriage was not consummated, to prescribe the appropriate remedies, and there is no record of his doing so. Nor is there reason to believe that anyone saw his journals but the physicians

* *Guillery* = instrument of pleasure.

41

who succeeded him in 1628; in fact no interest was taken in them until the middle of the eighteenth century. Added to this is the knowledge of Louis's attitude towards little girls before he reached his teens. He had had a passion for some four or five, whom he kissed and petted. His behaviour to this group, one not markedly childish, had been that of a lover, to the amusement and approval of his entourage. It seems, therefore, that his first intimacy with his wife, whether fully carried out or not, nauseated him, in restrospect at least, as indeed it must have repelled and frightened her; for she did not object, on personal grounds, to his avoidance not only of her bed but also of her company during the next five months, during which time he supped with her once and never saw her alone.

Neither Anne nor Louis was sexually precocious; and their subsequent history shows that they shrank from lust. He was romantic, susceptible, born out of his time; she was frigid. Yet at the outset he had been much attracted by her looks and her gentle manners; if they had been of humble birth and thus left to themselves, these two unfortunate children might have arrived at a happy union. As it was, he did eventually become very fond of her, although later on her limitations and her frivolity irked him beyond endurance, so that he lost patience and turned away. Naturally Louis's treatment of his wife was put down to the influence of de Luynes. But de Luynes was not a skilled intriguer, and at this time took very good care not to be involved in the struggle for power now being waged between Concini and the Prince de Condé.

Condé's principal weapon was the national hatred of the Italian. On the other hand, Concini had so long been established that by the beginning of 1616 he had a large army, plenty of money to pay for it and a personal bodyguard of fifty men, who accompanied him everywhere. It was said that he might dispose of his wife in order to marry the Queen Mother, and his defence of Marie de Medici against the insolences of Condé had given him a certain prestige; also, it seemed to a number of people that Concini alone had the power to prevent civil war, and that when his rivalry with Condé came to a head, he was bound to win.

After another conference between Condé and his allies and Louis and the Queen Mother, the Prince agreed to dismiss his troops on condition that the 'greybeards' Council', headed by

Sillery and Villeroy, was dismissed and replaced by younger men, of whom the most notable was Richelieu. In the summer of 1616 Condé's momentary triumph over Concini was crowned by the Italian being deprived of certain properties and retiring to his Normandy estates.

Condé then reopened his campaign for the throne by planning to kidnap the King. Louis was warned, and ordered his cousin's arrest. Between the factions of Condé and Concini he stood alone and almost powerless—for the fall of the one was bound to restore the other—but he decided to deal with his most dangerous enemy first. It was essential that Condé, who thought of Louis as a backward schoolboy, should be taken by surprise. So the plans were made; and on July 31st, 1616, Condé, having returned to Paris in triumph, visited the Louvre and entered the gallery where Louis was standing by the window with his gentlemen.

It is now axiomatic that hardship and deprivation, of whatever kind, may develop character but do not necessarily improve it. Louis still appeared to be a frank, amiable, kindly boy. In a reign of five and a half years, passing from bewilderment to humiliation, he had at last realized that he was not, as he had been told, subject to God alone, and that his mother and Concini were combating Condé for the continuance of their own power. Thus his only protection was a disingenuousness which had become instinctive.

Seeing Condé, he began, 'Good day, my lord Prince. I am going hunting, will you accompany me?' 'If it please Your Majesty, you must excuse me,' his cousin replied. 'I am about to tell the Queen my mother that I am after a stag as soon as I have heard Mass at the Capuchins',' Louis went on. 'Farewell, my lord—' and preceded Condé to the Queen's apartments, indicating that the Prince should follow him.

According to an eye-witness, Louis's casual geniality so deceived Condé that he followed him to Marie de Medici's cabinet and was there arrested. His relatives and supporters at once took flight, and Parlement approved his imprisonment. The Parisians, in order to show their preference for Condé, sacked Concini's palace to the tune of 75,000 crowns. This sum was reimbursed by the Queen Mother, and a fortnight later Concini returned.

For the next few months Louis continued to behave as if all was well, seemingly absorbed in his sports, his music and his painting; but the strain was too great. He could neither eat nor sleep, suffered agonizing indigestion and, in the small hours of October 31st, was discovered rigid and unconscious, his jaws so tightly clenched that they had to be opened with a knife. Recovering from what appears to have been an epileptic fit, he remained unwell, although he carried out his duties as usual.

Meanwhile, Concini's power and the resultant hatred of him, his wife and the Queen Mother reached their apotheosis. Louis knew that he himself had two weapons: the love of his people and the mystique of monarchy. All he needed was advice and encouragement as to their use. These were presently supplied by de Luynes; but it is doubtful whether this cautious young man would have taken any action if he had not been warned that his own life was in danger; for Concini had now become so powerful that he not only found himself able to dispense with the Queen Mother's support, but was planning to remove all Louis's entourage, either through arrest or assassination. De Souvré then joined Concini's faction; he was followed by Richelieu, who took care to remain in the service of Marie de Medici.

Concini, who had hitherto maintained the show of deference, now began publicly to humiliate and insult the King. His plan seems to have been so to degrade Louis as to destroy his regal prestige; then, having become a despised and negligible figure, he could be removed and imprisoned. News of his death would be calmly received and the eight-year-old Gaston installed under Concini's dictatorship.

The Italian opened his campaign by refusing to punish one of his pages who had murdered an attendant of Louis. He himself was now addressed by the semi-royal title of Monseigneur, and made it clear that, if he were ordered to leave the kingdom, would decline to do so. Meanwhile, he openly spoke of Louis as 'the idiot', remained covered in his presence and contemptuously offered to finance him when Marie de Medici failed to pay his expenses. Leonora co-operated by sending a footman to tell Louis not to make so much noise when he was playing billiards in the gallery below her apartments, as she was in bed with a headache. Concini followed this up by walking through the same gallery with his hat on, attended by a hundred gentlemen. Louis, with three, was standing by the window. Concini pretended not to see him and, still covered, passed on. Finally, at the carnival banquet of 1617, he raised his glass before Louis gave the signal to drink, drained it and was greeted by cries of 'The King drinks!' from his entourage.

These gestures appalled Marie de Medici. She begged Concini to leave France and settle elsewhere at her expense, warned him that he was in great danger and sent the Bishop of Carcassonne to plead with him. When Concini ignored these suggestions, her terror and irritation were diverted to Louis. In the course of his daily visit he stepped on one of her dogs and was bitten; as he stooped to staunch the blood she abused him for his clumsiness, and he left, muttering that she preferred her pets to himself.

It seemed, then, that the only means of defeating Concini and subduing the Queen Mother must be drastic to the point of violence. In the spring of 1617 de Luynes collected a group of conspirators, who agreed to arrest the favourite in the King's name. At certain moments—when he crossed the bridge connecting the main building of the Louvre with the Queen's apartments —he was attended by no more than half a dozen gentlemen, and thus could be seized without much difficulty. Yet it was obvious that his supporters would rush in to rescue him; and even if he were brought to trial, his judges would be bribed or threatened in his favour. There remained one solution—murder.

De Luynes's principal coadjutor was Déageant, who was bent on killing Concini, with or without the King's consent. They were supported by de Vitry, du Hallier and Guichaumont, all members of the lesser nobility. They now worked out a plan for what they preferred to call the arrest of the Italian, using de Luynes as their mouthpiece to Louis. De Luynes then approached his master with various suggestions for eliminating Concini, all of which he must have known to be impracticable. Should His Majesty leave for Amboise, there collect an army and march on Paris? Or should he wait in the capital until de Luynes with his forces came to the rescue? Or should he appeal to the people to restore his power?

Louis refused to consider these schemes. He wished Concini to be publicly arrested and tried for high treason. As the supreme representative of justice, he was determined to practise it. De Luynes seems to have pointed out that this would merely result in his own destruction and the enhancement of his enemy's strength. Louis said nothing. In the second week of April he interviewed the conspirators, and the plan of stopping Concini on the bridge, after barring the gates between him and his bodyguard, was put forward. Then someone said, 'But should he resist, struggle, attempt to escape?' 'Kill him,' Déageant replied. Louis made a violent gesture. 'No!' he exclaimed. 'One must prepare for the unexpected,' put in another gentleman. 'Above all, we must succeed. To fail would be worse than all else.' Silence fell while they waited for Louis's orders. He gave none, and they departed.

They then approached de Mesmes, Provost-Governor of the city, who said that he was more than willing to co-operate in Concini's arrest, but that he would have nothing to do with his murder. At the next conference, it was proposed that de Vitry should strike the first blow—Concini's resistance now being assumed—and he agreed, on condition that he was followed up by du Hallier and his friend Fouquerolles. The whole group then again interviewed Louis, and again de Vitry asked, 'Should he defend himself, what does Your Majesty wish me to do?' There was a short silence. Then de Vitry said, 'Sire, I shall carry out your orders,' and the conspirators retired. What they now described as 'the execution' was arranged for the morning of Sunday, April 23rd.

I I

At first glance, Louis's tacit consent to Concini's murder shows him as ruthless, cowardly and amoral. It would have been more in keeping with the standards of absolute monarchy if, instead of saying nothing, he had ordered the conspirators to kill him, in the manner of a Renaissance villain. But his situation was more complicated than that of Webster's Brachiano. At the age of fifteen and a half he was fighting not only for his prerogative, but also for his life; and if he believed, as seems more than likely, that Concini was his mother's lover, his position was one in which reason and piety then generally yielded to criminal assault, as in the case of Shakespeare's most celebrated hero. Finally, it was essential that he, an anointed king, the judge and father of his people, should emerge from this *coup d'état* with clean hands or, at worst, as an inexperienced youth, who, having once forbidden the murder, was overborne by his elders.

Some of those who rejoiced at Concini's death continued to say that he should have been disposed of according to law, disregarding the fact that circumstances made this impossible; but they were in a minority. In seventeenth-century France murder was taken for granted. Two thousand duellists were killed every year; and in Paris fifteen to eighteen people were assassinated by bands of robbers on five nights out of seven.

So it was that Louis's only anxiety concerned the efficacy of the conspirators' plan. If it failed, they had a chance to escape, while he would almost certainly perish; and he had to wait, unprotected and inactive, while they set about the business together.

On the morning of April 23rd Louis breakfasted at eight and played billiards till ten o'clock, the hour at which Concini was due to visit the Queen Mother. He did not appear and Louis, accompanied by de Luynes, went to Mass. At twelve thirty he was told that Concini had just arrived and was in Marie de Medici's apartments. When it was proposed that Concini should be arrested there, Louis said, 'Nothing must be undertaken in the presence of the Queen my mother. Tell the Marquis that I wish to see him in the Armoury.'

The messenger hurried away, only to find that Concini had left the palace by another entrance. A little later it transpired that he had been warned, and would not return. Louis then went to dinner. During the meal de Luynes suggested breaking into Concini's house and arresting him there, but de Vitry rejected this plan. Finally it was arranged that de Luynes should send a man Concini trusted but who was now attached to the conspirators, to assure him that he was in no danger; so the attack was put off till the next morning. Louis, having observed his usual routine, was in bed by ten o'clock.

After a sleepless night he got up very early and ordered his coach, as if for a hunting expedition. He remained in his bedchamber, while de Luynes's messengers came in with their reports. At ten, Louis was told that Concini, accompanied by some fifty gentlemen, was on his way to the Louvre. Louis went down to the long gallery and began a game of billiards with de Luynes. The next messenger told them that de Vitry, with twenty men, swords and pistols hidden by their cloaks, was moving towards the bridge leading to the Queen Mother's apartments. The next three minutes must decide the issue.

As arranged, Louis broke off his game, and sending to tell the coachman that he was about to leave, went to his bedchamber as if to change his clothes. A third messenger burst in, white-faced. 'It has failed! The Marquis's men overcame ours!' Some time ago, Louis had made up his mind to die fighting. 'Bring me my sword and carbine,' he said, and, one in each hand, left the bedchamber, crossed the ante-room and the great hall, and had reached the head of the staircase leading to the bridge, when he met another of de Vitry's men. 'Sire, it is done! He is dead!'

Louis ran back to the great hall, now filled with the shouting, cheering courtiers who had seen Concini fall. The windows were flung open, and he appeared on the balcony. Among the crowds in the courtyard below were de Vitry and his companions, all unhurt. 'I thank you, I thank you!' Louis called. 'Now I am king!'

In the confusion following the murder—Guichaumont struck first, followed by de Vitry and du Hallier—most of Concini's attendants fled, rushing past the guards and thus giving the impression that Louis had been killed and that they were taking over the palace. As he passed from one balcony to another, the rapture of his people came near to destroying the impassivity which had become instinctive. His eyes filled with tears; he laughed, then pressed his hand to his mouth. Until this moment, he had not fully taken in the passionate love and loyalty from which Concini and the Queen Mother had managed to isolate him. As it flowed over him he grew calmer. His first order was to recall his father's ministers, Villeroy and Sillery, whom Concini had removed. 'I will govern with their help alone,' he announced, as soon as he could make himself heard.

He was then approached by de Vitry, who said, 'The Marquis resisted arrest, therefore I had to kill him.' This euphemistic statement exculpated the speaker, who, putting his hand on Concini's right arm, had said, 'I arrest you, in the name of the King.' 'I?' exclaimed the Italian. 'Yes, you,' was the answer, upon which Concini, according to an eye-witness, *appeared* to be about to draw his sword and was then shot five times, dying as he fell.

Within the next half-hour the Queen Mother and Leonora Concini were told of the murder. Marie de Medici showed no emotion, merely remarking that, having reigned for seven years. she should now await a heavenly crown. Leonora set about collecting her jewels, which she hid beneath a mattress. She was taken to the Bastille, tried for sorcery and high treason, and beheaded a few weeks later. Richelieu lost his secretaryship, but was allowed to remain on the Council. The rest of the Concini faction were dismissed from their posts and given short terms of imprisonment.

The celebrations then began with fireworks and Louis's triumphal progress through the city. Escorted by four hundred gentlemen, he rode to the church of the Grands-Augustins, where he and de Luynes heard a Mass of thanksgiving. He had given orders that Concini's body was to be taken to St-Germain-l'Auxerrois, there to await secret burial. Somehow, it was discovered, carried off and torn in pieces by the mob, the heart being cut out and eaten. Meanwhile, a general holiday throughout the kingdom was proclaimed.

Before going to bed that night Louis had reorganized his Council, arranged for his mother to be confined to her apartments and forbidden access to her daughter-in-law and her other children. Her messages imploring an audience were ignored for a fortnight; she was then told to retire, with Richelieu, to Blois.

On the afternoon of her departure Louis, in a white satin doublet and scarlet hose and accompanied by de Luynes, was announced. He bowed and uncovered while his mother read out the statement she had been told to prepare. 'Sir,' it began, 'I have done my best worthily to carry out my regency and the administration allowed me by you.' There followed an apology for any 'inadvertent' errors, thanks for honourable retirement and a plea for the continuance of the King's goodwill. With an immovable countenance, Louis replied, 'Madame, I am come to bid you farewell, and to promise that I shall care for you as a son should. It is my wish that none but myself shall rule. Now I am king.' He then gave instructions for her journey to Blois and thanked her for her services to the state. Marie de Medici asked if her Intendant, Barbin, might be released. This interruption to an arranged programme took Louis by surprise. After a pause he replied, 'Madame, I have already told you that I will endeavour to please you, in this, as in all else.'

The Queen Mother began to cry. Then she came up to Louis and kissed him—for the first time in his life. He tried to speak and failed. Gaston, Christine and Henrietta Maria were ushered in to say goodbye. All wept as their mother embraced them. Louis said nothing; his eyes filled with tears as the Queen staggered to the window and, leaning against it, gave way to gasping sobs. He bowed and went out, followed by de Luynes, whom Marie caught up; holding on to his sleeve, she begged him to plead for Barbin. As de Luynes hesitated the King's voice, suddenly high and shaking, was heard. 'Luynes! Luynes! Luynes!'—and the favourite, deeply embarrassed, withdrew.

An hour later the Queen Mother's coach, followed by Richelieu's, left the Louvre. Louis watched till it disappeared. Then he turned to de Luynes and said, 'Let us go now to Vincennes.' With his wife, he remained in the château while the Louvre was put in order, redecorated and cleaned. So all trace of the old regime was removed. At about this time Héroard said something of the enormous burden he must carry. Louis replied, 'No—it was much harder to pretend to be a child than to do what I do now. I was made to whip tops at the Tuileries. It is time that I took charge.' Next day, at the Council meeting, he made it clear that he intended to listen and take advice. Each minister rose and spoke before he did; no interruptions were allowed. A few hours later, mercy was asked for a man wrongfully imprisoned and condemned by Concini. 'I must first ask my Council,' said Louis. 'If they approve, he will be released.'

FOUR

I

In the months following his *coup d'état* Louis not only took on the whole duty of a ruler, but began to show a gayer and more social side. For the first time since his childhood he found pleasure in feminine society; yet less in the Queen's than in that of her ladies. The most attractive of these was Mademoiselle de Maugiron. Now Louis's visits to his wife, made twice daily, created a romantic friendship between himself and this lively girl. The Queen became angry and alarmed, and Mademoiselle de Maugiron was dismissed, with the result that Louis resorted more than usual to de Luynes, whom he endowed with a dukedom, a large portion of Concini's properties and a wife—Marie de Montbazon, daughter of the Duc de Rohan. This young lady, later famous as the Duchesse de Chevreuse, was a flirt and a mischief-maker. Her friendship with Anne of Austria was one of the Queen's greatest misfortunes.

By the beginning of 1618 the European powers perceived that Louis's assumption of kingship was not being followed up by his conduct as a husband. The Spaniards began to say that his neglect of their Princess was an insult to themselves and their empire; the negotiations for the marriage of the Prince of Piedmont with Madame Christine were delayed; and Urban VIII sent his Nuncio, Cardinal Bentivoglio, to confer, first with Father Arnoux, Louis's confessor, and then with the King himself. If the King and Queen of France did not soon found a dynasty, their realm would be split by the Condé faction and thence by the Huguenots; thus the Catholic faith would be endangered, the rise of the Protestant powers a threat and the peace of Europe in jeopardy. Something must be done; and Father Arnoux opened the campaign.

Naturally the good priest's adjurations increased Louis's shrinking from the bride he had tried, so disastrously, to please. He changed the subject, became evasive, embarrassed and, finally, silent. As Arnoux continued to urge him he stammered out that there was plenty of time, and concluded the interview.

It was now Bentivoglio's turn; he was more direct, even peremptory; the result was the same. At last Héroard took a hand: why did His Majesty never see the Queen alone? Louis replied, 'She excites me,' as if ashamed, a confession to which Héroard found no answer. A more drastic remedy was then planned.

On January 20th, 1619, Louis's half-sister, Mademoiselle de Vendôme, was married to the Duc d'Elbœuf. The King was present at the bedding of the young couple and remained — probably at de Luynes's suggestion — to watch d'Elbœuf perform the duties of a husband, which he did so successfully that as soon as she was released, the bride sat up and said, 'Sire, do likewise with the Queen, and you will do well.' Louis made no reply.

Five days later he and de Luynes were supping together after hunting all day. They ate and drank heartily. De Luynes then accompanied the King to his bedchamber to attend his undressing. At the door he turned, came back to the bedside and said, 'Come, Sire — we must now go to the Queen.' Louis refused. De Luynes was adamant. A heated argument ensued. Then de Luynes stood over his master, tearing off the bed-clothes and forcing him to his feet. Louis struggled and protested: de Luynes persisted. Louis burst into tears.

De Luynes took no notice. Preceded by the valet with a can-delabra, he pushed and dragged Louis as far as the Queen's apartments, opened the door of the bedroom and shut it behind him. Louis remained with his wife till the small hours. Next morning both appeared radiantly happy, and for the next few months were always together. The news flashed round Europe. Spain was appeased, the Emperor approving and the Pope benignant. The only undesirable aspect was the triumph of de Luynes: what a pity that a nobody from the provinces should have succeeded where the highest nobility and clergy had failed!

In March the Nuncio asked the Queen, 'And how does the noble Dauphin?' Anne blushed and said nothing. Héroard inter-vened. His Majesty was overdoing it. 'A pause of fourteen days is desirable,' he said. A few weeks later word went round that Anne was pregnant. It was not so; but the young people's delight in each other's company continued, and Madame Christine's marriage to the Prince of Piedmont was celebrated. Then news came of the Queen Mother's escape from Blois; she was on her way back to Paris. Louis left Anne at St-Germain and summoned his Council to the Louvre.

Marie de Medici — who was now so fat that she broke the ladder provided for her escape from the castle — had been planning a revolt against her son; if he did not use force, there would be civil war. Her troops, headed by the Duc d'Épernon, were at Loches, and she joined him there. When they reached Angoulême those of Louis were ready to meet them. Richelieu intervened and persuaded the Queen Mother to abandon her campaign. Peace was signed, and on September 4th, 1619, she, Louis and Anne met at Montbazon's château of Couzières. Marie de Medici was in tears. Louis said, 'I have been wishing to see you for a long time,' and after talking to her alone, drove with her and the young Queen to Tours. On his return to Paris he released and received the Prince de Condé. Meanwhile the Queen Mother remained at Angers, and very soon Louis realized that she was planning another rebellion. He ordered her to come back; she refused. Again Richelieu attempted to make peace, but failed.

In December all these troubles were subordinated to the news of the Queen's pregnancy. Louis's joy found expression in music, in lyrics ('The sunlight pales before my Amaryllis, the lilies bloom'), and they renewed the fulfilment of their loves. He composed a ballet for the Twelfth Night festivities and ordered a banquet for the Knights of the Holy Ghost, at which she was to be the guest of honour. She appeared looking pale and wasted. Ten days later she miscarried and became feverish, then delirious. For three weeks she was dangerously ill.

Louis stayed with her night and day. No one else was allowed to nurse her. Returning to consciousness, the poor girl lost heart; she would rather die; she could struggle no longer. Forcing back his tears, holding her hand, Louis said, 'Take courage. There is nothing I would not do for you, if it cost me the half of my kingdom.' When she refused the loathsome potions pressed upon her, he knelt by the bedside, imploring her to make the effort for his sake. As she managed to swallow them and he left the room for a little rest, she murmured, 'The King loves me indeed—' and a few days later began to mend. During her convalescence she clung to him, kissing his hand. He left her to make a tour of the northern fortresses, returning for another honeymoon in the palace of Fontainebleau. Then her recovery was celebrated by a great tournament in the Place Royale.

Anne took her place in the royal gallery, which had been hung with violet velvet and embroidered with golden fleurs-de-lys, to watch her husband, in white satin, on a white charger, lead his team of thirty nobles to run at the ring. They lost the first round and won the second and third. The fourth was a draw; in the three following they won again. As the cheers broke out Louis turned to greet Pluvinel, his former riding-master. Smiling, the old man pointed towards the gallery, where the Queen stood, holding out the prize of a diamond ring. She had been so anxious for Louis to win that she was shaking, laughing, crying, all at once. He ran up the steps and flung his arms round her. As his courtiers saw the shy, awkward husband transformed into a gallant lover they cheered again, and the delighted Parisians burst into roars of applause. A few weeks later, sending for her to join him in the provinces, he scribbled one of many similar little notes: 'Come, come as happily as you will be greeted by him who passionately longs to see you.'

Then the shadows fell again. Marie de Medici had raised an army in Normandy, Vendôme another in Brittany and Anjou, d'Épernon a third in Saintonge. In Poitou, the Huguenots, under de Rohan, were killing their Catholic neighbours. Paris was in danger. At nineteen, Louis faced a civil and religious war.

His Council advised a parley, quarrelled and shrank from action. As the grumbling voices died away he stood up and said, 'Among so many hazards we must meet the nearest, that of Normandy. We should depart forthwith, and not wait in Paris while my realm is in danger and my faithful subjects are oppressed.' On July 7th, 1620, he set off for Caen. 'A thousand perils await Your Majesty there,' he was told. 'Perils here, there, on land and sea—let us make for Caen!' he replied. Ten days later the rebels surrendered, and he returned to Paris. Yet it was not the end. The wars of religion had begun.

II

If it is true that the successful ruler of the seventeenth century had to be brilliant, subtle and ruthless, then Louis XIII was not a great monarch. He was conscientious, brave, affectionate and, although modest and sensitive, very far from being weak or undecided. No King of France, not even his successor, worked harder; his refusal to spare himself was the despair of Héroard, as of all his doctors. On his journeys throughout the wars of the 1620s he never spent more than three or four nights in one place. Indeed, Héroard's journal and the records succeeding it show not only that Louis was always on the move, but that he travelled in conditions of the utmost hardship. He shared his soldiers' rations, was up and about before dawn, sometimes reviewed his troops for eight hours at a stretch and often spent sixteen to eighteen hours in the saddle, whatever the weather or the dangers. He trusted his officers and treated them as professional equals. His restlessness helped him to enjoy military life; but in his early twenties he missed his wife, as he did the time devoted to the arts, dancing (in which he excelled) and his hobbies and sports.

In Paris his routine was invariable and strenuous. He got up between six and seven, held a short *lever* and spent a long time in his bath. Sometimes he helped the valets to make his bed; then he breakfasted, took a short walk and heard Mass, after which he visited the Queen, held a Council, dined, hunted or played games, attended to business, saw the Queen again and was in bed by ten or eleven, thereafter rising to spend the night with her and returning to his own rooms in the small hours. Between receptions and after supper he appeared in ballets he or others had composed, or listened to concerts and plays performed by his own company or by travelling Italians.

He was still beardless, simply and elegantly dressed (his efforts to lessen his courtiers' expenditure were not popular) and had begun to lose his boyish good looks; but those seeing him for the first time felt that his rather large nose, pale complexion and too full lips were made up for by his athletic carriage, natural grace and informal geniality of address. His stammer sometimes enforced reserve; that did not affect his alertness or his courtesy. Every now and then, he was shy, but no longer awkward. He could be stern and was as outspoken in reproof as in praise. The coarseness and obscenity then in use disgusted him; but he enjoyed salted wit, and was not averse to mild practical joking. Those attempting to flatter, cringe or deceive got a crushing, sometimes an angry, reception.

Beneath this carapace of princely dignity and easy charm, Louis's deeper nature was developing on idealistic and dedicated lines. His duty and his religion were allied; that combination urged him to achieve unity throughout his kingdom. A devout Catholic, he yet hoped to practise his father's tolerance towards his Huguenot subjects. They themselves, operating on the belligerence of the Catholic majority, defeated the King's struggle for a peaceful co-ordination. As long as those dissenting from the national faith obeyed him and were loyal to his interests, Louis worked for their religious freedom; when they made alliances with the Protestant powers who threatened the prosperity and European status of France, he had no scruples about invading their territory and destroying their fortresses. He perceived, as many of his contemporaries did not, that rebellion, of whatever kind, within the realm, would bring back to it the appalling chaos and hideous suffering which his father had partially subdued.

Louis was naturally merciful and, when he could, cancelled or mitigated the ghastly punishments of his day, just as he saw to it that the humblest of his people were fairly treated. For he came to know, as no king of any country had ever known, the poorer classes, in his ceaseless journeys from one province to another; then he would put up at a farmhouse, help with the cooking and talk to the hosts in his jerky, kindly way, seldom forgetting a face or a name.

Above all, he had enough sense and humility to be aware of his limitations. He knew that he was neither an experienced diplomat, nor a skilled economist, nor a cunning exploiter of others' weakness; so it was that, in the second half of his reign, his personal authority seemed to be subordinated to that of Richelieu. In fact, they worked together, their respective talents complementing one another, much as did those of Queen Elizabeth and William Cecil, with this difference: Louis was fond of very few people, and at first the great Cardinal was not one of them.

Indeed, Louis's need for disinterested affection, his sensitivity and his physical frailty (he seldom had a whole year of perfect health) combined to make his life one of overwork, painful effort and recurrent disillusion. He was instinctively trusting, perpetually seeking love and constantly denying himself its consolations. Such a person, especially one in his position, is bound to be used and even betrayed by those on whom he depends. This was the case of Louis and de Luynes.

The favourite in no way resembled the degraded *mignons* of the Valois. But his triumph in the *coup d'état*, his high position as Constable of France and lord of vast estates had begun to estrange him from the King, who had, of course, done far too much for him. De Luynes could now ignore the youth he had rescued and, as it were, set on his feet as a husband; he may have thought that, because he had forced his master into certain activities, he was negligible. Without de Luynes, Louis's development might have been delayed, or less complete; as it was, finding happiness in his marriage, he no longer clung to the man he had raised to the highest office; and so he became aware, with a bitterness he never forgot, that de Luynes, having climbed on his shoulders, was now absorbed in his own splendour.

Shortly after putting down a rebellion near the Spanish frontier and thus uniting Béarn and Navarre in one faith and under one rule, Louis was talking with Marshal de Bassompierre as de Luynes, attended by his guards and gentlemen-in-waiting, came into the hall of the castle of St-Jean-d'Angély. 'See,' said Louis, 'the King enters.' De Bassompierre did not grasp the satire; in shocked tones, he replied, 'Sire, it is the Constable favoured by his master who displays *your* magnificence, and *your* rewards.' 'You do not know me,' said Louis. 'He thinks that I owe him so much that I should make him king. But he will never be that whilst I live.' He went on to complain of his friend to the Marshal, who warned de Luynes. This had no effect of any kind.

In fact de Luynes, having long ceased to be an asset, was now a liability. Timorous and muddle-headed, he had neither the liking nor the gift for active service. He appeared at his best in the incongruous periods of relaxation when the combatants summoned their wives and mistresses, organized concerts, ballets and tournaments, and picnicked in luxurious simplicity within a few yards of stinking corpses, burnt-out cities and smouldering ruins. In arbours of green boughs, waited on by gold-laced flunkeys, the Queen and her ladies, their glittering brocades and satins spread over a patch of meadow or a river bank, would dine to the music of lutes and viols, while their cavaliers, in bloodstained or powder-blackened finery, renewed the intrigues and the gallantries of the Tuileries and the Louvre. Louis would leave the trenches, still heaped with the bodies of his officers, to stage a mock battle in which fruit and flowers were the missiles, while the peasants hovered at a distance, staring at the great folk, and farmers' and merchants' wives came to present his courtiers with local delicacies.

In such idyllic interludes de Luynes still exercised some power; he and Louis would sup and chat together, as in the past; but when he failed to carry the siege of Montauban and made an ignominious and unnecessary retreat, he degraded his master more than himself. The King's waning affection turned to anger and disgust. He could not deprive the Constable of his honours and places in the midst of battle; while he waited to do so, de Luynes caught a fever, dying in the last week of December 1621.

For a short time Louis was cast down; but his responsibilities were too numerous, his decisions and plans too urgent to indulge a sorrow which must have been tinged with relief. The body of de Luynes was embalmed and dispatched to the nearest of his estates; as the black-draped chariot rumbled over the roads, his valets diced and played cards on the coffin.

Still Gascony was not subdued; the Protestants of La Rochelle were in revolt; and those of Basse-Guyenne were planning the establishment of a republic on the lines of the United Provinces of Holland. But Paris was safe; Marie de Medici had returned, apparently submissive and under the guidance of Richelieu, to the Louvre. In March 1622 Louis joined her there, to find his wife pregnant again, in excellent health and inseparably attached to the widowed Duchesse de Luynes, who married the Duc de Chevreuse a few weeks later. Then came disaster: another miscarriage, caused by Anne's subjection to the giddy high spirits of her new friend, who, encouraging her to run and slide in the slippery galleries of the palace, let her fall, and with her the hope of an heir.

Louis was infuriated, less with Madame de Chevreuse (who had tried, unsuccessfully, to flirt with him) than with the Queen. They had been married eight years, four in the fullest sense, and it was clear that she was fertile and reasonably healthy. Now, through an idiotic caprice, she had not only endangered the establishment of a dynasty, but the peace of a kingdom; for as long as she remained childless there was always danger of a *coup d'état*, either from Marie de Medici on behalf of the fourteen-year-old Gaston, or from Condé, whose Catholicism would not prevent him siding with the Protestant rebels. Louis began to see that his wife's pretty face and caressing ways concealed a selfish, frivolous stupidity. She made a gracious, even an impressive, public figure: but that was all. She preferred Madame de Chevreuse's fooleries and the giggling interchange of jokes and stories of that lady's circle to her duty as a queen. His anger turned to weariness and boredom; when he left Paris to renew the campaign in Royan and Toulouse, he was thankful to be free of her.

Louis remained at the head of his armies and in constant danger from March 1622 till January 1623. At this time he told de Bassompierre that the failure of de Luynes to raise the siege of Montauban had cost him many tears; there should be no more favourites in his life. Meanwhile, his staff, enraged by the appointment of de Puysieux, Sillery's son, to the Secretaryship of State, contrived a cabal against him and de Bassompierre, with which Louis had to deal, in the midst of his military duties. The King's tolerance encouraged de Condé to take advantage of his rank. He and his entourage would enter Louis's quarters unannounced, or even send for him, to discuss some triviality. 'God! what a trouble these men are!' Louis burst out to de Bassompierre. 'If they want to pass the time, they come to plague me, and for nothing.' 'They desire Your Majesty's advice,' said the Marshal. 'What advice?' Louis went on. 'They come at their pleasure, not at mine. Let them come when I send for them, asking my good leave. I will appoint my hour, not theirs.' Having established his authority over the Prince, he turned to deal with the local magistrates, who waited on him with a written complaint of his soldiers' cutting down trees for their camp-fires. Louis said, 'You can throw those statements in the fire. The woods and the men are mine, I'll hear no more!' He then wrote dismissing Madame de Chevreuse and her chief ally, his half-sister, Mademoiselle de Verneuil, from the Queen's service; a few weeks later they were reinstated, at Anne's instigation.

In May, joining the Marshal outside Royan, Louis said, 'Bassompierre, I am new here. Tell me what I must do in order not to fail,' and having been instructed, took charge. Several times he climbed out of the trench to make a reconnaissance, to the horror of his staff; later, as he rode away, a shot seemed to graze his helmet. 'Good God, Sire!' de Bassompierre exclaimed, 'that came near to killing you!' Louis, who had not moved, said simply, 'No, it came nearer to Monsieur d'Épernon' — and rode on. 'I have seen many other like actions on his part,' de Bassompierre, no flatterer, noted afterwards, 'and I never knew a man, nor a king, bolder — not even Henry IV.' A few days later, seeing one of his colonels falter and hearing him give the wrong order, Louis told him, 'If you cannot do better, I will break you, as I would a coward or a thief.' He was rather taken aback when, having threatened a defaulting engineer with dismissal, he was bluntly told, 'It's true, Sire, you should have done so.'

In appalling heat Louis reached Toulouse, where he became very ill with the tuberculosis from which he died twenty-one years later. He stayed in bed for a week, then struggled up, only to collapse again after he entered Béziers, emaciated, feverish, coughing, a ghastly figure. Here the heat was worse, but he managed to go on, taking Lunel after a long and bitter siege. Other triumphs followed, all too costly, and on his return to Paris he reorganized his Council, receiving Richelieu, who now obtained the cardinal's hat for which he had been angling for two years. So began the career which seemed, in the eyes of Europe and in those of most historians, to set the servant above the master. In March 1623 two more actors took the stage, bringing further complications, all disastrous. The future Charles I, then Prince of Wales, visited the Louvre, attended by his father's favourite, the inept but irresistible George Villiers, Duke of Buckingham.

FIVE

I

FROM Louis XIII's point of view, relations between France and England had not been satisfactory. Since his majority that nation of heretics had encouraged—sometimes openly, sometimes *sub rosa*—the rebellious elements in the Huguenot districts of his kingdom, and in November 1621 James I went so far as to send Lord Carlisle to negotiate between Louis and those of his Protestant subjects he had not been able to subdue. Louis's military situation forced him to submit to this humiliating intervention, for which de Luynes was partially responsible; and now the King's resentment of English insolence was renewed by the meteoric appearance of Buckingham and Charles, whose unofficial visit (they were on their way, incognito, to win the Spanish Infanta) enlivened his Court at his expense.

No one was much impressed by the stiff, diminutive Prince of Wales, whose stammer must have made his conversations with Louis an ordeal for both of them; but the magnificent Duke made his usual effect. The men's unwilling and envious admiration enhanced the women's ecstatic submission to his charm, his beauty and the jewelled splendours of his dress.

In his two-day visit Buckingham made what would now be called a dead set at the Queens and their ladies. He appeared in a ballet at the Louvre, gallantly approved the dancing of the thirteen-year-old Henrietta Maria and entranced Anne of Austria with his schemes for the Prince's courtship of her little sister, which was to be in the best romantic tradition—troubadour yearnings, moonlit rendezvous, amorous approaches, all in the manner of her favourite novelists.

Before the departure of the all-conquering Duke, Louis, no novel-reader, told him that, if he returned via Paris, he would not be received; when his wife and her entourage continued to talk of the fascinating Englishman, he announced that henceforth no gentleman was to visit her in his absence, a precaution which merely encouraged her schoolgirl rebelliousness and supplied Madame de Chevreuse ('*la Chevrette*') with material for further intrigue. His foolish embargo not only widened the gulf between them, but was taken by her as a personal insult. Deeply hurt by its implications, she fell back on Spanish pride, sulked, pouted and complained. Louis's coldness thereby increased; they continued on very bad terms, and in June 1623 she was found unconscious on the floor, bleeding from the mouth, nose and forehead. The Venetian ambassador reported apoplexy; others suspected a third miscarriage.

When the Queen went to St-Germain to convalesce, Louis again dismissed the Duchesse de Chevreuse. Anne wept and implored. Louis withdrew, inarticulate, miserable and exhausted. Between 1619 and 1623 he had covered the provinces of Orléans, Aunis, Saintonge, Guyenne and Gascony three times, and those of Touraine, Anjou, Picardy and Languedoc twice, appearing also in Normandy, Béarn, Nantes, Provence, Dauphiné, Comtat-Venaissin and Lyons. He had led his armies in five battles, successfully besieged as many fortresses and subdued a quantity of towns and estates. It was time he had a holiday; he spent it hunting in the district then known as Versailles-au-Val-de-Galie.

The woods lying between this flat, marshy country and St-Germain-en-Laye were full of game: foxes, deer, partridges, wolves. The open spaces contained a few cottages and two inns, all of the humblest kind. Here and there the marshes dissolved into ponds from which opaque vapours rose. *Galie*, the local name for the tracks of wild beasts, may have taken Louis's fancy; it is more likely that hunting in the neighbourhood with his father had brought him many happy hours and, later, soothing memories. Above all, the Val-de-Galie provided solitude and freedom; in the months succeeding his estrangement from his wife he returned to it again and again, and finally resolved to build a hunting-box there, on a scale which would enable him to live as a country squire. So the little château, long afterwards described by St Simon as a card-castle, came into being. A portion of the original building is still to be seen, enclosed in the overpowering and gorgeous palace of Louis's superb successor.

Between the summer of 1623 and the autumn of the following year Louis's dream of a woodland refuge was realized. An elegant yet solid red-and-white structure, it contained only fifteen main rooms; the three-storeyed central portion, twenty-four metres long and six in depth, was flanked by square mansarded towers and looked down over a miniature *perron* and a formal garden. The forest so enclosed it that the first *coup d'œil* must have given an impression of enchantment, of personal discovery and, to its owner, of possessive rapture. The privacy denied to kings—'those unhappy beings', Louis called them—was here achieved in exquisite beauty, in romantic peace, in shadowed isolation. Here he could relax with the selected entourage of those who shared his tastes; in such small, unpretentious rooms, hung, for the most part, in green, no minister, no ambassador could be received; here, after hours spent in dripping woods or steaming heat or frozen snowdrifts, he could play cards or billiards, and compose his songs and Masses with a group of young men who were neither politically minded nor constricted by protocol nor tediously sycophantic. The Versailles of the 1620s combined the amenities of a club and a comfortable home, 'of which,' de Bassompierre contemptuously remarked, 'the simplest country gentleman could not have boasted.'

In fact, the original château was exactly what the restless, over-taxed, secretive young King required. In it he could be himself. That self was oddly at variance with the public image adored by his subjects, and bore no resemblance to the gay, mischievous, friendly little Dauphin in whose chatter and high spirits his father and his courtiers had delighted. No King of France, not even 'our Henry', was more loved by his people, throughout his life; none was less understood. Louis's melancholic, capricious, rather sinister side was hidden from all but a few; and they never accustomed themselves to his violent changes of mood.

For this strange, generally impassive being seemed sometimes to revel in the macabre and the grotesque, in the manner of his Habsburg ancestors. He had been seen to imitate the dropped jaws and rolled-up eyes of dying men. In one ballet he appeared as a monstrous, hideously deformed old woman; in another as an Olympian deity, glittering and serene. Then the schoolboy prevailed, and he would become absorbed in some handicraft; then the artist, working at music, sculpture, painting; then the student, poring over medieval histories; then the huntsman, or the dedicated priest-monarch, or the journalist, writing anonymous reports of public events, or the military expert, technically equipped, inventive, meticulous. In some of his activities he failed, and knew that he did so; in one respect, that of easy gallantries and casual friendships, he had no success at all. A solitary, he disliked strangers. So it was that, as he reached his twenty-fourth year, he seemed to retreat behind the enormous shadow of Cardinal Richelieu.

The former Bishop of Luçon was thirty-nine when Louis, rather unwillingly, admitted him to the Council. They had in common one disability—for the Cardinal's physique was even frailer than his master's—and one ambition, that of restoring France to her former status. In a very short time Louis perceived the range of Richelieu's talents and valued him accordingly, while Richelieu, determined to retrieve the influence he had lost by his adherence to the Queen Mother, made it clear that Louis's authority was to be absolute and undeviatingly supported by himself.

The immediate result of this alliance was the Cardinal's predominance over every other minister; they all became negligible. Within a year he was supreme. Louis worked with him in almost perfect harmony and full appreciation of his genius, which was protean; so the patronage and support of such writers as Descartes, Corneille, Régnier and Malherbe fell to the man who founded the French Academy, partly because Louis's tastes rather inclined towards music and painting than literature.

No two men could have been more unlike. To the end of his life Louis was an idealist and a patriot. Richelieu saw the greatness of France as the basis of his own domination; and he would have found it difficult to say which he despised more, his fellow-men or their women-kind. Of the latter he remarked, 'One might think that these odd creatures cannot do harm because they do no good, yet I solemnly protest that they are more likely to ruin a kingdom than anyone else.'

He must have been thinking of Marie de Medici when he said this; having achieved his position through her pleading with the King (he had promised to restore her former power) Richelieu, gradually and with submissive courtesy, eliminated her from the political scene: yet in such a manner that she could not form a party against him. This arrangement was what Louis most desired. Filial loyalty and the lingering hope of gaining his mother's affection made it impossible for him to eliminate her himself.

The Cardinal's relations with the young Queen were more difficult. As soon as she realized that his policy rather tended

LOUIS XIII IN MATURITY

towards European combinations than towards dependence on Austria and Spain, she became hostile; and she resented his influence over Louis, in spite of the fact that it was as much in Richelieu's interests as in hers that she and her husband should found a dynasty. She did not trust him; no doubt she felt his contempt for her sex. Yet she was as helpless as her mother-in-law; she could do nothing against the pervasive, subtly exercised power which, screened by Louis's regality, coiled octopus tentacles round every department of state.

The process of this joint administration was exquisitely smooth. After prolonged study of some problem, based on information supplied by a carefully chosen force of agents, the Cardinal would make a précis of the matter, either orally or in writing, and place it before his master. Discussion followed, then a pause for thought, and then a request for Louis's orders. And here the element of equality, imperceptible to so many, was created. If Louis had been stupid, conceited or heedless, he would have asserted himself in Richelieu's despite, just to show he was master. In fact, when he did not approve, an alternative had to be evolved; but on the whole, he and Richelieu saw eye to eye, because they were both intelligent, practical, and moving—for different reasons—in the same direction. Furthermore, Louis was beginning to realize that he must sometimes spare himself. His public and military duties and his fluctuating health made delegation of certain activities essential. In the same way, Richelieu found it highly convenient to refuse an offer or reject a scheme by sheltering behind the authority of the monarch. So a quantity of much-needed reforms, affecting the whole administration of the country, were not only put in hand but carried out, to the disgust of those who now began to yearn for the good old days of murderous duelling, unfairly developed properties and the jurisdiction of an inept and over-privileged aristocracy.* The Cardinal could afford to despise popularity; Louis's love of his people and his dedication to their welfare made him dependent on it.

It was generally supposed that Richelieu's influence on the King turned him towards a consistency of conduct bordering on harshness. This was far from being the case. Before he reached his teens Louis had said to Héroard, 'I must not only be just, but *do justice,*'

---

* In 1627 François de Montmorency-Bouteville killed Bussy-d'Amboise, another famous duellist, who was his twenty-second victim.

so emphatically that the doctor recorded the words in awe and wonder. When he was sixteen, a lady whose husband had been condemned to death for duelling knelt at his feet imploring mercy, and was told, 'I owe my subjects justice, and in this case I must put justice before mercy.' So those who failed the state, whether through treachery, incompetence or misfortune, were cast out, imprisoned, or, in the worst cases, executed. Louis's most celebrated remark — 'I could not be a king if I allowed myself the indulgence of private feelings' — although made after the Cardinal's rise to power, was merely a summing up of the principles he had followed since childhood. Louis paid, in secret misery, for all his orders for imprisonment or execution. Richelieu saw the gates close and the heads fall with perfect serenity.

II

By the summer of 1624 Louis's mistrust of Richelieu had disappeared. Their most urgent concern was to prevent the Spanish dominion of Europe, as it was that of all the Protestant powers. They began by insuring the independence of the much disputed Valtelline territory and went on to arrange the marriage of the fifteen-year-old Henrietta Maria with the Prince of Wales. In May 1625 Charles, having succeeded his father, sent Buckingham to fetch home his bride. The Duke at once began to court Anne of Austria.

The genius of a great novelist has recorded for all time, and not altogether inaccurately, Buckingham's effect on the Queen. She was technically innocent; in no circumstances would she have committed adultery. But although she rejected his inflated gallantries, she was flattered by them, and seems to have seen herself as the virtuous heroine of an *amour courtois* romance: as the faithful wife of a neglectful and unappreciative husband. That the famous scene of temptation need never have taken place was Louis's first thought. He knew his own inadequacy; and he could not forgive Anne for having allowed the beautiful and dashing favourite of two kings first to speak with her alone in a garden at night, and then to enter her bedchamber without leave. Her defence was equally reasonable. She had called for help as soon as the Duke began to make love to her, and had ordered him out of her room. ('She is at least faithful from the waist down,' remarked one of her ladies.) What more could be expected?

Louis remained suspicious and hostile. Further mischief was made by Marie de Medici, who thought that she might regain power if the young couple were permanently estranged; meanwhile, the younger Queen blamed Richelieu for her husband's attitude. She felt herself unjustly persecuted and spied upon, and was further chagrined by the departure of Madame de Chevreuse, whom Louis sent to England in his sister's suite. That lady then became the mistress of Lord Holland. A year later she, with others of Henrietta Maria's entourage, was sent back to France by Charles I, on the grounds that she had influenced his wife against him.

Anne of Austria tried to revive her husband's love. She might have succeeded if she had become pregnant, or freed herself from the trivial gossip of her women, or attempted to share his private interests. She was incapable of so enlarging her horizon; and she deeply resented Louis's friendship with François de Baradas, a dull and simple young man, whom the King had made his Chief Whip (*écuyer de la petite écurie*) and First Gentleman of the Bedchamber. There was no question of Baradas influencing his master in any way; and Richelieu employed him to report on the King's daily life.

At this time the Cardinal's actions were those of a careful guardian. Louis's reserve made it difficult to find out what his thoughts and wishes were; and Richelieu was sufficiently in advance of his age to grasp the connection of mind and body in the case of a delicate and sensitive person. 'Your Majesty's temperament,' he told Louis, 'so rules your physique that the slightest emotion affects your health and may disrupt your powers.' If Louis died or became an invalid — both recurrent possibilities — then the whole equilibrium of the state was endangered. His heir-presumptive, the eighteen-year-old spoilt darling of the Queen Mother, had had his eye on the throne for some years. And Richelieu knew that his accession would be an unmitigated disaster.

For Gaston was a frivolous, conceited, false, brainless fop, whose only talents were those of mimicry and indoor games, interspersed with petty intrigues against his brother. He had a good figure and dressed well; this rather drew attention to than concealed his adenoidal tendencies—his mouth was perpetually ajar—his pendulous features and blank, protuberant stare. He had already proved himself a nuisance of the first order; yet the King was an affectionate brother, and had never competed with him for their mother's favour. When Louis was sixteen and Gaston eight, and they were supping with her, Louis hesitated to ask for one of the marzipan apples which Gaston was devouring; so he whispered to the boy to pass him one secretly, and ate it at the sideboard. This incident partially illustrates the family scene, in the sense that Louis always wanted to please Gaston and his mother, if he could do so without sacrificing his integrity; their joint machinations now made this impossible; and the question of Gaston's marriage further complicated the situation.

In his sixth year Henry IV had contracted him to the richest heiress in Europe, a Guise cousin: Mademoiselle de Montpensier, Princesse de Dombes. Their marriage had been delayed lest his children should precede the King's. Now, in order not to lose this great prize, arrangements were made for the wedding to take place at Nantes, where the Court spent the summer of 1626.

Until then, neither Richelieu nor Louis knew that a cabal had been formed round Gaston, headed by his Governor, Marshal d'Ornano, the Comte de Chalais (Louis's Master of the Wardrobe), his two half-brothers, Alexander and Caesar de Vendôme, and the ubiquitous Madame de Chevreuse, who was now de Chalais's mistress. They had planned a *coup d'état* in which Richelieu was to be assassinated at a dinner-party given by Gaston; Louis would then be declared incapable of sovereignty and forced into monastic retirement while his marriage was dissolved, upon which Gaston would marry Anne of Austria, or, failing a dispensation, one of the Vendômes. There was a possibility that Louis's murder would follow that of his minister.

The first step was made by Gaston, who told his brother that he did not wish to marry Marie de Montpensier. In this he was supported by Anne, who was appalled at the thought of his bride having children before she did. She was, of course, entirely innocent of any design against her husband; but her attachment to Madame de Chevreuse, and thus to de Chalais, involved her, unwittingly, in Gaston's schemes, or rather, in those of d'Ornano, who was the moving spirit in the affair.

68

The Marshal had reckoned without Richelieu's spy system, which was by now perfected. As soon as d'Ornano had been arrested, the Cardinal confronted Gaston with his discovery. Cringing and protesting, Monsieur gave away the names of all the conspirators except de Chalais, assured Richelieu of his loyalty to his brother and declared himself ready to marry Mademoiselle de Montpensier. The Court then moved to Nantes, where Alexander and Caesar de Vendôme were seized and imprisoned. On July 12th Gaston, having been reconciled to the King, was approached by de Chalais and Madame de Chevreuse: now that he had regained his position, why should they not continue with the plot?

He agreed, thought better of it and confessed to the King, with the result that de Chalais was arrested and his mistress banished to Lorraine. On August 5th Gaston's marriage to Mademoiselle de Montpensier was celebrated. A few days later de Chalais was told to prepare for death—Louis refused to sign the order for the preliminary process of torture—and spent the night in prayer. It then occurred to Gaston that he might save the man he had betrayed by having the headsman kidnapped, and in the early morning of the 19th he, with his axe, disappeared. A condemned criminal, formerly a butcher, was called in; unnerved by the crowds and by the presence of de Chalais's mother, the understudy struck thirty times before killing his victim.

Richelieu heard the details of the scene without emotion. The King, who had known de Chalais since childhood, was in agony; unable to eat or sleep, he continued to brood over the plot, in which he believed his wife to have been involved. Richelieu, aware of her enmity towards himself, decided that she should be taught a lesson. So the Queen of France and daughter of the King of Spain was summoned, like any ordinary suspect, to answer to the charges of conspiracy and high treason. She asseverated and proved her innocence, adding, 'What could I have gained by such a change?' Richelieu, who wanted only to frighten her, advised Louis to accept her defence. But the breach between husband and wife was complete. He could not entirely banish his suspicions: and she never forgave them.

In September the Court returned to Paris. Gaston, now Duc d'Orléans, was heard vowing vengeance on the Cardinal, whose guard of musketeers was increased by the King. Louis then took refuge at Versailles, to find that Baradas was assuming the airs of a great man and neglecting his duties. Richelieu suggested that he should be replaced by an under-sized, grotesquely plain nineteen-year old, Claude de Rouvroy, known as the Flea, a skilled huntsman with no ambitions beyond the chase. He was friendly and gay, and Louis became mildly attached to him—'first,' he told another courtier, 'because he always knows where the game is, and secondly because, when he blows his horn, he does not spit into it.' Two years later de Rouvroy was made First Gentleman of the Bedchamber and Duc de Saint Simon. His only son, the greatest of all memoirists, was born in 1675.

Meanwhile, the activities of Madame de Chevreuse ('I do not care for innocent pleasures,' was one of her most celebrated catchphrases) followed the usual pattern. She had become the mistress of Charles, Duc de Lorraine, and was urging him to continue the rebellion begun by the Vendômes. By this time Louis and Richelieu had a more urgent problem on their hands. The Duke of Buckingham, incensed at his dismissal from the French Court, had sent forces to the help of the Protestant rebels in La Rochelle and elsewhere. Two French ships were captured. At a Cabinet meeting the ministers agreed with Richelieu that, 'while the Huguenots remain in France, the King has neither mastery within his kingdom, nor glory beyond it.' In January 1627 war between France and England was declared.

SIX

I

EIGHT years after Louis told Héroard that he avoided his wife because she 'excited' him, he was sleeping with her regularly, although he no longer loved her. He was bent on his duty as a king; but that he was able to possess her may be accounted for by her attitude towards himself, and towards men in general. She now knew and could exercise her powers of attraction. When Richelieu made advances to her, she rejected them; yet her description of this curious scene indicates a certain triumph. Quite apart from her desperate need of a child, she loved Louis; and their estrangement was not made up for by his spending the nights with her, for this had no effect on his cold and formal approach in the daytime. She blamed Richelieu for her unhappy situation, not realizing that the King suspected her of intriguing with Spain and thus weakening France's position, which had now become extremely precarious.

Between January 1627 and September 1630 Louis fought two wars, one against the Anglo-Huguenot forces of La Rochelle, and one against the Spaniards and their Piedmontese allies in the Italian Alps. In both he was victorious. The English were as ignominiously routed after Buckingham's murder as before it. In their attempt to disembark from the Île de Ré they lost four thousand men, and forty English banners were captured to hang in Notre Dame. The French were so eager to invest Ré that Louis, remaining to command the mainland forces, had to ration the number of volunteers. To the cries of 'And I, Sire? Am I not to go?' he replied with a smile, 'Do you want to leave me all alone here?'

In the autumn of 1628 the English attempted another invasion. When they saw the fortifications of La Rochelle, the sailors mutinied and sailed away, leaving their starving Huguenot allies to submit to Louis, who once more promised them religious freedom in return for their loyalty to himself, thereafter entering Paris in triumph.

71

He did so with a heavy heart. Héroard had died in the preceding January at the age of seventy-eight; Gaston's wife, having given birth to the child later known as La Grande Mademoiselle, had left him a widower, and Louis himself had been very ill. During the anti-Spanish campaign of the Pas-de-Suse his health improved, and he received the homage of his defeated brother-in-law, the Prince of Piedmont, with encouraging graciousness. When the Prince knelt to kiss his boot, Louis turned to embrace the sister he had not seen for ten years with a radiant face. That peace was signed in April 1629, followed by one with England a few days later.

Still the Huguenots of Montauban and Languedoc were in revolt, and Louis, leaving Richelieu to continue the Spanish campaign, took the field against the Duc de Rohan, defeating him in June of this year. After a progress through Provence he returned to Fontainebleau in September, to find that Gaston and Marie de Medici had made a pact to eliminate Richelieu. When the Cardinal joined his master he defeated them by offering, with a burst of tears, to resign. Louis assured him of his loyalty, 'to my last breath', summoned Gaston—who had retired, in the sulks, to Orléans—and patched up a peace between the minister and his family.

In April 1630 Louis left Paris to defend the frontier fortress of Pignerol against the Spaniards; he was in excellent health and spirits, for Anne was pregnant. Surely, after eleven years of disappointment, he might hope for an heir. In May she miscarried, and Louis, after four months' strenuous campaigning over a large area, fell desperately ill of dysentery at Lyon, where Anne joined him. On September 21st his life was despaired of; he sent for his confessor and said, 'If you believe that I am in danger, do not hesitate to say so, for I am not afraid to die.' Two days later he became delirious and began to vomit blood; he was then given the last sacraments. He asked the doctors—who were bleeding him regularly—what chance he had. 'There is nothing more to be done,' was the answer, and again he prepared himself for death. He then sent for his courtiers and the Queen, asked their forgiveness for any injuries he might have done them, and signed to Anne to come to the bedside. He kissed her and tried, in vain, to speak. As a last resort, he was bled from the arm. The doctors said that he must die before nightfall.

That evening the fever diminished, and Louis asked for food. He continued to mend, and by October 11th was convalescent, although very weak. Anne chose this moment to urge the dismissal of Richelieu. 'I am sorry that I have been harsh with you,' said Louis, 'but I can come to no decision until I have made peace with Spain,' and that night succumbed to another attack of fever. By the end of October he was well enough to leave for Fontainebleau, and to speak to Gaston. 'We are good friends now,' he wrote to the Cardinal, 'but I fear it may not last.' Finally he reached the haven of Versailles, where he improved so rapidly that he was able to hunt, St Simon told Richelieu, 'as merrily as if he had never been ill.' During his brief holiday Marie de Medici and Gaston began their final campaign against their great enemy. This time the odious Cardinal should not escape.

They had many powerful allies, for Richelieu was more hated and feared than most reformers; and few, if any, of his contemporaries could have been expected to see that his reorganization of the kingdom, supported by the royal authority, would finally make France a great power and destroy for ever her subordination to the Habsburg empires. Louis alone valued his services at their proper worth; he disregarded, or perhaps did not always perceive, the Cardinal's ruthlessness and hypocrisy. Richelieu could be agreeable, even charming; he was an expert soldier; he shared the King's aesthetic tastes; but he was cold, calculating and self-interested. So it followed that he was detested not only by such despicable intriguers as Marie de Medici and Monsieur, but also by those patriotic and high-minded servants of the state who saw in his policy the destruction of what they most valued, and were prepared to effect his downfall at any cost to themselves.

Richelieu despised them all. Apart from a few hangers-on, Louis was the only person who had his trust and loyalty. He knew that the King was weak as far as his mother and brother were concerned, and that he would not punish or exile them unless forced to do so. He therefore made it his business outwardly to remain on good terms with both.

On November 9th, 1630, Louis returned to Paris. After his daily visit to his mother he saw Richelieu and asked him if he and she were good friends. Something in his manner seems to have disquieted the Cardinal; but he replied reassuringly. Neither he nor Louis then knew the extent or the strength of the cabal formed against him; headed by Marie de Medici and Gaston, it included, among others, Anne of Austria, the King's most distinguished general Louis de Marillac, his brother Michel who was Keeper of the Seals, Bassompierre, the Duc de Guise and several of Anne's ladies, who formed a liaison between her and Philip IV, the natural supporter of any plot which would bring down his most stubborn enemy.

On the morning of the 10th Richelieu, having decided to make his customary visit to the Queen Mother at the same time as Louis, went to the Palace of the Luxembourg, to be told that she had taken a purge and could see no one. Increasingly perturbed, he sent for Michel de Marillac, and received the same formal excuse. When he reached his own palace, he found it deserted. The antechambers were empty. Then he knew the worst. Louis had agreed to his removal.

He returned to the Luxembourg. On the stairs he met Michel de Marillac. 'Sir! They told me you were ill?' Marillac made no reply and the Cardinal hurried on; he saw no pages, no gentlemen-in-waiting. He tried the doors leading to the Queen Mother's apartments; all were locked. He was shut out. To go back to his own rooms would be to find himself under arrest.

Then he remembered the little staircase leading from Marie de Medici's bedchamber to the chapel. He ran up it; the door opened. He drew aside the curtain. There was the King, with his mother. Smiling, Richelieu advanced and said, 'I will wager that Your Majesties were talking of me.'

Marie de Medici muttered a denial. Then she burst into a torrent of abuse. Purple-faced, gesticulating, her voice breaking into a scream, she let fly at the traitor, villain, thief—accusing him, among other crimes, of planning to marry his favourite niece to Monsieur. *That* creature—a nobody—everyone knew what she was; but they were all to go—his friends, his dependents, all!

She came up to him, waving her arms, her face close to his. He tried to speak; it was useless. He knelt, weeping. She stood over him. 'Crocodile tears—!' (Her language, he noted, was such as he had never heard from any woman.)

At last Louis broke in. 'But Madame—Madame! You torture me—you offend me—' He stopped, white and shaking.

Suddenly silence fell. Marie de Medici was panting for breath. The Cardinal wiped his eyes, and said quietly that he would admit to any fault, if he might only resign. 'I am not well, I cannot continue,' he went on. 'What does Her Majesty wish? How may I serve her?'

The furious woman turned away. As Louis began to intercede for Richelieu, she rounded on him. 'You put a servant above your mother!' Louis said to Richelieu, 'You may go.'

In the courtyard Richelieu waited, watching Louis's coach. He appeared, said 'To Versailles,' and drove away, without a look or a sign. It was all over. Richelieu went home and prepared to fly.

As the coach rumbled out into the Rue de Vaugiron, Louis told the man to take him to the Hôtel des Ambassadeurs, where he was staying until the alterations to the Louvre had been completed. He went to his cabinet. St Simon alone was in attendance. 'Lock the doors,' said the King, and as the young man obeyed flung himself into a chair, tearing off his doublet so violently that the buttons rattled to the floor. St Simon dared not speak. 'Where is he?' said Louis at last. 'But Sire—here,' St Simon replied, and went to find the Cardinal.

Richelieu was setting off for Le Havre, when he was told to wait on His Majesty the next morning at Versailles. He knelt; Louis, who was standing with his gentlemen, raised and kissed him. Then he said, 'You are my faithful and loving servant. I know that you are not undutiful to the Queen my mother.' He added that Marie had been misled by a cabal, of which he now knew all the details. 'Continue to serve me as heretofore,' he concluded, 'and I will protect you against your enemies.'

The Cardinal produced another burst of tears and a second offer of resignation. The result was excellent. There could be no question of a parting, now or ever. He spoke of the Queen Mother's vengeance, and was reassured. So ended the famous Day of Dupes. Richelieu had lost his power for exactly twenty-four hours.

Vengeance followed: but not that of the Queen Mother. Michel de Marillac was deprived of his post and imprisoned. His brother Louis was recalled and, with de Bassompierre, sent to the Bastille. Meanwhile, Gaston had fled to Orléans, with a million livres' worth of valuables, given him by Marie de Medici; from there he formed an army and prepared to march on Paris.

Louis, having dismissed some half-dozen of the young Queen's ladies, went to the medieval fortress of Compiègne. There he was pursued by his mother. Another appalling scene ensued. Louis refused to listen; then he gave orders that she was to be confined to her apartments and, returning to Paris, summoned the Parlement, to whom he announced his support of all Richelieu's reforms. He added that anyone who joined or adhered to Monsieur was guilty of high treason and would suffer death. They protested. He was adamant, and they gave in.

Returning to Compiègne, he told his mother that she must retire to Moulins. She refused. Gaston then appeared in Paris and, bursting into Richelieu's apartments, began to shout and bluster. 'If you were not a priest — !' But, somehow, his dagger was not drawn from its sheath, and he went away. He was next heard of in Lorraine, with the Duc de Guise.

In the months that followed the Marshal de Marillac was accused of betraying his country to Spain and was beheaded. The Queen Mother, screaming, 'If you wish me to leave Compiègne, you will have to drag me out by the hair!', shut herself up and, in July 1631, escaped to the Spanish Netherlands. She and Gaston then prepared to invade. The Duc de Lorraine came to plead with Louis for him. The King replied enigmatically, and Lorraine returned to help Gaston collect an army. Louis made Richelieu Duke and Peer of France and Governor of Brittany. He never saw his mother again.

So he triumphed — alone. Richelieu had become the symbol of his victory. Throughout France, his people acclaimed the master and the servant. Anne of Austria, bereft, frightened, bewildered, prostrated herself, begging his favour. Louis was kind but distant. He allowed her to accompany him everywhere, and continued to treat her with cold politeness. Then it was observed that he was paying marked attentions to one of her ladies, the exquisitely blonde Mademoiselle de Hautefort. He was always talking to her in the Queen's ante-chamber. When she fell ill, he sent to inquire every day.

II

With Louis's final separation from his mother his life entered another phase. Now he was no longer divided between filial and monarchic loyalties. The open enmity of Marie de Medici eliminated moral conflict, while adding to his burdens. Yet his health improved as his activities increased; his energy became demonic. The records of his journeyings—which involved sieges, battles, conferences, Parliamentary meetings and processions—show that he travelled all day and almost every day, seldom stopping for more than twenty-four hours in one place, heading his armies one month, holding a bed of justice the next, and galloping at break-neck speed for hours at a time in order to conduct an advance, discuss terms with an ally, crush an uprising or reward a supporter. His correspondence with Richelieu, with provincial potentates, with those patricians whose wavering loyalty was one of his greatest problems, with foreign ministers and the heads of states, shows an extraordinary grasp of essentials, as of the European complications in which the fortunes of France were involved. For the Thirty Years' War, which began when Louis was sixteen, was now shaking his realm; and Gaston's intermittent efforts to bring in the Spanish against him enhanced his difficulties. Finally, the resolve of those nobles whose rule, with their ideas, dated from the Middle Ages, to prevent the central control and modernization of the country, made civil war inevitable and constant.

The disagreeable aspect of this modernization—taxes, regula-tions, cruel punishments—was attributed to Richelieu, whose power was upheld by the King's stern absolutism and unremitting assiduity. If Louis had had time to think about himself, he would have been sunk in gloom and bad temper; he seldom gave way to either; but now his impassivity concealed iron resolution and harshness. He was no longer agonized or even disturbed by the execution of men he had known all his life. Unmoved, he rejected the pleas of weeping relatives and desperately imploring friends. His cold yet courteous replies—'There can be no mercy for a traitor'—'I am sorry, but he must die'—were calmly uttered and submissively received.

Still he could not rest. As soon as he had a moment's freedom he was off and away with his huntsmen till nightfall, in all weathers. In other intervals he saw to new buildings, talked with architects, chose tapestries, sat to portrait-painters and studied plans, pausing to compose a new ballet or inspect an invention. He was always available and on view; his palaces in Paris and the provinces were crowded with sightseers; he took off his hat to them all; he had a word or a mild joke for the humblest.

If Louis had not been supported by his people's love he might not have sustained the loneliness, the hardships and worries which increased every year. In January 1632 Gaston secretly married Marguerite de Lorraine, the sister of Louis's greatest enemy, and obtained money for an invasion from Philip IV. In June Louis seized the Duchy of Bar, which enabled him to bring Charles of Lorraine to his knees. Then the Spanish attacked Trèves, and Louis hurried to help the Elector. When Gaston opened his campaign in Languedoc, Louis sent the Duc de Montmorency, the richest and most powerful of his vassals, to take the field against his brother. But Montmorency joined Gaston (who failed to supply the troops he had promised) and was defeated, captured and beheaded in October, while Monsieur, having once more submitted to Louis, fled to his mother in Brussels.

Louis's alliances with Gustavus Adolphus of Sweden and with the states of Saxony, Savoy, Tuscany, Mantua and Montferrat were a strong but by no means an invulnerable defence against the Habsburg powers. In November Gaston combined with Charles of Lorraine to raise Languedoc, Champagne and Normandy. Once more, Louis defeated them, and became master of Alsace; and once more, his brother withdrew. Then Richelieu, who had been seriously ill, made one of his few mistakes. Hoping to win Anne of Austria's favour, he allowed Madame de Chevreuse to rejoin her entourage—a pointless and dangerous gesture. When Louis visited his wife, he found her hostile and defiant. She and her ladies continued to abuse the Cardinal, one of whose diseases was haemorrhoids. They called him Rotten-Arse—was it not apt? Louis turned away, towards Mademoiselle de Hautefort. Her response was too bold; when she indicated that the note he was expecting would be found between her breasts, he picked up a pair of tongs to remove it. ('What an idiot!' exclaimed Madame de Chevreuse, when she heard the story.)

This recoil gave Saint Simon the impression that all his master needed was a go-between. After the King had been speaking at length and, it seemed to him, passionately, of Mademoiselle de Hautefort, he said, 'I will be Your Majesty's ambassador, and arrange the affair for you.' Louis stared at him; then, in his severest manner, he replied, 'It's true that I am in love with her, that I seek, talk and think of her, I cannot help it, being a man. But it is weak, and as my station makes it easier for me to succeed, so I must take greater care to avoid sin and scandal.' As St Simon stood abashed he added gently, 'I forgive you, because you are young—but never talk so to me again, if you wish me to go on liking you'—and walked out of the room.

To describe this reproof as that of a prig would be to lose perspective. Although Louis desperately needed a mistress, his adherence to God's law and his marriage vow was even more necessary, if he were to retain his self-confidence. Also, his resistance to Mademoiselle de Hautefort's charms may have had something to do with his growing awareness of her character. He knew that he was not attractive to women; and presently he perceived that it was not the man but the king in whom she was interested. Later he realized that she, with Madame de Chevreuse and his wife, made fun of his shyness and lack of gallantry; yet for nearly two years he was subjugated by her beauty. So, as his loneliness increased, he fell back on his care for St Simon's education, and became more dependent on that rather simple youth's response. 'You must not address the Duc de Bellegarde in that fashion,' he would point out, and help his protégé to rewrite the letter, as he would have helped the son for whom he longed—as indeed, he would have advised or trained the brother who was not only destroying all his work, but who, through Madame de Chevreuse, had installed a traitor in his household. This was Châteauneuf, now Keeper of the Seals, whom the Duchesse had persuaded to report all Louis's plans to Spain.

In April 1633 Châteauneuf was discovered and imprisoned. In the following year Gaston's marriage became known and was annulled by Parlement. For the fourth time Monsieur, hoping to cancel the annulment, submitted himself to Louis and was received by him and Richelieu in October 1634.

It was impossible for the King to punish or imprison his brother as long as he was heir-presumptive. The probability that Louis might die leaving no son to succeed him had to be taken into account, and thus Gaston must be induced rather than forced into a semblance of loyalty, in the hope that he would abandon his Spanish allies. Up to now Louis and Richelieu had known that they might withstand but were not likely to defeat the Habsburg powers, partly because their armies were not yet up to standard, and partly because the national finances were still in a precarious state. During the winter of 1634-5 they both worked at these reforms, while Richelieu, with the help of his famous 'Grey Eminence', Father Joseph, and the former papal Nuncio, Cardinal Mazarin, formed an anti-Spanish league with Sweden, Germany and Holland. At the same time, he put a spy in Gaston's household, the Comte de Chavigny, who became Monsieur's Chancellor. His reports indicated that Gaston was more interested in confirming his marriage than in Spanish intrigue; but Anne of Austria was wholly committed to the Habsburgs, and doing all she could to warn them of her husband's plans.

Yet she and Louis kept up an almost impenetrable façade. She accompanied him on most of his journeys and all his public appearances. They took the waters together, entertained and presented seven-hour-long ballets, in which Louis danced the principal parts; he continued to visit her twice daily. In May 1635 he declared war on Spain, and still she continued to work against him. His knowledge of her treachery must have estranged them; yet it seems that he sometimes spent the nights with her. She complained of his neglect; but chiefly on account of his coldness of manner. Then his private life was revolutionized. He fell passionately in love with a gentle, pious and innocent girl of seventeen—Louise de Lafayette, who had been one of the Queen's ladies for some five years.

SEVEN

I

LOUISE DE LAFAYETTE was the daughter of an ancient and noble house, whose properties had dwindled to a small estate in Auvergne. One of her cousins, the Marquise de Sénécey, was Mistress of the Robes, and she was the sister-in-law of Marie-Madeleine de La Vergne, the author of *La Princesse de Clèves*. Her upbringing had been strict and her tastes were those of a country-woman. A round-faced, snub-nosed brunette, her only beauty was her large dark-blue eyes; her serious expression gave her a slightly formidable air. She was devoted to the Queen and extremely puritanical; but when Louis began to notice her she fell in love with him.

He first became aware of her at a ballet, for which he had composed the music and the choreography, and which celebrated the opening of the shooting season. On March 20th, 1635, he, the Queen and their Court rode out to the forest of Chantilly, and he saw that Louise was an accomplished horsewoman. During the course of that single day his love attained full strength. He could think of no one else; and as the weeks went by he perceived that he had found his ideal in a woman who shared his tastes (he had never before come upon one who liked talking about hawks and hounds) and who loved him for himself. From the beginning of their short relationship to its melancholy end, she not only refused to make use of him, but tried to free herself from the sin of loving him so well. Her piety went as deep as his; and her unsophisticated, simpler nature made her shrink from his advances, although he became dearer to her than anyone else in the world. Yet, knowing that this world was but a preparation for the next, she would not commit fornication with the forlorn, ailing man whose one hope of happiness was in her power.

As soon as their situation became apparent, Louise and the King were surrounded and spied upon by those determined to profit from it. At first, the Cardinal favoured her — she was unlikely to stand between him and his master—and, through Madame de Sénécey, urged her to yield; the Queen was resigned, trusting in her loyalty; and Louis himself, sympathizing with her scruples, set out to win her with gentle and patient persuasion.

After some happy days at St-Germain, Louis's courtship was interrupted by the war with Spain. For four and a half months— from April till August 1635—he travelled on military duties. Then the Queen and her ladies joined him at Monceaux, where Louise fell ill, and in his letters to Richelieu he sent agitated reports of her progress. He did not see her again till he returned to spend Christmas at St-Germain. He then discovered that she disliked and mistrusted Richelieu. Not only so: she implored Louis to heal the breach with his wife (she did not know that Anne was betraying him to his enemies) and to receive the Queen Mother. Richelieu, informed of these persuasions by Louise's confessor, Father Carré, tried, without success, to win her over. Louise, finding her situation intolerable, decided to extricate herself by turning towards a higher power. She told Father Carré that she wished to become a nun.

It seems that the King had been counting on her subjugation. In the misery and longing of absence he had consoled himself with the vision of Louise, radiantly installed in the enchanted solitudes of Versailles, always there waiting for him, understanding, loving, the gift of happiness in her hands. Surely she could not deny him; their love was divinely inspired; and he could no longer endure the burden of kingship without her, his *alter ego*. So he reasoned and implored. She withstood him, in agony for them both. She would never love anyone else; therefore she must go. Then, appalled by the thought of all she would lose, and doubting the reality of her vocation, she put off her decision, avoiding Louis whenever she could bring herself to do so and seeking guidance from an apparently Sphinx-like deity. There seemed no solution, or at least none that she could face.

By this time Louis's armies were fighting on four fronts—the Escaut, the Rhine, the Alps and the Pyrenees—so that his activities were proportionately increased. In October 1636 Gaston, having formed another plot to murder Richelieu, lost his nerve at the last moment and fled to Blois. A month later the fortress of Corbie was taken from the Spaniards by the French, and Louis, returning to Paris, attended the first performance of *Le Cid*. He then left to deal with the rebellion raised by Gaston, and dismissed St Simon, who had become insolent and overbearing; so he was even lonelier than before.

In January 1637 Richelieu, informed by Father Carré that His Majesty was more than ever enthralled by 'the little creature', decided to eliminate her, and told Carré to influence her towards convent life. Still she could not make up her mind; and then the tortured King turned upon her. She was playing with him; if she wanted to be a nun, she had better become one, and end this miserable suspense. They parted, and he wept all night. Next day, when he visited the Queen, she dared not look at him. He pursued her into the ante-chamber, where they talked, in company but unheard, for nearly three hours.

The King's health, which had again broken down, improved; he believed that he and Louise would achieve happiness in the end. In February, having dealt with peasants' revolts in Normandy and Gascony, and finding that the Queen and her ladies had left St-Germain, he went to Orléans to receive the egregious Gaston's fifth submission. He returned to Paris to be told that the Lafayettes were urging Louise to restore the family fortunes by becoming his mistress. Warned by Boisenval, one of Richelieu's spies, that the King was wearying of her, Louise asked her parents' leave to take the vows.

In fact, Louis was still passionately in love; and he now had a supporter in his newly appointed confessor, Father Caussin, whom Richelieu had instructed to detach the King from Louise. But Caussin, a Jesuit, had principles and ideas of his own; and he hated the Cardinal. When Louis spoke of his love for Mademoiselle de Lafayette, adding, with characteristic restraint, that if she entered a convent it would sadden him, Caussin replied, 'I see no danger, Sire, in your attachment, so long as it is confined to its present limits. And before you permit the young lady to enter a convent, you should seriously consider her vocation.' The King then told Caussin to discuss the matter with Louise. The priest warned her against precipitate action, asked her if she realized what giving up the world would entail, and concluded, 'You might not care to carry a cross that may be heavier than you think.' 'Since childhood,' Louise replied, 'I have considered becoming a professed religious. Had I desired marriage, the King would have found me a wealthy husband. But I had other interests than my own.' When Caussin told Louis that Mademoiselle de Lafayette's vocation seemed to be genuine, the King burst into tears. 'It's true that I love her very dearly,' he said, 'but if God has called her, I will not stand in her way. Rather than that, I will leave her now, and never see her more.'

Louise then arranged for her reception at the House of the Visitandines de Sainte-Marie in the Rue Saint-Antoine. Still it was not too late; Louis had the right to forbid her entering that or any other order. He was greatly tempted. Piteously, he burst out to Caussin, 'What haste is there? Can she not wait a few months, till I leave for the army? Then separation might not be so painful; now, the very thought of it kills me.' Deeply moved, Caussin agreed that delay would not be wrong. Then Louis said, 'Leave it be. If I caused her to lose her vocation, I should regret it all my life. But nothing has ever cost me as much as this sacrifice —' and again broke down.

On May 9th, 1637, Louise and the King spoke together at St-Germain. 'If this were not a true vocation,' she said, 'I would not leave you, not for all the world. If you wish it, I will wait until July.' 'You know very well', Louis replied, 'that I will never restrict you for love of myself. Do what you think right.' She said nothing. He could bear no more, and left for Versailles.

From there, writing to Richelieu of his agonized longings, 'which overwhelm me, above all when I am alone,' Louis gave permission for Louise's retirement to the Visitandines. On May 19th he returned to St-Germain to attend the Queen's *lever*, the tears running down his face. Louise forced herself into calmness, so as not to add to his sufferings. When the *lever* was over she went to the window to watch him drive away. 'I shall never see him again,' she said, and began to cry.

She was wrong. In the twilit world of the religious life they met and spoke together, often for hours at a time. From behind a grille her shadowy figure appeared at his command, untouchable, remote, as if summoned from the grave. His gentlemen stood apart; no one heard what was said. One day, as he left the convent, he met one of his courtiers, who tactlessly began, 'So, Sire, you have been to see the poor prisoner?' 'No,' said the King, 'It is I who am in prison —' and rode on.

War, revolution, illness, treachery, overwork — these he had borne, and would continue to bear. It was the appalling loneliness, the hideous blank, the misery of loss that defeated him. He considered abdication and retirement into a monastery; then he knew that he must go on. His visits to Louise, meagre though they were, helped him to endure the weeks of absence, when, leading his armies, he seemed to be courting death. And there was always Versailles, the fairy-tale castle in the forest, where he had dreamed of their life together ...

Richelieu was considerate and subservient; he could afford to be. He even encouraged his master to cast his eye again on Mademoiselle de Hautefort. Mechanically, Louis did so, and turned away. Now he began to rebel against the Cardinal's pervasive, ceaseless vigilance and to resent his power, forgetting that, if Richelieu had not sometimes taken full charge, he would have had fewer hours with Louise. Why, for instance, had the Cardinal suggested that the Queen should be made Regent during his absence at the front in November 1636?

Richelieu had laid a trap. In August 1637 he presented the results to his master. The Queen had used her regency to convey all the military secrets she could obtain to her brother. Her letters to Philip IV, conveyed by the King's valet, La Porte, written and dispatched from the Convent of Val-de-Grâce, were now in Richelieu's possession. In the presence of the Chancellor and the Archbishop of Paris, the Cardinal summoned Anne of Austria to answer to the charges of espionage and high treason.

She began by swearing to her innocence on the Sacrament. The Cardinal replied by producing her letters. She broke down, begging for mercy. Gravely, Richelieu assured Her Majesty that she would be exonerated in return for her solemn promise of loyalty. 'How good Your Eminence is to me!' she sobbed out. 'Give me your hand.' 'I did not presume to take it,' Richelieu told Louis. 'Out of respect, I left Her Majesty, rather than approach her.'

Louis then interviewed his wife in the presence of his confessor and, having obtained the names of her accomplices—La Porte, Madame de Chevreuse, two nuns and the Lady Abbess of Val-de-Grâce—formally forgave her. A month later, they were together at Fontainebleau, and in October attended a service of thanksgiving for his victories over the Spanish. Their rather grim relationship was then resumed. Lovelessly, he continued to sleep with her throughout the autumn of 1637.

On the afternoon of December 5th the King visited Louise and stayed with her longer than usual. Their conversations were secret; but during the twenty-two years that elapsed between his death and hers she let fall certain details which were later revealed. She continued to urge Louis to dismiss Richelieu, to abandon his heretic allies and to affiliate himself with Spain; these projects hung on a complete and permanent reconciliation with the Queen; it was as if Louise believed that their union would never be fruitful while they remained on bad terms. Louis pointed out the impracticability of these suggestions; but whether they disagreed or not, he always came away soothed by the talks which were his only consolation; and it seems that his continued frequentation of the Queen was partly due to the influence of Louise.

On this occasion a great storm burst as he was leaving the Rue St-Antoine for Versailles. He decided to wait: but the rain continued, and he told Guitaut, the Captain of his Guard, that they must proceed, whatever the weather. Guitaut protested: the horses would be bogged down and their legs broken — why not stop at the Louvre? Louis, knowing that the Queen was there and longing for solitude, objected; Guitaut dwelt on the sufferings resulting from the journey, and the King yielded. Guitaut then sent one of his officers to warn Her Majesty, so that when Louis, soaked and shivering, reached the palace, he was welcomed by a radiant wife, blazing fires, a good supper and a change of clothes. One formality was lacking. His private apartments, unoccupied for some months, were not ready, so he spent the night with the Queen. He left early next morning, his impassivity tinged — as always after a parting from Louise — with gloom.

The result of this joyless union was that Anne of Austria conceived for the fourth time in a marriage now entering its twenty-third year. In January 1638 her pregnancy was announced; the child moved in June; and on September 5th a Dauphin, Louis the Gift of God, who reigned for seventy-two years and brought France her greatest glories and her bitterest ruin, was born.

So the dynasty was saved. As far as Louis's private happiness was concerned, this long and passionately desired event profited him nothing. The Queen's pregnancy had failed to rouse him from his habitual depression; her complacency, her attempts to recreate their youthful loves, not only failed to move him, but were so irritating that he could hardly bear to remain with her. Her falsity, her silliness, the harm she had done, could not be ignored; and her idiotic questions, he told Richelieu, were more infuriating than ever. Now his visits to Louise no longer consoled him; he took no pleasure in the development of his intelligent and attractive son; he was desperate. Once more, he turned to Marie de Hautefort.

She encouraged him: but so delighted in teasing and quarrelling that she made him very unhappy. When they were on good terms he called her the Inclination; more often, she was the Creature. His letters to Richelieu were full of complaints of her cruelty and her insolences. She made a point of dwelling on the virtues and charms of the Queen; her praise, which he knew to be meaningless, nearly drove him frantic. Yet he persisted with his painful courtship of this acid siren, as with his marital duties. In December 1639 Anne became pregnant again; in the following September their second son, Philippe, was born.

This event was followed by a series of military triumphs, so that 1640 was known as the Year of Victories. At last, everything Louis had worked for had come to pass. It was too late. He continued to do all that was required of him; yet now his only happiness lay in trivial distractions: hunting, music, ballets. His illnesses — gout, indigestion, a perpetual cough, insomnia, headaches — made most days and nights a torment. At thirty-nine, he was an ageing, exhausted invalid, whose children got on his nerves, whose only confidant was a man even sicker than himself and thus a constant anxiety. So it was that his passion for Mademoiselle de Hautefort became morbid and selfish; he forbade her to marry, yet did not establish her as his mistress. She then turned upon him — he was a tyrant, a fool. He begged her to be kind, and settled a fortune on her; still she abused him; and still he could not resist her.

And still the war went on, sometimes badly, sometimes without result. Now, with two healthy sons, watching the Spanish power begin to disintegrate, feeling his people behind him and the national economy on the mend, Louis was more wretched than at any time in his life. But another change had begun — his penultimate phase. In November 1639 he was subjugated by a beautiful, worthless youth, who became a symbol of evil, degradation and disaster.

Louis XIII was not a great king; but he tried, all his life, to be a good one. To that end he deliberately sacrificed his hopes of personal happiness. The advent of this unpleasant catamite has destroyed his posthumous renown. At the bar of history Louis the Just stands condemned as a contemptible weakling. Three decades of courage, piety and unselfishness have been overshadowed by a relationship which lasted for two and a half years.

II

Henri d'Effiat, Marquis de Cinq-Mars, was just eighteen when Louis made him his Grand Master of the Wardrobe. Their story is hatefully familiar: the tired, sickly, middle-aged man and the heartless, stupid, greedy youth, whose cruelty feeds on the sufferings of his benefactor, and whose arrogance thrusts him towards his own destruction.

For Cinq-Mars, formerly one of Richelieu's protégés, had a capacity for ingratitude and forgetfulness which eliminated all sense of self-preservation. He seized the position of reigning favourite without decorum and without respect, while his insolence staggered the most cynical and sophisticated observers — even Richelieu himself. They saw their master, the crowned and anointed descendant of St Louis, the absolute monarch, the fearless commander, cringe and complain and plead, and yet continue to cling to an idle, petulant, conceited young man, whose chosen companions were expensive prostitutes and vulgar rakes, whose ambitions centred on the variety and richness of his wardrobe, and whose conversation was inept, tedious and obscene. Yet Louis, an acute and careful judge of human nature, persisted in his attempts to educate and reform this creature; he tried to lure him away from gaming-houses and brothels; he hoped to restrain his expenditure; he believed that he might eventually guide him towards religion, intellectual interests and — most pathetic delusion of all — some affection for himself. Cinq-Mars rebelled, sulked, grumbled, and escaped to the welcome of Marion Delorme and the toss-pots of the Marais. Louis waited for him to come back; then there were reproaches, expostulations, further demands, despair on one side, contempt on the other. The King's report of one dialogue epitomizes this destructive relationship.

LOUIS. His Eminence says that you wish to please me, but you do not do so in the matter of laziness.

CINQ-MARS. I cannot change, or do better than before.

LOUIS (angrily). For a man of your sort, who thinks he ought, as you have told me, to be given the command of an army, indolence is an insurmountable obstacle.

CINQ-MARS. I never wanted a command. I never said so.

LOUIS. Yes, you did. Laziness is typical of the Marais, where they live only for pleasure. If you mean to behave as before, you had better go back there.

CINQ-MARS. I am quite ready to go.

LOUIS. You should not speak so to me.

CINQ-MARS. I never wanted to be Grand Master, and I am not going to change my manner of life.

LOUIS. If you remain in this mood, I would rather you did not see me.

CINQ-MARS. I shall be very pleased not to. (And walks off, disappearing for several days.)

Louis's accounts of these scenes, most of which took place in public, resembled those of an hysterical schoolgirl enslaved by a predatory governess, and were all addressed to Richelieu. The Cardinal read them without pity, waiting, calmly, for the inevitable end.

This began when Cinq-Mars demanded a royal bride—preferably the Princess of Mantua. Then, irked by the unbroken power of his former patron, he followed the old pattern, even less skilfully than his predecessors, by forming a plot to murder him. (It is hardly necessary to add that Gaston was involved in this scheme.) All was discovered, just as the King was reaching the point of nausea. 'I spit him out!' he said. But Cinq-Mars was too vain, too grossly self-absorbed to see that Louis's violent obsession had turned to an equally violent disgust. After an interval of horror and incredulity the King was relieved at the news of the young man's guilt. Cinq-Mars was tried, condemned and beheaded in September 1642.

Louis and one of his courtiers were playing chess on the morning of the execution. The King glanced at his watch. Then he said, 'I wonder how the Grand Master looks now'—and went on with the game.

The influence of this colourless Antinous had no effect on the King's public life, or on the national fortunes. While the miseries of war increased, all danger of France being swallowed up by the Habsburg powers had been removed. Everywhere the Spanish forces were falling back; cities, fortresses, whole districts submitted to those of Louis. His navy swept the seas; his colonial empire was enlarged. From the Pole to the Tropic of Capricorn, from great Canadian lakes to the Red Sea and the Indian Ocean, the fleurs-de-lys were acclaimed sometimes worshipped, as the insignia of a god. Louis's European rule was now established on the frontiers of the Rhine, the Escaut, the Tagus and the Po; he was Count of Roussillon, Barcelona and Cerdagne. The rebels within his kingdom—Huguenots, the famous Bare-Foot gangs, recalcitrant clergy, treacherous nobles—were being subdued. And in July 1642 another old enemy disappeared. Unregretted, almost penniless, Marie de Medici died in Cologne.

Meanwhile the King's personal supervision was maintained. Within a week he still covered hundreds of miles, sleeping on the ground, calming officers' disputes and receiving the homage of his new subjects with quiet geniality. The only tribute he rejected was speechifying. 'Master Provost,' he said to one orator, 'your addresses are perfection—they are short.'

He had more work than ever before, for Richelieu was dying. In the autumn of 1642 the two friends talked together for the last time, and it was agreed that Mazarin should succeed his patron as principal minister. On December 4th Richelieu, required to forgive all his enemies, murmured, 'I have had none but those of the State—' and ceased to breathe. Monsieur, exclaiming, 'My enemy has left the world!' took the opportunity to make yet another submission, to which the King replied, 'It is no longer possible. I have already forgiven you six times. Henceforth, I wish to see the effects of your promises. I shall not believe in your word.'

Far from being lost without Richelieu, Louis seemed to work more freely, although he himself was beginning to fail. His relations with the Queen had further deteriorated, for he suspected her, not without reason, of having encouraged Cinq-Mars to intrigue against him with Philip IV. Aware that she must shortly begin her regency, Anne so worked upon the Dauphin as to put him against his father. Louis thought that his heir was being spoilt by his mother and her ladies. When he was severe (he never

whipped little Louis), the child defied him and ran screaming to
the Queen. Then the weary King controlled his impatience and,
remembering his own childhood, found time to play with his son
and bring him toys, so that they became, he noted, 'the best
friends in the world'. For a while he considered removing him
from his mother's care; but that meant separating him from
Philippe, and he did not want him to be lonely. Louis had no
patience with his younger son, whom the Queen dandled, stuffed
with sweets and dressed in girl's clothes, and who whined and
pirouetted alternately. It was not much of a family life; but he was
too tired and too ill, now, to improve matters. Meanwhile,
Mazarin was all that could be desired, almost all that Richelieu
had been, although his master could not quite forget the late
Cardinal's introduction of him to Anne of Austria—'I am sure
Your Majesty will like him, as he so greatly resembles His Grace
of Buckingham.'

By the beginning of January 1643 Louis knew that he had not
long to live, and was thankful for it. He also knew that the treatment of the doctors succeeding Héroard had shortened his life,
and told them so. This would not have troubled him if he had not
thought it his duty to survive until the Dauphin reached his
majority; then he had intended to abdicate and retire to Versailles
with four Jesuit fathers, there to hunt and do penance for his sins,
of which the greatest, he felt, was his treatment of his mother.
Another, deeper anxiety was for his 'poor people'; but now his
two-year plan for their rehabilitation and for peace with Spain
must be put aside. These hopes abandoned, he made a will
enforcing the control of his ministers over the regency of Monsieur
and Anne of Austria. He then released and pardoned a number of
rebels, and allowed certain exiles to return to France, one exception being that of Madame de Chevreuse. Within an hour of his
death nearly all these arrangements were rescinded by Gaston and
the Queen.

For a few weeks his indomitable spirit prevailed. On February
21st he settled at St-Germain, never to leave it again. Still he
attended Council meetings and received ambassadors. On April
2nd he was too weak to attend the Maundy Thursday ceremonies,
and the four-year-old Dauphin washed the feet of the paupers
selected for that purpose. Next day, supported by two of his
courtiers, the King walked in the gallery for the last time.

After he had been put to bed, there was still a great deal to do; interviews and receptions succeeded one another in the intervals of purging and bleeding. Saint Simon was allowed to return; weeping, he knelt by the bed to receive his master's instructions about the funeral. Glancing towards the windows, the King said, 'The road to St Denis is rough—my body will be much shaken.' On April 21st the Dauphin, having been publicly baptized, came to see him. Struggling out of the mists of exhaustion and pain, Louis said, 'My son, what is your name, now?' 'Louis XIV, Papa.' The King flushed up; he said sharply, 'Not yet—' and turned away.

A few days later he received the last sacraments; then he called for his musicians, who sang and played to him. It was thought that he could not live through the night; next morning he rallied and remained clear-headed and calm, although in considerable pain, till May 8th, when he collapsed again. He had revived a little, and was talking to one of his ministers, when there came a burst of laughter from the ante-chamber. 'That must be Monsieur and the Queen,' he said.

He was wrong, as far as his wife was concerned. She was in the deepest distress; throughout her treacherous and senseless machinations she had not ceased to love him. The stupidity and arrogance which destroyed their relationship were beyond his comprehension.

On May 14th, the thirty-third anniversary of his father's murder, he became delirious; he was leading a charge: once more, his troops were victorious. He asked what time it was, repeating the question at intervals. The whole Court was then admitted to watch him receive Extreme Unction. His sons and the Queen knelt at the head of the bed; his confessor, Father Dinet, was at the other side. In a supreme, agonizing effort, Louis removed a small gold crucifix from his neck and gave it to the priest. 'For Sister Louise-Angélique de Lafayette,' he whispered.

The atmosphere in the crowded room, thickened with incense, made it difficult for him to breathe. The stench was appalling; but he seemed unaware of it, and to be following the prayers. Towards two o'clock he murmured 'Jesus— !' and lost consciousness. Still the chanting, the weeping, the coming and going of courtiers, ministers, physicians and priests continued; and still his breathing could be heard. Half an hour later—almost at the same

92

moment that his father had sunk beneath the assassin's knife—he looked towards Father Dinet. He was speechless; but the thought of Louise and his instinct for secrecy were united in a final gesture. He put his finger to his lips, and died.

Louis XIII was the last King of France for whom his people wept. That tribute, and the comments of the rather dim-witted Claude de Saint Simon, combine in his most fitting epitaph. 'When I saw the coffin lowered into the vault,' said the ex-huntsman, 'I wanted to throw myself in after it. That incomparable King, brilliant, pious, modest and loyal,' he added, 'was a hero, a son worthy of Saint Louis. To me, his memory was and always will be, precious and sacred.'

PRINCIPAL SOURCES OF INFORMATION
with dates of the most recent editions

Baschet, A.,   *Le Roi chez la Reine* (Paris, 1864)

Bassompierre, Marquis de,   *Mémoires* (Cologne, 1665)

Batiffol, L.,   *Au Temps de Louis XIII* (Paris, 1904)
Louis XIII à Vingt Ans (Paris, 1910)
Le Louvre sous Louis XIII et Henry IV (Paris, 1930)

Canu, J.,   *Louis XIII et Richelieu* (Paris, 1946)

Champigneulle, B.,   *Le Règne de Louis XIII* (Paris, 1943)

Clermont-Montglat, Marquis de,   *Mémoires* (Paris, 1836-8)

Erlanger, P.,   *Louis XIII* (Paris, 1946)
L'Étrange Mort d'Henri IV (Paris, 1957)
Cinq-Mars (Paris, 1962)

Fontenay-Mareuil, Marquis de,   *Mémoires* (Paris, 1819)

Griffet, H.,   *Histoire de la Règne de Louis XIII* (Paris, 1738)

Héroard, J.,   *Journal* (Paris, 1868)

La Porte, P. de,   *Mémoires* (Geneva, 1755)

Motteville, Mme de,   *Mémoires* (Amsterdam, 1723)

Nolhac, P. de,   *Création de Versailles* (Versailles, 1901)

Orléans, Gaston d',   *Mémoires* (Paris, 1838)

Réaux, Tallemant des,   *Historiettes* (Paris, 1929)

Richelieu, Cardinal,   *Mémoires* (Paris, 1836-8)

Rossignol, C.,   *Louis XIII avant Richelieu* (Paris, 1869)

Saint-Simon, Duc de,   *Mémoires* (Paris, 1951)

Siri, V.,   *Memorie Recondite* (Paris, 1765-7)

Tapié, V.-L.,   *La France de Louis XIII et de Richelieu* (Paris, 1952)

Vaunois, L.,   *Vie de Louis XIII* (Paris, 1947)

Wedgwood, C. V.,   *The Thirty Years War* (London, (1938)

THE ELECTRESS SOPHIA

(OCTOBER 1630 — JUNE 1714)

Certaine fille, un peu trop fière,
Prétendait trouver un mari
Jeune, bien fait, et beau, d'agréable manière,
Point froid et point jaloux : notez ces deux points-ci.
Cette fille voulait aussi
Qu'il eût du bien, de la naissance,
De l'esprit, enfin tout ; mais qui peut tout avoir ?

JEAN DE LA FONTAINE

ONE

I

On February 14th, 1613, Elizabeth Stuart, only surviving daughter of James I and Anne of Denmark, was married to Frederic V, Count-Elector Palatine of the Rhine. Bride and groom were exactly of an age—sixteen and a half—and made a pleasantly contrasting pair. He was swarthy, elegant and rather shy: she was vivacious and white-skinned, with dark eyes and golden hair. In spite of the fact that Frederic's title dated from the tenth century, there were some, Queen Anne amongst them, who considered that the Princess was marrying beneath her and had been sacrificed to the Protestant interest—for the Palsgrave, a Calvinist, was head of the Evangelical Union founded by his father. He was also very rich, moderately intellectual and extremely high-minded. Within a few days of their meeting he fell in love with the exuberant, rather dominating Elizabeth, her father's 'little Bessie' and the nation's idol, who, all her life, had been indulged, petted and admired.

Elizabeth and Frederic entered their capital of Heidelberg on June 7th, and were happily settled in a peaceful and prosperous kingdom for six years. In July 1617 the Catholic Archduke Ferdinand of Styria, heir of the late Austrian Emperor Matthias, was crowned King of Bohemia. In August 1619 the Bohemian Protestant majority revolted, deposed him and asked the Elector Frederic to reign over them. After some hesitation and many misgivings, he accepted. Although both he and Elizabeth were genuinely persuaded that they were thus striking a blow for the Protestant cause, she had not forgotten her mother's sneers about a Princess of England becoming 'Goody Palsgrave', and he had been much affected by her declaration that she would rather eat sauerkraut at a king's table than feast on luxuries at that of an elector. Also, the existence of three children, with another on the way, may have enhanced their dynastic ambitions and influenced them against the warnings of the Electress Dowager, who, dreading the vengeance of the Catholic powers, urged them to refuse, as did James I.

In October 1619 they were crowned, and installed in the Edissa Palace of Prague. ('He is but a Winter King, and will go with the melting snows,' the Jesuits assured their congregations.) In the following year the Austro-Spanish armies advanced through the Palatinate and routed the Bohemian troops in the battle of the White Mountain. Elizabeth and Frederic took refuge in Germany, eventually settling in Holland, which became their headquarters for the rest of their married life. In October 1630, the ninth year of her exile, Elizabeth gave birth to her twelfth child and fifth daughter. She could not think what to call her. Finally, slips of paper were inscribed with various names and jumbled together; the first drawn was that of her long-dead sister, Sophia. Elizabeth had already lost her eldest son, Frederic-Henry, who was drowned at the age of fifteen, and Louis, who died in infancy. Her thirteenth and last child, Gustavus, was born in 1631, the year of his two-year-old sister Charlotte's death.

So the Princess Sophia became the pet of three elder sisters, Elizabeth, Louise and Henrietta, and five brothers, Charles-Louis, Rupert, Maurice, Edward and Philip—but not of her mother. The Queen of Bohemia preferred her collection of dogs and monkeys to her children, and was too much absorbed in her husband to share the interests of her very remarkable and rather undisciplined brood.

Soon after she was weaned Sophia was sent to Leyden to be brought up by her father's old governess, Madame de Ples. She had just passed her second birthday when news came of his death from plague in Mainz, after a last, unsuccessful and costly attempt to regain his kingdom. At this hideous (but by no means final) blow, the Winter Queen's indomitable courage gave way; then she tried, for her family's sake, to control her grief. 'Though I make a good show in company,' she wrote to an old friend, 'yet I can never have any more contentment in this world, for God knows I had none but that which I took in his company, and he did the same in mine; for since he went from hence he never failed writing to me twice a week, and ever wished either me with him or he with me.' So she would not—or could not, for she was not well off—send for the younger children, and Sophia remained in Leyden till she was ten; she grew to dislike the place more every year. A pretty, headstrong, clever little girl, she was always in trouble for disobedience, or ill-timed laughter and mimicry. In her famous memoirs she gives a detailed account of this grim period in her life.

Madame de Ples was assisted by her two spinster daughters. All three were severe, humourless, fanatically pious, and so ugly as to frighten most little children. Gustavus, who was nervous and delicate, may have suffered more from them than Sophia did. In 1633 Charles-Louis and Rupert, aged sixteen and thirteen respectively, left Leyden to fight under Prince Henry of Nassau against the Spaniards, thereafter finishing their education at the court of Louis XIII, while Elizabeth and Louise joined their mother at the Hague; so the nursery party consisted of Sophia and the four youngest brothers. Although the boys' tutors were less strict than the governesses, all five children were brought up under the most rigorous Calvinist discipline. They spoke and corresponded with one another in French and English; they learnt Scripture history, prayers and the Catechism in German, thus becoming trilingual before they reached their teens.

Every morning Sophia was called at seven o'clock and, still in her nightgown, went to Fräulein Marie to say her prayers and read a passage from the Bible while that lady cleaned her teeth; she spent so long over this process that Sophia learnt to repeat her daily portion without any subsequent recollection but that of the grimaces made by the governess. At eight thirty she was dressed, and studied Latin, Dutch, Italian and mathematics with visiting masters till ten; then came her favourite lesson, dancing; she was summoned to dinner at eleven.

She entered the dining-room last, to find her brothers standing in line, backed by their tutors and gentlemen-in-waiting. She curtsied deeply to the Princes, more slightly to their attendants, and again to the governesses as they entered with their ladies. With another curtsy she removed her gloves and handed them to a maid-of-honour; turning back to the table, she curtsied once more, and yet again after washing her hands; another salute followed grace, and the ninth and last was made before sitting down.

Although she detested this ceremony and the dullness of the meals (these varied only with the days of the week), Sophia's awareness of the hierarchical system was thereby so inculcated as to become instinctive; and although she was immensely bored by the bi-weekly theological discourses of visiting ministers, she grew up a militant anti-papist. This conviction was enhanced by an inward scepticism; very soon, all forms of faith seemed rather ridiculous. Also, she came to despise her divinity teachers as soon as she realized that she need only rattle off the correct answers to a series of questions in order to give satisfaction, just as she learnt by heart, without the faintest interest, Pibrac's *Fifty-Four Precepts of Good Conduct*, a famous educational work of the sixteenth century. Rising from dinner, she rested till two thirty, resuming lessons till six. She supped at six thirty and went to bed at eight, after more prayers and Bible-reading. Fortunately, her governesses were so short-sighted that it was easy to hide from them, and easier still to play tricks of which she felt rather ashamed as she grew older; they were not worthy of a princess, and she never described them.

As the Palatine brothers reached their teens they left Paris to travel—Charles-Louis and Rupert moved to England, and stayed at the court of their uncle Charles I from 1635 to 1637. Only Sophia and Gustavus remained in Leyden. They were devoted companions; as his health made it impossible for him to lead an active life, they became inseparable. During one of their visits to the Hague, Sophia heard a Dutch lady say to the Queen, 'He is very beautiful, but she is thin and ugly—I hope she does not understand English?'

Sophia was too fond of Gustavus to feel jealousy : but the remark haunted her : was she really the only plain member of a handsome family? She never forgot the pang of self-disgust, nor the feeling of hopelessness. 'I thought my misfortune irreparable,' she said, forty years later. Then she could think of nothing but Gustavus. All his life he had been in constant pain, for which the doctors found no remedy. As he reached his ninth year his sufferings became acute, and were increased by epilepsy; after months of agony, he died in January 1641. His mother was desperately miserable; he had been the prettiest and the gentlest of all her children. Sophia's grief was tinged with furious resentment; she could neither forget nor forgive the doctors' stupidity: for the autopsy revealed that for years the poor little Prince had been afflicted with the stone. She would not admit that an operation would almost certainly have killed him, and all her long life she avoided, whenever possible, the ministrations of the faculty, attributing her wonderful health to this precaution.

She could not remain alone at Leyden and, shortly after her tenth birthday, joined her mother at the Hague. So a different life began: a happy, busy time. Sophia had a moment's remorse for her naughtiness to the Ples family. 'I loved the good old creatures out of habit and gratitude, and without sympathy,' she recalled. It was glorious to be free of them and their dreary lessons. There were treats and parties every day, her brothers and sisters spoilt her, her mother allowed her to romp and tease, and they were all, always, on the move, either to the Queen's country palace of Rhenen, or making expeditions. And also, there were her mother's courtiers, ready and eager to indulge her — the gentlemen especially ...

II

The little Princess whose position in the continental hierarchy was so humble that only her nearest relatives took any interest in her future, was exceptionally fortunate throughout her childhood and adolescence. Her first nineteen years were spent in the most civilized country in the world; and her circumstances, those of an impoverished but privileged refugee, brought her into contact with the creators of a unique and highly evolved regime. If she had been brought up in any other European court she would have dwelt apart, leading a more or less artificial existence. That provided by Holland, the largest and richest of the seven United Provinces of the Dutch Republic, was one in which simplicity and comfort, beauty and usefulness were so blended as to stimulate and develop her better qualities; she shared its amenities with all classes but the poorest.

Sophia was especially lucky in that her hosts and protectors, the family of Orange-Nassau, held a high position in the state. She learnt from their methods of administration, as from their circle and habits, a sense of proportion and an acuteness of vision seldom found in other young persons of her rank. Its head, Prince Frederick-Henry, who divided his authority with the Grand Pensionary of the Republic, was known as the Stadtholder; he was also Captain and Admiral-General of the forces and First

Magistrate. After the King and Queen of Bohemia settled at the Hague, he gave them a large town mansion, besides the establishment at Rhenen, both of which he redecorated and furnished on a magnificent scale. When Sophia arrived her mother was still able to sustain a commodious and stately manner of life, partly through the generosity of the Nassaus, and also by means of the allowance settled on her by Charles I. At her husband's death, he had begged her to return to England; she refused, on the grounds of giving her children a continental education, and also because she felt it would be easier to arrange suitable marriages for them from her own court, which was visited by most Protestant potentates and a number of foreign ambassadors. Few travellers toured the Republic without paying their respects to the Winter Queen; she kept open house. John Evelyn, then an unknown young gentleman, received by her on the ninth anniversary of her husband's death, was duly impressed, both by the black-hung presence-chamber and the agreeable discourse of its owner and her children.

That owner, formerly Donne's 'She-Sun' and Wotton's 'eclipse and glory of her kind', was now in her forty-sixth year and, although still attractive and lively, no longer a beauty. The famous amber-coloured hair was brownish-black, her skin had become weather-beaten, her nose, always rather large, drooped a little and her eyes, never her best feature, were slightly sunken. She moved gracefully and her manner retained all its old fascination, so that she was still known as the Queen of Hearts to admirers of both sexes, who lent her money and sacrificed their interests to hers. In fact, Elizabeth of Bohemia was one of those women who, accustomed to adulation since infancy, continue, unconsciously, to assume its existence in everyone they meet, with the result that they generally receive it; her courage, her rather crude humour, her gay informality of address, and the fact that her misfortunes had made her something of a legend, created an atmosphere of devotion in a court which subsisted largely on hopes and the patience of unpaid tradesmen.

In this circle of uncritical loyalists, the Queen's children made a dissentient group. They loved but refused to bow down to their mother; nor would they always subscribe to her whims. Three of them—Rupert, Elizabeth and Louise—were brilliantly clever, and thus often recalcitrant. Charles-Louis ('Timon'), very conscious of his position as Elector-Palatine and head of the family, disliked her interference and was pained by her unconventionality; Maurice, a milder edition of Rupert, was equally independent; Philip and Edward, both wild and rebellious, ignored her demands; Henrietta gave no trouble; and Sophia, that very sharp child, observed, with an oddly adult detachment, that Her Majesty was capricious, vain and sometimes rather silly.

These withdrawals did not so much distress the Queen as bewilder her. Herself an outdoor, energetic woman, she could neither understand nor appreciate the tastes and temperaments of her two eldest daughters. She had been well educated and was moderately cultured; but the fact that the Princess Elizabeth, who was now twenty-three and should long since have been married, was more interested in her correspondence with Descartes and preferred the study of philosophy and mathematics under his tuition to marriage plans and the trivialities of a circumscribed court, curbed her mother's natural sympathy and made her very impatient. The classical beauty of this Princess — '*La Grecque*' — was sometimes marred by the effects of a poor circulation; her indifference to her red nose so annoyed the Queen as to prevent her eldest daughter appearing at the appointed times. When Louise once asked Elizabeth why she drew back, she demanded, 'Do you want me to go with this nose?' to which her sister replied, 'Am I to wait till you get another?' to the delight of the ubiquitous Sophia.

That young lady's pleasure in her sisters' and brothers' company never failed, although she was slightly taken aback by Louise's total disregard of appearances. Certainly, she was remarkable; she painted almost as well as her master, the great Honthorst; indeed, it was difficult, sometimes, to tell her work from his: but her clothes — thrown on! And her hair, like Elizabeth's absent-mindedness, became a subject of much family teasing.

Princess Henrietta, now in her sixteenth year, was fair-haired, exquisitely pink and white and large-eyed, with no pretensions to culture; her hobby, that of making delicious sweets, gave her eleven-year-old sister more satisfaction than Louise's painting (some of her portraits were imaginary — very odd!) or Elizabeth's philosophical explorations.

Sophia soon discovered that Rupert ('*Robert le Diable*') who had just returned to the Hague after a campaign ending in three years in an Austrian prison, was his mother's favourite. His moody humours, his flouting of her wishes, his contemptuous relegation of her duller contemporaries, were far outweighed by his sombre beauty, his protean talents (he spoke six languages, drew almost as well as Louise and had already achieved European repute as an engineer and a soldier) and his uncertain attitude towards herself; he reminded the Queen of her own days of glory. So she forgave him and Maurice, remonstrated sharply with Edward and Philip, was exacerbated by, while admiring, Elizabeth and Louise, indulged Henrietta and Sophia, and encouraged her courtiers to spoil the youngest Princess, who was a natural comedian. Very soon Sophia was exploiting her reputation as a romp; her pranks provide a characteristic example of seventeenth-century humour.

These revolved round the Queen's dogs and monkeys, of which there were some two dozen, uncontrolled in every sense and encouraged by Sophia to set about her mother's visitors. The elegant Prince de Tarente fled before them; young Zulestein retaliated so brutally that Sophia taught him a lesson by dipping her handkerchief in the Queen's close-stool and throwing it in his face. (This was considered highly amusing.) Then there was Monsieur Marigné, who sent Sophia a letter from the monkeys, asking her to be their queen. Sir Henry Vane followed this up by a proposal of another kind, supposedly from Count Contarini. The Princess replied by giving the Englishman a box, in which, she said, there was a ring for her admirer. Sir Henry opened it to find a dog's mess and a rude rhyme in which the young lady compared his chin to a lamp-post.

When the Queen of Bohemia went to hunt at Rhenen her sons resumed their travels, and, as she found the evenings rather dull, her daughters got up private theatricals. Sophia was bitterly chagrined when they told her she was too young and too short to take the principal part in a French version of the *Medea*. She at once learnt the whole piece by heart, and so was allowed to play the confidant, aided by *chopines* and the prompting of a professional actress.

Then they all left for Honslaerdyck to receive Queen Henrietta Maria, and the Princess Mary, who at the age of ten had been married to Prince William, Frederick-Henry's eldest son. Sophia, who had heard much of her French aunt's beauty, was somewhat taken aback to see 'a thin little woman with shrunken arms, and teeth sticking out from her mouth like guns from a fort'. She was better pleased to hear an English courtier say, 'When the Princess Sophia has grown a little, she will surpass all her sisters,' and began to consider her own assets. She longed to be taller; but her brown curls and large dark eyes were all that could be desired: and she knew that she carried herself well.

As she reached her teens she gave up romping and began to think of marriage. At this point, Lord Craven, her mother's most faithful admirer, came into the picture. So far, all the plans for the elder Princesses' alliances had fallen through, mainly for financial reasons. Sophia also was dowerless; nevertheless, Craven and the Queen thought that a marriage with the Prince of Wales might be arranged. He and Sophia were exactly of an age; and her Calvinistic training would be no barrier, quite apart from the fact that she was not naturally pious.

In 1644 the future Charles II, then in his fifteenth year, was wandering about the West of England; nominally General of the Western Association, he remained under Prince Rupert's command. His aunt and her advisers still believed that the Royalists must eventually triumph, as did Queen Henrietta Maria, who was planning his marriage to an heiress, preferably to another cousin, Anne-Marie de Montpensier, later known as La Grande Mademoiselle. A more suitable alliance was that put forward by the Prince and Princess of Orange-Nassau with their eldest daughter; her mother, the formidable and ambitious Princess Amalia, had always resented her husband's support of the Palatine Stuarts, and as soon as she realized that Sophia might be preferred to her own child, set about trying to destroy her reputation. The girl was an undisciplined coquette—had she not been heard to describe the Prince of Wales as 'a delicious morsel'? So Amalia instructed the fifteen-year-old Prince William-Henry to frequent the Queen of Bohemia's court with a view to compromising Sophia, in spite of the fact that he had only just begun married life with the Princess Mary. He was not unwilling: for Sophia was far prettier and livelier than his rather dull little bride, whom Queen Elizabeth described as 'deadly lazy'. Sophia, apprised of this scheme by one of the young Prince's gentlemen, retaliated by leaving the room whenever he visited her mother. William-Henry then asked her, Prince Philip and the Landgrave von Salm to take part in a ballet, for which daily rehearsals would be necessary. Philip haughtily refused, but not before von Salm had told Sophia that she might well govern the Orange-Nassau heir, and through him the whole province of Holland. 'So might your wife,' Sophia coolly replied, 'but that she is more virtuous than you are' — and the intrigue came to nothing.

Sophia, her mother and the Princess Elizabeth all fell ill in June of this year, recovering to find that Prince Charles-Louis had left for England in order to affiliate himself with Parliament, to whom he apologized for the royalism of Rupert and Maurice. The Queen was appalled; but she dared not protest, for she was now dependent on Parliament for her allowance. In 1645 she was further cast down by the news that Prince Edward had apostasized in order to marry a Catholic, Anne of Gonzaga. Then Prince Philip, who had been fighting for the Venetians against the Turks, returned to the Hague to find that a Monsieur de l'Épinay, renowned for his gallantries, had made advances to his mother. He did not wait to challenge the Frenchman, but attacked him when he was unarmed, with the result that de l'Épinay died a few days later. Elizabeth forbade Philip her presence, and he joined his brothers in England, thence departing to fight for the French; he was killed in 1650. The Queen was less concerned about the Épinay scandal than about Parliament's reduction of her revenue and Charles I's dismissal of Rupert, whom he cashiered and disgraced after the siege of Bristol; he and Maurice then joined the French army in Flanders.

As the fortunes of her family declined, Sophia continued to enjoy herself — specifically with a young German Prince, Ernst-August of Brunswick-Lüneburg, who visited the Hague at this time. They played and sang together — she was much struck by his elegance and the beauty of his hands — and he then continued his tour; he wrote to her often, mostly about music. She made inquiries, and having discovered that he was the youngest of four sons, with little hope of an inheritance, broke off the correspondence.

She was equally prudent when in September 1648 the Prince of Wales, almost penniless, rejected by La Grande Mademoiselle and proscribed by the victorious Parliament, arrived at the Hague. She took a great fancy to him, and they were soon on the best of terms, 'as cousins and friends'. Sophia knew, as did everyone else, that this ugly, amusing youth had a mistress, Lucy Walter, known as Mrs Barlow, who was expecting his child. When he came to walk with Sophia and concluded a gallant approach with 'You are handsomer than Mrs Barlow—I hope soon to see you in England,' she told her mother, who was delighted; for the Queen much preferred her nephew's company to that of her own children, and so chose to interpret his advance more favourably than her daughter did. Then the Princess heard that Charles's courtiers were saying that she might persuade Lord Craven to finance him —and nothing had been said about marriage. Next time the Prince asked her to walk with him she made the excuse of a corn on her foot. 'My real reason,' she recalled, 'was to avoid him, having sense enough to know that the marriages of great kings are not made up by such means.' In January 1649 her cousin became a king, although not a great one. His father's execution horrified Europe and crushed her mother. Sophia took it calmly, merely noting that the new King avoided her in the presence of his latest supporters, the Scots Covenanters. This withdrawal gave her further proof of the Queen's foolish optimism and her own perspicacity.

So the picture of a rather smug, cold-hearted young woman seems to emerge. Yet although Sophia was neither amorous nor impulsive, she had a loyal and affectionate nature. She was devoted to her sisters and to Charles-Louis, always her favourite brother. Her cool head and acute judgment were combined with a natural gaiety and an unfailing interest in other people. When Parliament cut off her mother's allowance, leaving her and her daughters dependent on charity, Sophia remained serene. 'In those days,' she says, 'my temperament was so cheerful that the misfortunes of my family did not affect me, although sometimes we were hungry, and had to feast, like Cleopatra, on diamonds and pearls.' In other words, the Queen of Bohemia, after reluctantly pawning a few jewels, clung to the remainder, while continuing to entertain, with the result that the Princesses were cold, shabby and underfed. Lord Craven, whose great wealth Parliament had been unable to confiscate, was their chief support; he took a father's place in Sophia's life, and they shared jokes and catch-phrases. 'It was not surprising', she goes on, 'that I did not mind being poor, because the shopkeepers let me have what I needed—and I trusted in Providence to pay them.'

This carefree attitude gave her independence of mind; in other respects her standards were high. The iron discipline of Madame de Ples had not only enforced her natural resilience but made her increasingly critical of her mother's vague hopefulness and casual freedom of manner. Sophia's sense of dignity and rank was as instinctive and perdurable as her common sense. She knew that if she did not look after her own interests, nobody else would, and she was determined not to submit to the fate of her sisters. For Elizabeth, having refused the King of Poland and the Duke of Neuburg on religious grounds, was now past the marrying age and losing her beauty. Louise had privately betrothed herself to the Marquess of Montrose, who left her to raise the Scots Royalists and met his death at the hands of the Covenanters. Henrietta was too childish to think beyond needlework and cookery. So Sophia decided that she herself must look round for a suitable husband. Her only ally was Charles-Louis, who in 1649 succeeded his father to the Electorate of the Lower Palatinate, as a result of the Treaty of Westphalia. He promised Sophia that he would send for her as soon as he was installed, which he did in the following year, shortly after his marriage to Princess Charlotte of Hesse-Cassel.

Elizabeth of Bohemia did all she could to prevent her eldest son accepting this partial inheritance; because the Lower Palatinate amounted to half his father's kingdom, she urged him to insist on his full rights. When the prudent young man ignored her suggestions and fell back on the support of the English Parliament, she tried to stop Sophia's departure, on the grounds that, if she remained in Holland, her marriage with Charles II might somehow be achieved. Both Sophia and her brother knew that this was a daydream. The Princess therefore respectfully indicated that her mind was made up, adding that her journey to Heidelberg would be arranged and paid for by Lord Craven.

In March 1650 she set off, as if acting out the old nursery game played by her brothers and sisters at Leyden — 'going home to Heidelberg'. To Sophia, that city was rather a goal than a home — and the setting for her career. She left the Hague in high spirits, resolved to enjoy every moment of the journey.

TWO

I

THE new Elector Palatine, now in his thirty-fourth year, was calculating, patient, energetic and ruthless. Such persons are usually cold-hearted; Charles-Louis's temperament combined an instinctive kindness with a sensuality which sometimes bordered on violence; yet his intuition generally turned the results of these impulses to his own advantage.

He was the best-looking of an unusually handsome family: tall, slender and dark, with the high-bred, finely cut cast of feature most often seen in Gothic statuary. His manner was stately, and he could be pompous; yet this seeming reserve would suddenly give way to a rather juvenile exuberance. Perhaps his deepest feelings were for his inheritance. Although he could have had but the vaguest memories of the country he left in his third year, he had sacrificed all that his family held most sacred in order to regain a portion of it. In the eyes of his mother, of Rupert and Maurice, and of his uncle Charles, he had been a traitor. The English Parliament, while using him, realized his disingenuousness; and the rest of his family, Sophia excepted, took his hospitality only when driven to do so. She and Henrietta called him Papa, trusted his judgment and admired his efforts to restore his decimated kingdom.

For now Charles-Louis had need of all the determination of which he was capable. He found the Palatinate in an almost hopeless condition, for which there appeared, at first, no cure. He was in the position of a doctor who, called to attend a moribund patient, can produce only the most primitive and inadequate remedies.

The castle of Heidelberg was a fair example of the general situation. In the early part of the Thirty Years War, which began when Charles-Louis was a year old, it had been besieged and occupied by opposing forces, and was now a structure of skeletal beauty. A contemporary print shows it dominating a landscape devoid of life. Forests, meadows, farms and villages have been flattened into a grim uniformity; the Rhine might be the Styx, the mountains those of the moon.

The spirit of the people, some of whom had been reduced by hunger to cannibalism, rose to welcome their Elector. The city fathers conducted him to his birthplace, of which the porphyry floors, the gilt pillars, the painted ceilings of what had been one of the most splendid palaces in Europe had disappeared; the walls had cracked; the windows were glassless. He settled in a house near by and began the gigantic, the heart-breaking task of rehabilitation.

The effect of this devastation on Sophia was, ultimately, beneficial. She had never known luxury until, during her journey, she was entertained by the Duke of Neuburg, the Landgrave of Hesse-Cassel and the Elector of Cologne, with a magnificence which made her new home seem pathetically humble; cheerfully, she accepted its conditions. When she was met at the frontier by a carriage without seats drawn by a pair of horses who refused to move, she walked through the mud to a windowless house, merely noting the excellence of the cooking.

Her brother and sister-in-law then appeared and conducted her to Heidelberg. After an hour or so Sophia came to the conclusion that the Electress Charlotte must be a very silly woman. She was handsome enough: but she grumbled about everything, got herself up ridiculously and could talk of nothing but her trousseau, which was at the same time extravagant and dowdy. Within a few days she confided to Sophia that she had not wanted to marry Charles-Louis, and gave her the list of her rejected suitors, one of whom was Prince Ernst-August of Brunswick-Lüneburg.

Her brother then took her aside and said, 'My wife has many good qualities, but she has been badly trained,' going on to ask Sophia to take her in hand. By this time the young lady was beginning to wish herself back at the Hague. She observed that her brother's standards of seemliness were constantly sacrificed to his passion for his wife, whom he embraced in public; quite often, they were seen locked in each other's arms. Surely, Sophia thought, such a love must be eternal and serene; then she observed that Charlotte and Charles-Louis quarrelled without ceasing. He made scenes whenever she encouraged their courtiers' attentions; she replied with outbursts of rage. At night they were reconciled;

during the day she whined and sulked in the intervals of hunting and playing cards. Sophia concluded that what she needed was a good thrashing.

She was thankful when Princess Elizabeth and Prince Edward arrived, thus partially healing the breach caused by Charles-Louis's disapproval of Princess Henrietta's marriage to the Prince of Transylvania, which had been arranged by her eldest sister. Elizabeth considered the alliance quite good enough for a dowerless sixteen-year-old; Henrietta cried at the thought of leaving home; Charles-Louis protested at this degradation of their name; the Queen of Bohemia took alternate sides. Henrietta no sooner saw her Hungarian prince than she fell in love with him; five months later she was dead.

Elizabeth, who had left the Hague as the result of a dispute with her mother about the Queen's encouragement of Monsieur de l'Épinay, had been living with her aunt, the Electress of Brandenburg. Her grief at the death of Descartes made her more than usually critical; and she had even less use for her sister-in-law than Sophia had. This annoyed Charlotte, who complained to Sophia, as did Edward, of Elizabeth's curt answers and moody humour. Later, Sophia realized that she should have stood up for the sister who was worth all the rest of the family put together; but a sudden influx of visitors distracted her, and she plunged into a round of gaieties with a party of young people. She dressed up, danced, made expeditions and revelled in the attentions paid her, particularly in those of the Prince of Holstein, who drank her health so deeply that he choked and was sick all over the table—what more amusing tribute could there be? And then it made his elderly spinster cousins so jealous; and one of his gentlemen, who bowed whenever she looked at him, was even more ridiculous. She was further set up by a proposal, her first, from a Portuguese nobleman; refused, of course; but it amounted to a triumph. Then all was gloom and horror. She fell ill with smallpox, recovering to find her beauty gone.

It was not so, as subsequent reports on her appearance prove. Although her youthful glow may have sunk, her delicate features and her large dark eyes were unaffected; and her charm of manner was perhaps enhanced by a shade of timidity. Her attractions were emphasized when Prince Ernst-August reappeared, and began to court her in earnest. They played and sang together as before; and Sophia started to think seriously of marriage. But first—had the Prince's situation changed?

In 1641 Ernst-August and his brothers, Christian-Louis, George-William and John-Frederick, had come into their respective inheritances through the death of their father, the reigning Duke of Brunswick-Lüneburg. In 1648 Duke Christian took over the government of the largest and richest principality, that of Celle, and George-William that of Calenberg, with its principal town of Hanover. The two youngest received money, but no land. Duke Christian remained at Celle, and in the course of the next ten years drank himself quietly to death. Duke George, a gay and accomplished young man of cosmopolitan tastes, departed to Venice, where he set up a mistress and was presently joined by Ernst-August, who now resumed his correspondence with Sophia. She found his letters as charming as ever; but realizing that he was not in a position to ask for her hand, she presently ceased to answer them, because 'I was afraid people would say I had grown too fond of him.' Nevertheless, his admiration had restored her self-confidence and her determination to wait until she could marry well, in spite of the fact that her sister-in-law's behaviour had become more impossible than ever after the birth of the heir, another Charles, known in the family as Karellie, and a daughter, Elizabeth-Charlotte, born in 1652. The pet-name of this baby, an exceptionally attractive and intelligent child, was Liselotte. Sophia became her Lady Governess and grew very fond of her.

Her devotion to her brother and his children helped Sophia to endure the crazy onslaughts of the Electress, who now accused her of an incestuous relationship with Charles-Louis, and desired him to stop going to her apartments. The Elector replied by visiting his sisters every evening, attended by all his gentlemen. Sophia ignored the Electress's diatribes; but when she discovered that her sister-in-law was libelling her in letters to their relatives, she decided to accept the next person who offered for her.

This was Prince Adolph, younger brother of the King of Sweden, a rather sinister widower, whose reputation as a wife-beater was at first concealed from Sophia. The match was made up, the terms agreed, and plans for a private wedding, as being less expensive, put in hand, while Sophia braced herself for marriage with a man she did not expect to like. Then the King of Sweden broke off the alliance on the grounds of his recently completed agreement with

THE ELECTRESS SOPHIA AS A GIRL

Cromwell, much to Sophia's relief, and her brother's disappointment. He did not want to part with her; but he was beginning to
feel that he could no longer let her stay, for his difficulties, both as
husband and ruler, had become almost insuperable. While
Charlotte made scenes every day, his mother wrote twice a week,
asking him to pay her debts and instal her at Frankenthal, formerly part of her dowry, regardless of the fact that this property
was still in Spanish hands. When Charles-Louis replied that he
could only offer her a residence at Heidelberg, she refused; it must
be Frankenthal or nothing. She then changed her mind and
prepared to join him, but was prevented by the Dutch, who would
not let her leave until their bills were paid. Once more she wrote
to Charles-Louis begging for money; when he did not answer she
sent Lord Craven to plead her cause, at the same time complaining
of Elizabeth's and Sophia's neglect. Her state of mind was partially
due to the disappearance of Prince Maurice, who had been lost in
a storm off the Virgin Islands and was never heard of again. For
many years it was thought that he had been captured and sold as
a slave.

By this time Prince Edward had left Heidelberg and was living
in France. He was replaced by Rupert who, in 1656, suddenly
descended on the Elector and demanded his share of the kingdom.
When Charles-Louis replied that the allowances he made him
and Edward, and the support of Elizabeth and Sophia, were all he
could afford, Rupert had to suppress his rage, as he did not wish
to leave Heidelberg. Then Ferdinand IV, King of the Romans,
proposed for Sophia; just as the terms were completed, he died.
And all the time, the Electress continued to rave and complain.

Elizabeth took refuge in philosophical studies, and affiliated
herself with the newly restored University of Heidelberg, where
her teachings were much in demand. Both Sophia and Charles-
Louis were now desperate. He then solved part of his problem —
but in such a manner as to add to her difficulties.

I I

For some time Charles-Louis, nauseated by his wife's neurotic
egoism, had been taking refuge in the arms of one of her ladies,

Louise von Degenfeld; her beauty also attracted Prince Rupert, whose advances she rejected. He continued to court her, and one of his letters, reproaching her with coldness, was inadvertently given to the Electress who, much flattered, waited for Rupert to appear and coquettishly began, 'I do not know why you should upbraid me, nor doubt of my affection.' The Prince blushed and seemed so embarrassed that the Electress, turning again to the letter, perceived the mistake. She then scolded Louise, who replied that she was perfectly indifferent to His Highness.

A few nights later the Electress discovered Louise and Charles-Louis in bed together in the room adjoining her own. With screams of rage she rushed upon the girl, who took refuge behind Charles-Louis. In the ensuing struggle he managed to prevent his wife tearing at his mistress's face, but not before she had got hold of Louise's little finger and bitten it to the bone. By this time the room was crowded with attendants, and the Electress was removed by her ladies. Next morning Charles-Louis promised that he would give up Louise, and assured his wife that he had not broken his marriage vows.

Charlotte then forced open Louise's desk, to find her husband's love-letters which, together with a number of jewels, proved his adultery. She summoned Louise, who appealed to Charles-Louis to protect her, upon which the Electress sent for Sophia and Elizabeth. The sisters came in to see Charles-Louis standing between the two women, while Charlotte, marching up and down, stormed and gesticulated. 'Princesses!' she shouted, 'Do you see these jewels, the price of a whore? Why were they not given to me?'

Sophia, overcome by the absurdity of the remark, burst into peals of laughter—as did her sister-in-law, who now succumbed to hysteria. 'You should return those,' said Charles-Louis, indicating his presents. 'Take them!' screamed his wife, and threw the jewels all over the room, while Sophia continued to laugh and Elizabeth stood by in disgusted silence.

Charles-Louis then took Louise to his cabinet, which he locked, returning to sup with his wife, who seemed to be calming down. A few days later the Electress discovered that Louise had been placed in a room above her husband's apartments, whence he climbed up to her by a ladder. She seized a knife, made another rush at her rival and was held back by her ladies. Charles-Louis then established Louise in a house near Frankenthal, where he spent all his free time. Very soon those wishing to see him privately visited him there. One of the first was Count Hammerstein, the emissary of Duke George-William of Hanover, with an offer for Sophia. The Count added that before asking officially for the Princess's hand he must be certain that the reports of her beauty and intelligence had not been exaggerated, and that there was no question of her still being betrothed to Prince Adolph. Reassured on both points, he presently described his master's situation.

George-William's subjects had insisted on his marrying; if he did not set about founding a dynasty, they would cut off supplies. The Duke did not want to settle down—he spent most of his time abroad, chiefly in Venice—but now he agreed to take a wife, and had chosen Sophia, subject to her brother's approval. Hoping to stimulate the Duke's rather sluggish approach, Charles-Louis told Hammerstein that although his sister was still unofficially engaged to Prince Adolph, George-William might win her if he were serious in his intentions. 'It depends upon you,' he concluded, 'whether that other marriage takes place or not.'

Shortly after receiving Hammerstein's report George-William and Ernst-August visited Heidelberg on their way to Venice. Sophia, always practical, now found that she preferred Duke George, as being livelier and more sophisticated than his younger brother. As soon as the preliminary gallantries had been gone through, he asked her if she was still betrothed to Prince Adolph. Receiving a satisfactory answer, he continued, rather perfunctorily, to court her, and then said, 'Have I your leave to ask the Elector for your hand?' 'I did not reply like the heroine of a romance,' Sophia recalled, 'for I at once said yes.'

The contract of marriage was drawn up, and the brothers made ready to leave. At the last moment George-William asked the Elector to keep his betrothal a secret from the Hanoverians—'because,' he explained, 'if they know I am committed, they might not increase my allowance.' Meanwhile, Sophia perceived that Ernst-August was not pleased about the marriage, because he feared that she might estrange him from his brother, to whom he was devoted. She had a feeling that all was not well, for other reasons; but the contract was signed, and shortly after the Dukes' departure George-William's portrait arrived and was hung in the Presence Chamber.

Determined to make the most of his last months of freedom, George-William set up a Greek mistress on his arrival in Venice, from whom he caught venereal disease. Undaunted, he continued to revel in the gaieties of the city. His increased allowance enabled him to stay on; his letters to Sophia became shorter and colder: then they ceased altogether. She was angry, humiliated and very anxious, for she had reached her twenty-seventh year: was she to share the fate of Louise and Elizabeth? She managed to retain her outward cheerfulness, and with it her dignity; this self-control was rewarded by another proposal.

Without warning, Father Manari, the self-appointed envoy of the Duke of Parma, appeared at the Elector's court. Sophia's portrait had taken his master's fancy; but his offer depended, naturally, on her conversion to Roman Catholicism. To win over a Palatine Stuart would be a triumph for Manari, an ambitious young man, who now produced the picture of Ranuccio II and a courteous letter from his mother, as one assuming the Elector's acceptance on behalf of a sister past the marrying age.

Sophia was delighted. If the rumour of her abandoning George-William (and the Protestant faith) for Ranuccio reached Venice, then surely her recalcitrant lover would hurry back to claim her; so Father Manari was kept in suspense while she and Charles-Louis waited for the outcome. At worst, it would be better to reign as Duchess of Parma than to remain where she was: for now Charles-Louis was talking of a separation from his wife and a morganatic marriage with Louise; if either or both took effect, Sophia's position would become untenable.

By this time, George-William had come to the conclusion that he could not face matrimony, with Sophia or anyone else; so he suggested to Ernst-August that he should marry her instead; in return, he would give Ernst-August his Hanoverian estates, while himself receiving an increased allowance and solemnly promising never to take a wife, so as to stand down from the succession. Ernst-August was more than willing to oblige; but he pointed out that, as the youngest brother, he ought not to agree until Duke John-Frederick had been consulted. When John-Frederick joined them George-William outlined the proposed arrangement, adding, 'You will suffer no injury by it, since, if I die, you will succeed to my Duchy as next in line.' John-Frederick flew into a temper. 'Why should you give up the Princess to my brother and not to me?' he demanded. 'I should be a fool to agree!' George-William, equally enraged, turned John-Frederick out of his palace and was only just restrained from throwing him into the Grand Canal.

It was then agreed that Ernst-August should return to Hanover in order to discuss the new arrangement with his brother's ministers; on the way he fell dangerously ill. George-William joined him in Vienna, and after some delay they reached Hanover together.

George-William at once informed his Council of his scheme, adding that he had decided never to marry and would give them a written promise to that effect. Ernst-August would continue the dynasty on condition of an allowance which would enable him fittingly to support a wife and family. Unwillingly, the ministers agreed, and Hammerstein was instructed to proceed to Frankenthal to put the new terms before the Elector. Having done so, Hammerstein pointed out that, although George-William would retain the title of Duke of Hanover, the property would be Ernst-August's, and as, by the Treaty of Munster, he would eventually become Coadjutor-Bishop of Osnabrück, that estate would be settled on Sophia as part of her dowry; meanwhile she would receive the honours of the future Duchess of Hanover and Osnabrück. He added that Duke Christian, the eldest brother, was not only childless but unlikely to live very much longer; Duke John-Frederick, who was still a bachelor, had become a Catholic in 1651, so that he could not succeed; George-William had agreed never to marry. Thus Sophia's children would eventually inherit all the Brunswick-Lüneburg estates, with the dukedoms of Hanover, Osnabrück and Celle. 'She will be', Hammerstein lyrically concluded, 'the mother of our country.'

The cautious Elector replied that, although the prospects sounded well, he did not trust George-William to keep his word; what if he broke it, and had a family? 'There is nothing to fear,' Hammerstein assured him, 'His Highness is so debauched that he is incapable of children. That is why he wants his brother to marry the Princess.'

Still Charles-Louis withheld his consent. 'I will write to my sister and ask her opinion,' he said. He was about to do so when news came of another defection in his family, one so grave as temporarily to eliminate all other considerations.

Of the Queen of Bohemia's thirteen children, seven were dead and five had left home. Only the Princess Louise remained to share the penury and the constrictions of a meaningless existence. She was thirty-five; her lover had been executed; her mother alternated between bursts of complaint and the 'wild humour to be merry' which must have been almost as trying as her periods of depression. Without the brothers and sisters who had enlivened hardship and defeated ennui, Louise was thrown back on her painting, a pursuit tolerated but not consistently encouraged by the Queen, who still behaved like a spoilt beauty, as obstinately regardless of her circumstances as of her appearance. For with age had come ugliness, even distortion; and one day, when her mother's indomitable complacency may have been more than usually infuriating, Louise began work on her cruelly satirical portrait of the Winter Queen.

Elizabeth is shown sitting at her dressing-table, attended by three pretty young ladies-in-waiting. Their fresh looks and elegantly simple dress emphasize their mistress's withered yet bumpy features, the dated elaboration of her gown, her Jacobean ruff and peacock fan. As if to drive home the absurdity of the sitter's attitude towards herself, the table is littered with objects symbolizing the hopeless struggle against decay: a paper smeared with rouge, spectacles, a grubby account book, some pills—and a set of false teeth.

This brilliant example of *genre* painting, now in the Herrenhausen Museum at Hanover, partially illustrates a development in the artist which staggered her contemporaries. Wearily turning away from the dust-heap of her mother's court, Louise found refuge in an inner, a spiritual life. She studied, she compared, she came to a conclusion—and so to a resolve. Early in the morning of December 27th, 1657, she disappeared; and presently a letter to the Queen was found in her room. Louise intended to become a Catholic; and she was now on her way to France, to be received into the Church which offered the fulfilment she desired. So the Queen of Hearts was quite alone; her only companion had deserted her for a creed which in her eyes stood for evil mumbo-jumbo and eternal damnation.

The triumph of her Catholic, the horror of her Protestant relatives, left Louise unmoved; she found permanent happiness in the convent of Maubuisson, of which she eventually became the Abbess, dying there fifty-two years later. Every effort was made to reconvert her; letters flew from the agonized Queen to her family.

She upbraided Prince Edward, her apostate son; she implored Charles II to remonstrate with Louise; she sent lamentations to Charles-Louis.

Sophia seems to have received the news of her sister's break-away with indifference. All this fuss was, to her, one more example of what she most deplored — waste. Whether of money, emotion or endeavour, this became, in her view, the real, the ultimate disaster. She despised the outward forms of the old faith, while the practices of Lutheranism and Calvinism sometimes struck her as equally absurd; but that yoke was more adaptable and could, at a pinch, be evaded altogether. Dignity, prosperity, a suitable and secure position — these were the goals of her supremely reasonable ambition. She had no use for conflict, or for wild rebellion, or — most foolish of all — romantic yearnings. So it was that when she received the Elector's letter about the transfer of her hand, she replied that she did not need his recommendation of Ernst-August as a more reliable character than George-William. 'I care only for a good establishment,' she wrote, 'and if I find it with the younger brother, then I shall have no difficulty in relinquishing the one for the other. My pleasure', she correctly added, 'lies in doing what you think is best for me, and I am wholly in your hands.'

So another contract was drawn up, followed by a compli-mentary exchange of letters between Sophia and Ernst-August. The wedding was to be celebrated in Heidelberg, the consumma-tion of the marriage in Hanover. It only remained to dismiss poor Father Manari, who was later found drowned, whether by accident or not, no one knew ('Italians are naturally passionate, and it may have been suicide,' remarked Sophia), to plan the bride's trousseau and select her attendants. In the first week of September 1658 Ernst-August arrived; and Sophia made another of her practical decisions.

The ludicrous and degraded spectacle of her brother's married life (which caused the more fastidious Princess Elizabeth to retire to a Protestant convent in Westphalia) had not been wasted on Sophia. She drew from it the conclusion that affection, rather than passion, must form the basis of a successful union. When she and her bridegroom met again she was 'very pleased to find him likeable, because I had made up my mind to love him'. So she did love him — had he not brought her what she most desired? For forty years she continued to do so, unperturbed, tolerant, philosophical, loyal. Ernst-August was dull, kind, genial and not more selfish than most princes. Sophia's receipt for marriage was that of her eldest brother's favourite song, *'Quand on n'a pas ce que l'on aime, il faut aimer ce que l'on a.'*

She was married in such splendours as Charles-Louis could afford—a silver brocade dress with a 'prodigiously' long train, and a diamond tiara. The processions, the banquets and balls continued for several days. Then Ernst-August left for Hanover alone, in order to receive his bride at the frontier with the honours befitting her rank and position. By this time she realized that he had fallen in love with her. 'My sentiments,' she recalls, 'went rather further than the liking he had originally inspired, for I began to feel what must form the basis of true love.' Charles-Louis accompanied her to the frontier, where she shed a few tears. 'There would have been more,' she adds, 'if my heart had not been elsewhere ... '

This noun, a new addition to Sophia's discreetly selective vocabulary, was characteristically apt. Her heart, that warm yet manageable organ, would always be found in the right place.

THREE

I

SOPHIA'S journey to Hanover was ceremoniously prolonged. At each principality—Mainz, Frankfurt, Cassel—its ruler received her with formal courtesy; she was feasted during the day and watched ballets and fireworks at night. Although sharply critical—one Landgrave had dirty hands and another provided uneatable bread—she enjoyed every moment of her progress.

The seventeenth century was not an age in which the appreciation or even the awareness of 'scenery' had a place; the connotation of the word was purely theatrical. So when the new Duchess exchanged the Rhine for the Leine she made no comment on the contrast between the setting of her brother's kingdom and that of her husband's. The flat bleakness of the northern landscape, its seemingly endless stretches of heather and marsh, the opaque atmosphere, the sparse, blunt coppices did not strike her as dreary and monotonous after the gorges and mountains of Heidelberg, because the red-brick, timbered and painted farmhouses, the neat cottages, the solidly spired churches, the well tilled fields stood for what she had learned to value most—comfort, order and careful administration. When she entered the medieval city of Hanover to the sound of cannon, trumpets and cheering crowds, that encircling prosperity merged into the stateliness of tall, high-gabled houses and civic buildings, ample bridges and the great bulk of the Leine Palace, all set against a richly interlacing background of lime avenues, knot gardens and fountains, each of these last with its group of stout nymphs and amiable cherubs. All was perfection—disciplined gaiety, adequate splendour and respectful warmth.

As Sophia stepped from her coach she was greeted by the four Brunswick-Lüneburg Dukes, her mother-in-law the Dowager Duchess of Celle, and two cousins, the Duke and Duchess Antony-Ulric of Brunswick-Wolfenbüttel. While the prescribed series of salutes was being interchanged they observed a slight, pale, aquiline young woman, whose large eyes slanted slightly upwards, dressed in an amber satin gown—her best, presumably, for she wore it when sitting for all her early portraits—cut very low and clasped with brooches of pearl and aquamarine. Her dark hair was drawn back from a high forehead, falling in ringlets; her only other ornament was a necklet of large Roman pearls. She moved gracefully, and behaved with the smiling composure of one long experienced in public appearances, curtsying low or slightly, modestly holding back or serenely accepting precedence, as occasion required. Ernst-August was radiant, eager to show off his prize; George-William could not remove his eyes from her. When they entered the palace he took care to inform her that he personally had seen to the redecoration of her rooms and the fresh gilding of the bronze canopy under which her chair of state was placed. This pleased her best of all; it symbolized the perdurable wealth and status which had been her single aim.

And then there was love—for as soon as the banquetings and processions were over her honeymoon began. For the first time in her life, she found herself spending hours alone with a gay, indulgent, amorous young man, who asked nothing better than to admire and possess and pet her. Everything she did and said pleased Ernst-August; he revelled in the high spirits and good humour which enhanced his own; his jolly court was at her feet; her mother-in-law was graciously approving; his brothers were her servants. Then she came upon the serpent in this well-appointed Eden—the exuberant susceptibility of George-William.

That light-hearted *coureur de femmes* now found himself in the agreeable position of being able to flirt with the sister-in-law he had rejected as a wife, regardless of her embarrassment and his brother's annoyance. Ernst-August, remembering that Sophia had married for an establishment, did not at once perceive that she had fallen in love with him, and was indifferent to George-William. 'I so idolized him,' she says, 'that I felt quite lost when he was not with me. I remember with pleasure ... the passion he had for me.' She treated George-William with sisterly freedom; when he took advantage of this approach, Ernst-August became suspicious. He had always envied his brother's success with the sex, and now, seeing him join Sophia at cards, in the hunting-field or out walking, he was bitterly jealous.

It did not occur to Sophia that her husband could doubt her

love—it may not have been quite so ardent as, many years afterwards, she chose to think—and she continued to enjoy George-
William's company, to the point indeed of sitting by his bed when
he was ill and asking him about his Italian travels. On this
occasion, when Ernst-August had sulkily withdrawn and was
pretending to read, he heard her say, 'I am sure you would rather
be in Italy than here.' 'Since you came to Hanover,' George-
William gallantly replied, 'I wish to be nowhere else.' Sophia
laughed, and said, '*Quand on n'a pas ce que l'on aime, il faut aimer ce
que l'on a.*' Ernst-August, taking this to mean that she had put
up with himself in default of his brother, marched out of the room
and refused to speak to her for the rest of the day. In tears, she
implored him to tell her what the matter was, and eventually
reconciliation followed reassurance.

The two brothers then decided to take Sophia to Italy. When
they were a day's journey from Hanover, she came to the conclusion that she had better return; the situation was too difficult.
They would not go on without her, and went to stay with the
Dowager Duchess at Herzberg, where they were joined by Duke
Christian, now permanently drunk. The three inseparables then
left for Hamelin to hunt, and here George-William renewed his
courtship of Sophia. It seemed to Ernst-August that she encouraged him, and that the most dangerous moment was when
he himself fell asleep after dinner. So before settling down he
placed her opposite him and put his feet up on either side of her
chair. 'This procedure sometimes lasted for hours,' she says, 'but
I did not object, because I loved him.'

The whole problem could have been solved by Sophia telling
George-William to leave her alone; but, somehow, she could not
bring herself to do so ... One morning, he visited her while she was
dressing. She asked him to withdraw while she changed her
chemise, and locked the door behind him. He objected, and she
then told him that she had no intention of becoming his mistress.
'But', she complacently recalled, 'his passion and the Duke's
jealousy continued.'

Once more the brothers left for Italy, while Sophia set off to stay
with her mother at the Hague—only to find George-William
waiting for her at Leyden. In considerable alarm for her reputation, she begged him, 'for the love of God,' to continue his journey,
and he did so—not very reluctantly, for she was now pregnant and

no longer at her best. Thereafter, his fading penchant was dimly renewed in the intervals of more satisfactory affairs. Sophia also had other interests, the most absorbing of which was the education of her niece, the six-year-old Liselotte, who was brought to Hanover a few months after her marriage and remained in her charge for the next four years.

Sophia's devotion to Liselotte lasted all her life; the vast correspondence of their maturity partially illustrates the development of their characters. At a very early age Liselotte decided that she would like to be a boy, and having heard that this metamorphosis had once been brought about by jumping, she proceeded to leap and bound, a habit she retained long after she had given up all hope of changing her sex. No doubt her romping ways and quick wit reminded Sophia of her own childhood; and then, as they both settled in at the Hague, she saw her headstrong mother completely dominated by this clever, lively grandchild. 'She is very pretty,' the Winter Queen reported to Charles-Louis, 'and you may believe it ... for you know I care not much for children, but I never saw one I like so well as her, she is so good-natured and witty.'

Elizabeth's great-nephew, the fatherless Prince William Henry (later William III) then aged eight, also took a fancy to Liselotte, and during this visit they got on very well. (A year later he had reached the teasing stage, and Queen Elizabeth reported that Liselotte 'could not abide him'.) While Sophia was so often called upon that she had not, according to her mother, 'time to piss', the little Palatine Princess was taken to see her Dutch and English relatives. Sophia, who had always resented the haughty airs of the widowed Mary of Orange, did not accompany her mother and niece to the Binnenhof, merely remarking, 'Lizette, take care not to behave as you generally do. Follow the Queen step by step, that she may not have to wait for you.' 'Oh, aunt,' was the reply, 'you shall see how well I behave.'

The young lady's first sight of her Stuart cousin produced a characteristic interchange. 'Pray,' she asked William, 'can you tell me who is the lady with the fiery nose?' The Prince gleefully replied, 'That is the Princess Royal, my mother,' and Liselotte was momentarily silenced. Then she and William were sent to play; they were rolling about on a valuable Turkey carpet when the summons came for Liselotte to join her grandmother. She ran into the Presence Chamber, gave the Princess Royal's skirt a brisk tug, curtsied and then strode on before her, in order to keep up, 'step by step', with the Queen. She could not think what it was that made everybody laugh so.

When they got home Elizabeth said to Sophia, 'Lizette has made a delightful visit,' and described the scene. Both ladies laughed heartily, and Sophia said, 'Lizette, you have done well in revenging us on the pride of the Princess.'

This injudicious comment and the attentions of Queen Elizabeth's courtiers so worked upon Liselotte that her aunt had to put her down by saying, 'Your brother has a better face than you,' and the child burst into tears, to be reassured by the doting Queen. 'This is a sad business—yours is better,' she insisted, adding in her next letter to Charles-Louis, 'She is a very good child and not troublesome ... All the Hague is in love with Lisel ... She reminds me of my poor Henriette.'

Although there was not the slightest resemblance between the stout little Teuton with her round blue eyes and rosy, oblong cheeks and the exquisitely frail Henrietta, the Queen persisted with, 'She is not like the House of Hesse, she is like ours,' much to Sophia's amusement, who, watching her mother wait on Liselotte, only hoped that the child would not become hopelessly spoiled. She herself was soon eager to leave the Hague; her mother's dogs were more impossible than ever, Liselotte was always over-eating, and she longed to be at home with her husband. In March 1660 they left for Iburg.

By the beginning of May, when they moved to Hanover, Liselotte realized that her aunt was expecting a baby. When Sophia's labour began she was taken out into the garden and shown a doll in a rosemary bush, which, her governess said, was the newly-born child. Liselotte knew better. Hearing screams of agony from the bedchamber, she slipped back into the room and hid behind a screen. When at last a very different kind of baby— the son who, fifty-four years later, became George I of England —was taken over to the fireplace, the young lady revealed herself, and got a tremendous scolding; everyone was too rejoiced at the birth of the heir to give her the whipping she deserved.

Sophia was in ecstasies over the child who was to cause her so much unhappiness. 'He is as beautiful as an angel,' she wrote to Charles-Louis, adding that motherhood made no difference to her love for Liselotte, who had just given them all a great fright by nearly swallowing a pin. Then Duke George-William appeared from Italy with a pet dog for the little girl. A few weeks later he and Ernst-August set off for Venice, while Sophia and her niece went to stay at Heidelberg, taking with them the baby George-Louis.

Here they found the Elector divorced from his wife and morganatically married to Louise von Degenfeld, who eventually bore him fourteen children. They were presently joined by the two Dukes, and with them visited the Hague, to say goodbye to Elizabeth of Bohemia, who was leaving for England, where she died the following year. In October 1661 Sophia gave birth to her second son, Frederick-August, and settled down to perfect happiness in Iburg. 'I do nothing but sleep, eat and sing to the children,' she told Charles-Louis. Of the two babies, she thought the elder was her favourite: but she was too wrapped up in them both to be sure. Meanwhile Liselotte was getting on very well with her lessons; Ernst-August had given her a little cart, drawn by two dogs, in which she drove about the palace.

In December Ernst-August's triumph was crowned by his accession to the Bishopric of Osnabrück, which enabled Sophia to hold her own court. As 'Bishopess' she could not, she confessed, take herself very seriously. Both she and Ernst-August read and wrote letters in their comfortable pew, breaking off to laugh when the sermon was particularly absurd. They travelled about the principality in great style, taking the waters at Pyrmont, going down the Harz silver mines (Sophia was the first woman ever to do so) and attending performances by travelling players.

In August 1663 Sophia came to the conclusion that little George-Louis was really quite ugly; this discovery coincided with her husband's announcement that Hanover was wearisome, and his departure for Venice. Sophia agreed to join him at the frontier, after another visit to Heidelberg, where she would have preferred to stay; but 'I would have gone to the Antipodes with him, if he had asked me.' They expected George-William to be of the party. Then they heard that he was to remain at Cassel with the Prince and Princess de Tarente, and that he had fallen desperately in love with the Princess's French Huguenot lady-in-waiting, Eléanore d'Olbreuse, a beautiful and virtuous girl of twenty-five. This connection, which was to end twenty years later in hideous disaster, pleased his brother and sister-in-law. A quiet, well-bred mistress was just what the flighty George-William required. Hearing excellent reports of the young lady, they decided to ask her to Hanover, and were much amused when told that Duke John-Frederick also was seeking her favours. So, after prolonged sightseeing and entertaining in Verona and Vicenza, they reached Venice late one evening in May 1664.

Sophia was appalled. Nothing but water! She had never seen such a melancholy place. 'Do you not think it beautiful?' urged Ernst-August. She dared not say no, and he was so happy to be back that he did not observe her disappointment. What chiefly depressed her was the black gondolas and the mournful cries of '*prémi!*' — '*stàli!*' of the gondoliers; she might have been looking at so many floating sepulchres; and they shot by too quickly for her to catch a glimpse of the ladies her husband admired. Then their social life was inaugurated by a visit to a convent, and Sophia began to enjoy herself. The only trouble was that she constantly had to suppress the desire to burst out laughing. Everyone was so kind; but the ludicrous aspect of Venetian life made it very difficult for her to behave as became her position.

The nuns, who were most agreeable, although elderly and bearded, thought only of young men, and could talk of nothing but love; the churches were crowded with amorous couples. Fancy dress was the rule for the evening, when the Venetian nobility danced in the streets. In the daytime, chariot races were held on the sands of the Lido, each lady being accompanied by her *cicisbeo*. Ernst-August insisted on Sophia having one, and produced a Sicilian poet, whose costume was covered with paste jewellery. When she objected he found her another, more presentable escort, while he himself returned to his bachelor gallantries in what she describes as 'a more realistic manner'. She did not mind that in the least; but Italian cookery did not agree with her, she succumbed to malaria and was pestered by the attentions of a procuress, who wanted to arrange a rendezvous for her with the French ambassador. So she was thankful to return to Vicenza, where Ernst-August and the lady of his choice arranged another chariot-race, which ended in a pile-up of horses and drivers. This was followed by a concert and a mock debate on madness, which Sophia found almost as boring as the conversation of her husband's former mistresses.

They then proceeded to Milan, which she preferred; but a ball every night was really too much, and her callers, who often numbered a hundred at a time, were ineffably tedious. Her visit to the broken-nosed but still miracle-working Virgin of Loretto was highly enjoyable, although the smell of the oil-lamps made her feel sick; but a daubed painting, the work of St Luke, and a set of crockery used by Mary and Joseph, made up for this. Sophia and the priest who was showing these objects exchanged glances of amusement as he raked in the money.

After a short stay in Vicenza, where the food—cauliflower and anchovy salad at every meal— was terrible, they entered Rome incognito. Sophia would have enjoyed their visit more if Ernst-August had not settled down to cards each evening with the Princess Colonna, *née* Mancini, Cardinal Mazarin's niece. The Princess at once set about trying to convert Sophia, who took refuge in serious sightseeing. She went several times to St Peter's, found the Pope rather ill-bred, and had a brief altercation with the priest of Santa Maria della Vittoria, who told her that the battle of the White Mountain had been won for the Catholics through that Virgin's intercession. 'Such a great princess as yourself', he added, 'should give something to Our Lady.' 'I would,' said Sophia snappishly, 'if she had been on the other side'—and walked out between the banners taken from her father's army.

By this time, she was pining for home and the sight of her children. But the Duke could not tear himself away, and they continued their tour, returning to Venice for the carnival, while Sophia noted a few amenities. The puppet-shows in Siena were skilfully presented, Florentine sweetmeats and the Pitti Palace quite pleasing in their different ways, and the manners of the Bolognese most delightful; in Venice operas and masked balls made the damp endurable. Then at last, they began to make their way back, and Sophia was nearly killed on the St Gotthard pass. At Frankfurt they heard that Duke Christian-Louis was dead, and that John-Frederick had seized his estates in the absence of George-William, who could not be induced to break off his courtship of Mademoiselle d'Olbreuse. While Sophia settled in at Iburg, Ernst-August hurried over to Celle to protect one brother's rights by reasoning with the other.

I I

If Ernst-August had not been the kindest and most affectionate of brothers, he would have ceased to be on speaking terms with George-William at the time of his marriage; for then, having handed over Sophia with the promise of a large sum of money, that Duke had failed to pay up. Now, finding George-William deprived, Ernst-August rushed to his defence, and after prolonged and difficult negotiations the three brothers came to an arrangement which satisfied them all. George-William inherited the largest estate, and so became Duke of Celle. John-Frederick succeeded to the Duchy of Hanover: and Ernst-August added the Countship of Diepholz to the Duchy and Bishopric of Osnabrück. Thus, in view of one brother's Catholicism and the other's promise not to marry, the inheritance of Ernst-August's and Sophia's children still appeared secure. Although George-William had twice broken his word, it did not occur to them that he might do so again. Nor did they grasp that his way of life had changed, and that his actions were subordinated to the principles and desires of a young woman whom they at first looked on as an admirable influence.

Eléanore d'Olbreuse was the elder daughter of a Poitevin marquis. In her teens she had been one of the respectable beauties of the court of Louis XIV, and at twenty-five she was even more dazzling and still determined to retain her virtue. At the time of her meeting with George-William she had come to the point when she must choose between two careers: that of becoming the mistress of a man who would make her a good settlement, or marrying well. Her principles forbade the first choice; and her poverty might endanger, if it did not altogether remove, her chances of marriage. Her only ally was the Princess de Tarente, sister of the late Elector Palatine and Sophia's aunt. This lady, who wanted to see her protégée well established, advised her to yield to George-William. He was so besotted that, if she played her cards well, she would be sure of a good settlement. But Eléanore desired to be a wife; although she was greatly taken with George-William and soon became very fond of him, she would not become his mistress.

This refusal threw him into a frenzy. He would not leave

Eléanore, even to deal with the seizure of his estate; the negotiations were halfway through before he appeared. Then he asked Ernst-August and Sophia to receive her, and they agreed. He did not tell them that he had signed a deed in which he declared that, if she became his mistress, she and her children would inherit part of the fortune he had already bequeathed to those of Sophia and Ernst-August. Still she would not yield, and she and George-William were on the point of a morganatic marriage when Sophia wrote asking her to Iburg.

Sophia was delighted to oblige her brother-in-law. As long as he remained faithful to a mistress, there was no danger of his breaking his word about marrying and thus depriving her own children. When Eléanore, with her sister Angélique and their friends Mademoiselle de la Mothe and Mademoiselle de la Mansélière appeared, she received them with the utmost kindness.

Sophia was incapable of feminine jealousy. She took a great fancy to Mademoiselle d'Olbreuse and much admired her glittering dark beauty, her tall slenderness and quiet elegance. Her manners were perfect; she was neither spiteful nor frivolous, and seemed very intelligent. Sophia therefore did everything she could to bring about a permanent bond between her and George-William. Nothing but good would come of their setting up together for life; and there could, of course, be no question of marriage in view of her rank and his promise to Ernst-August.

Although Eléanore had been received with all the permissible marks of favour—on her arrival Sophia and George-William met her at the foot of the great staircase, thence conducting her to the private apartments for salt biscuits and coffee—etiquette forbade her sitting down to meals with the ducal family. She and Angélique looked on while they ate, and then, nauseated by the sight of greasy sausages surrounded by a mess of ginger and onions, retired to their rooms to cook something for themselves. This irritated Sophia, who made satirical comments on the sisters' little *cache* of saucepans. Meanwhile, Mademoiselle de la Mothe, a mischief-maker, for whom Ernst-August had taken a brief fancy, told him that Eléanore was holding back in order to force George-William into a legal marriage. When this was repeated to him by his brother, George-William replied, 'If she thinks that, then she may return whence she came, I should never commit such a folly. But if she comes to me, I will care for her while I live and give her a good pension after my death.'

In fact, Eléanore was far too sensible to insist on an impossibility. Her behaviour during the next ten years shows the evolution of a long-term plan, which was inaugurated, in November 1665, by George-William's written promise never to abandon her and to give her an allowance and a pension after his death. This 'anti-contract' eliminated their children from the inheritance of titles and estates.

After the deed had been signed by George-William and witnessed by Sophia and Ernst-August, the couple went up to bed 'without company or candles', according to Sophia. Next day Eléanore, in tears, told George-William that she might at least have been granted the title of a married woman, and suggested that of Madame de Celle. This was refused, and after some discussion she became Madame de Harburg. 'It is like a marriage of conscience,' remarked Sophia contemptuously. 'How can George-William think of nothing but love and hunting?' Thereafter Eléanore, although allowed a chariot with six horses, was not permitted to drive out with Sophia and Ernst-August, nor to eat with them, nor given a chair with arms; she could—a great concession—remain seated in the presence of visiting royalties.

She endured these deprivations for a short time; as soon as she became pregnant she persuaded George-William to leave Osnabrück for Celle, whence she wrote to a friend, 'ours is the happiest home in the world,' adding that the Duke had sworn to keep her always with him, that her settlement had been more than generous and that in his duchy she received the honours of a princess. ('This seemed to us pitiable,' Sophia recalls. 'One could only shrug one's shoulders at such folly.') In September 1666 Eléanore gave birth to a daughter, Sophie-Dorothea, and three months later Sophia's third son, Maximilian-William, was born at Iburg. Eléanore then arranged an alliance for her sister with Count von Reuss, and set about endearing herself to her husband's subjects, whose disapproval of anti-contracts and intriguing Frenchwomen was soon dissipated by her charm and tact. She drove out with her baby to tour the city and received an affectionate welcome. George-William, hitherto so neglectful, became a model ruler. He rebuilt part of the castle, installed a theatre (now the oldest in Germany) and improved the condition of his estates. He and his Madam, as Sophia called her, seemed to be leading an ideal life. They could do nothing for Eléanore's former companions, who remained at Hanover. Then they heard that Mademoiselle de la Mansélière had become the mistress of Ernst-August. Sophia's account of this incident is an odd mixture of pique and common sense.

She had nearly died during her last labour, dreaded another, and so was thankful to be temporarily free from her husband's attentions. In any case, why should she grudge him his pleasures? She then perceived that Mademoiselle de la Mansélière had not only fallen in love with Ernst-August, but was appalled at her own weakness. 'This virtue of hers,' says Sophia, 'mingled with a great love, made her very unhappy. She often fainted—and screamed.'

All this to-do (more waste!) began to get on Sophia's nerves; when she realized that rumour had outstripped fact and that Mademoiselle de la Mansélière, although emotionally involved, had not yielded to her husband's advances, she blamed Eléanore 'for spreading horrible falsehoods' about the poor girl and continued to treat her as a friend—after all, were they not both devoted to the same man? Nevertheless, la Mansélière's evening walks with Ernst-August on the terrace did not look well, and Sophia was relieved when the young lady asked if she might return to France. She then begged to see Sophia alone, and explained that she was leaving in order to 'clear her name'. 'For your own sake,' replied the Duchess, 'it would have been wiser to be more discreet. I know you have done nothing wrong, but it is just as foolish to show your feelings in public as to behave immodestly in private.'

Bursting into tears, la Mansélière fell on her knees. Sophia kissed her and slipped two enamelled bracelets over her wrist, upon which the sobs turned to howls ('terrible ... I had never seen her in such a state') and she was carried from the room. When she left Hanover it was said that she had done so to conceal her pregnancy—'a great lie,' Sophia recalled. 'Nevertheless, I was glad, for I feared that anyone favoured by the Duke might come to rule his heart and so lessen his love for me.' She sent la Mansélière a miniature of herself, and wrote to her regularly ('which I enjoyed, for she was an excellent letter-writer') as did Ernst-August who, in October 1668, suggested that the girl should be installed as Lady Governess to their newly-born daughter, Sophia-

Charlotte. 'That might put us in the wrong,' his wife replied. 'It is not enough for a woman simply to *be* chaste, she must also appear so.' A few years later la Mansélière died, and was summed up by Sophia as 'rather a *strange* person, with a fine spirit and troublesome lusts.'

Shortly after the birth of the daughter who became her favourite child, Sophia's nephew, Charles-Louis's heir, was betrothed to Ernst-August's niece, Princess Wilhelmina of Denmark, and they went to Heidelberg to celebrate the occasion. Sophia, once more pregnant, found the journey rather an effort; but Liselotte's rapture at their reunion made up for her fatigue. In October 1669 her fourth son, Charles-Philip, was born, and two years later the clouds began to gather. France invaded Holland, and Ernst-August was summoned to take the field against Louis XIV. Sophia, who was now carrying her sixth child, suddenly became aware that a plot was being engineered at Celle by Schütz, George-William's Chamberlain, whom she describes as 'corrupt, self-seeking and determined to rule a master incapable of ruling himself.'

The situation was not quite so simple as she supposed. Schütz may have been an intriguer; but he was also the instrument of Eléanore, who was now planning to ask the Emperor Leopold's permission to legitimize the five-year-old Sophie-Dorothea. This only child was already a great heiress; and her legitimization must be preceded by her parents being married. Ernst-August protested, and the negotiations with the Emperor were broken off; finally, through Schütz's agency, it was agreed that if Sophie-Dorothea married into a royal house, she would be given the right to strike the bar sinister from her arms.

Duke Antony-Ulric of Brunswick-Wolfenbüttel then asked for the little Princess's hand on behalf of his eldest son, a boy of twelve, upon which Eléanore again begged George-William to marry her. He dared not break his oath to Ernst-August, and compromised by making a further settlement on mother and daughter, to the rage of Sophia, who began to suspect 'Madam' of the most sinister designs. At this point, both brothers, with Sophia and Eléanore, were bidden to the Danish court, whence Sophia was to conduct her husband's niece to Heidelberg for the marriage celebrations.

In Denmark, what would now be described as the cold war between Sophia and Eléanore began. Although both women were officially ruled by the brothers, George-William and Ernst-August entered the struggle as unskilled and rather unreliable allies. Their devotion to one another made it impossible for them to scheme and attack and undermine as the women did. The cold hatred, the merciless resolve of the German-Stuart Princess and the French aristocrat produced a series of skirmishes which the two Dukes understood only in part. If Sophia and Eléanore had been stupid and feeble, the violence and horror, the tragic climax which their rivalry eventually produced might have been avoided, and a patched-up peace achieved.

They were not rivals in the ordinary sense. Sophia despised Eléanore; but she was beginning to assess, and so to dread, her possibilities. Eléanore, safely entrenched behind George-William's devotion, could afford to ignore Sophia's hostile reconnaissance of her weak points. It did not matter to her that the Queen of Denmark had not greeted her with a kiss, that Sophia now spoke of her as the Duke's whore, or—more derisively still—as *la Signora*, and thought her beauty faded. Her mirror, George-William's subjugation and Ernst-August's friendly manners reassured her; and she and George-William had a good laugh over the coarse food and rough drink of their Danish hosts. Sophia's riposte—'the truly great prefer plain roasts to French ragoûts'—was received with sophisticated scorn, and the Duchess of Osnabrück lost that round. When Eléanore heard that Sophia referred to Sophie-Dorothea as 'that bastard', she let it be understood that George-William had promised to marry her if they had a son, and that in any case all *religious* persons considered their relationship a marriage in the sight of God. 'Better in God's sight than in man's,' replied Sophia.

After taking the waters at Pyrmont, Sophia left for Heidelberg, where her fifth son, Christian, was born. As soon as she began to recover, her brother asked her to help him with the scheme nearest his heart—or rather, his ambition—the betrothal of Liselotte to Philippe Duc d'Orléans, Louis XIV's younger brother, whose wife, Charles II's adored Minette, had died, some believed of poison, in 1670.

It is possible that a few years earlier Sophia would have discouraged a marriage which seemed to hold no hope of happiness for her niece. She was now in her forty-first year, and her character had hardened, perhaps because life with Ernst-August had not been quite so idyllic as it seemed in retrospect when she wrote her memoirs, a decade later. Her criticism of others' frailties were more acid, and her severity about illicit unions was truculently harsh. The strictness of her upbringing and her pride of race had risen to combine in setting her on guard against any encroachment of what she would have described as the family honour. Her devotion to Charles-Louis and the memory of his first wife's impossible behaviour had enabled her to accept his second marriage; but she had become increasingly suspicious and hostile, not only about George-William ('He is the king of the *canaille*') but also towards John-Frederick, now married, whose wife had borne him a daughter, nearly dying in the process. 'God give her long life to bear only daughters,' said his sister-in-law. With the establishment of six children to be considered, she had become fiercely protective; and she knew that Ernst-August was still inclined to weakness when his brothers' interests conflicted with his own.

So it was that Liselotte's horrified resistance to marriage with a French Catholic homosexual, suspected (wrongly) of having murdered his wife, received no support from the aunt whom she trusted to protect her. Whatever the Duc d'Orléans's reputation — and it could hardly have been worse — he was the greatest match in Europe, while Liselotte was insufficiently dowered, rather plain, and in her twentieth year. The poor girl's dread of an enforced 'conversion' to popery, and her misery at leaving home, were ignored. Sophia and Charles-Louis united in their determination to link up the Palatinate with the rising might of Louis XIV. After a series of painful tutorials Liselotte was received into the Church she had been taught to think of as the epitome of superstitious decadence, and dispatched, in floods of tears, to a court she believed to be corrupt, frivolous and unclean. Sophia was sad to let her go; but there could be no question of her favourite niece and pupil, the granddaughter of a Stuart Queen, submitting to the fate of her spinster aunts. Louise, that brilliant eccentric, might be happy at Maubuisson with her painting and her nuns; Elizabeth, who had entered a German Protestant sisterhood of which she eventually became the head, might be satisfied with a life of discipline and study; but Liselotte was born and educated to be a great lady, to take the *pas*, in the contemporary phrase, of all but crowned heads, indeed of Sophia herself.

Sophia and Charles-Louis conducted her to the frontier, where she was received by Anne of Gonzaga, their brother Edward's widow. (He had died in 1663.) All cried bitterly — 'I never saw a more touching farewell,' Sophia recalled — and she and her brother returned to Heidelberg, where they were joined by Ernst-August in time for the carnival. Sophia enjoyed the parade, in which she appeared as Night, and the Electress Louise as Minerva. She and Ernst-August then left for Osnabrück. In the autumn of 1672 they went to Celle, thus giving Sophia the chance of a sortie into enemy territory.

In a long talk alone with George-William she taxed him with the recurrent rumour of his marrying Eléanore in the event of their having a son. Angrily, he denied it, and offered to force Eléanore to bear out what he said. Sophia was not to be tempted into an act of hostility which might later be used as a weapon against her. 'Pray say no more,' she said, 'I will accept your word for it,' and George-William, much impressed by her tact and tolerance, let the matter drop.

Still the rumours went on; and Duke Antony-Ulric renewed his proposal for the marriage of Sophie-Dorothea with his eldest son. Then open war was declared — war in which Ernst-August at last became an active participant. His good nature had been tried to its limits; he prepared to fight his brother — and the odious Schütz — on his own ground, that of his solemn oath never to marry.

He had reckoned without Eléanore. George-William talked of making her Countess of Wilhelmsburg; and she was again in touch with the Emperor about the legitimizing of Sophie-Dorothea.

FOUR

I

THE child whom Sophia declared to have been 'born in iniquity' was brought up as a Frenchwoman, not only through the influence of Eléanore, but because her father, eventually turning away from Italy to France, had modelled his court on that of Louis XIV. His daughter spoke German with servants and local dignitaries; with relatives and friends she conversed and corresponded in her mother's tongue.

Yet the daily routine in the castle of Celle still followed that of George-William's predecessors. His retainers were summoned by a trumpeter from the tower to meals in the great hall at nine in the morning and four in the afternoon. Punctuality was enforced, and when all were seated a page went round insisting on quiet and seemliness; swearing, discourtesy, throwing about or pocketing food were forbidden; none but the butler was allowed to enter the cellar; the Duke's squires were given beer and hot possets but no wine; accounts were carefully kept and salaries paid weekly. Thus German orderliness combined with French *savoir vivre* to create luxury and comfort without the stifling etiquette and the competition for favours which made life at Versailles so irksome to Liselotte. Sophie-Dorothea, although not very highly educated, was reasonably accomplished, growing up in a happy, lively home; she seems seldom to have been bored or repressed. Her parents were as devoted to her as to each other; and when the deaths of three infant sisters presently made it clear that she was to be an only child, their adoring love was so concentrated on her that she became rather wilful and self-absorbed. From her earliest years she knew that she was pretty; as she reached her teens she achieved great beauty.

Her surroundings, those of a fairy-tale princess, were picturesque yet stately; luxury and homeliness, baroque grandeur and medieval simplicity, were blended to provide a perfect setting. The gabled houses, the clean, narrow streets, the glittering curve of the Aller were subordinated to and yet complemented by the soaring outlines of the lemon-coloured castle, with its four cupolaed towers, long lines of windows and triply arched façade, all embowered in wooded slopes leading down to the grey-green encirclement of the river. Prosperity without pretentiousness, elegance unmarred by ostentation, all the comforts of modern life in ancient splendour—these were Sophie-Dorothea's heritage, as were the doting admiration of her father's subjects and the courtly attentions of his guests. If she knew that her position was anomalous, it could not have much disturbed her, for she also knew that she was an heiress whose hand was sought by neighbouring and distant potentates, while she was free to run and play as if she were a private person; so she grew up high-spirited, healthy and self-confident.

If she ever considered her aunt Sophia, it was as a slightly alarming but not unpleasant person, whose elder sons she met rarely and formally, and in whom she took no interest. The fact that the heir, George-Louis, her senior by six years, disliked her, was not apparent, for he had been more strictly brought up than she; in any case, they saw almost nothing of one another.

Throughout the early 1670s Sophia maintained her attitude of scornful indifference to the family at Celle (Countess of Wilhelmsburg—ridiculous! But nothing would come of that suggestion), and enlarged her own interests. She visited Elizabeth at her sister-hood—where, much to the elder Princess's embarrassment, she made a mocking attack on the theories of a popular preacher—and received Elizabeth at Iburg. They were very happy together, recalling old days and shared pursuits, one of these last being the study of philosophy; and it was at about this time that the great Leibnitz, formerly Duke John-Frederick's protégé, became known to and taken up by the Palatine sisters.

Sophia needed a distraction of this kind, for her relationship with Ernst-August was now complicated by his taking a mistress she could neither ignore nor dismiss. The arrival at Osnabrück of Clara and Catherine von Meissenberg, both beautiful and accomplished young women, had not, at first, disturbed her. But when Ernst-August established Clara by marrying her to his principal minister, Baron von Platen, she realized that unless she behaved with the utmost circumspection, she might have to share her power with the Baroness. Whatever jealousy and bitterness she

138

may have felt, she concealed; her pride, her affection for Ernst-August and her instinctive adaptability helped her to accept Clara von Platen not only calmly, but also graciously. Naturally she held the contemporary view that princes acquired a series of mistresses as a matter of course; such attachments, and the inevitable expenditure, were the insignia of rank. (In Sophia's eyes, George-William had betrayed his class, not only by treating his mistress as if she were his wife, but by remaining faithful to her; such behaviour was bourgeois and absurd.) She might well have despised Ernst-August if he had not observed the customs of his time. As it was, she allowed herself one withering remark about the Baroness's crude use of paint — thoroughly justified, in that the plastered red and white then in vogue sometimes caused death through lead-poisoning — and treated her as became her position.

If she did resent Clara's growing influence, she also made use of it; and she knew that Ernst-August would turn to herself in a crisis. When, a year or two later, Catherine von Meissenberg (who had married Count Busche) became the mistress of George-Louis, thus enhancing the Platens' status, Sophia made no objection, for by that time she had the whole situation in hand, and she and Ernst-August were on the best of terms, although she could not rejoice, as he did, at the birth of her seventh and last child who was named after his father. In this same year, 1674, she wrote to Charles-Louis, 'One cannot help loving one's children, but it would be better, fate willing, not to have so many.' She went on to describe her six-year-old daughter, 'Figuelotte', with adoring praise. She was perfect: pretty, clever and well-behaved. Sophia planned a great future for Figuelotte; already she was beginning to share her mother's tastes, and so consoled her for the departure of Ernst-August for the war. He was accompanied by George-Louis, who left for his first campaign in 1675. The Duke of Celle followed them, and the cost to both duchies caused much suffering. But, Sophia told her brother, 'George-William's bad household and bad conduct are more ruinous than war.'

Her censure was based on moral grounds. The people of Celle suffered less than those of Osnabrück and Hanover, because that principality was richer and better organized; but in Sophia's eyes their Duke had broken all the rules of good behaviour by obtaining the Emperor's leave for the legitimization of Sophie-Dorothea in 1675. Once more, Ernst-August was assured that his children's inheritance would not be affected, and was asked for his approval of a morganatic marriage between his brother and Eléanore. Unwillingly, he agreed. When he and George-William returned from a victorious campaign in the autumn of this year, his brother suddenly announced, 'I think I shall now marry,' adding that when he did so Eléanore would be given the title of Princess. At Ernst-August's and Sophia's furious protests he let the matter drop until February 1676; then, in answer to a letter from Sophia, he replied, briefly but vaguely, that she need not worry, because 'Madame de Harburg's' new title did not affect the succession. Two months later he and Eléanore were privately married.

At first, Sophia and Ernst-August believed and gave out that this was a morganatic alliance, that is, one sanctioned but not celebrated by the Church. It was not so. George-William and Eléanore were legally one, and their ten-year-old daughter was now officially contracted to Duke Antony-Ulric's heir, who was killed at the siege of Philipsburg in 1676, upon which her hand was transferred to his younger brother. Sophia and her husband were beside themselves; but worse was to follow.

As soon as the marriage became known, Eléanore was addressed by the Emperor's envoy as Duchess of Brunswick (and therefore of Celle) and prayed for in church. The ambassadors of other foreign potentates (that of Louis XIV was desired to lure George-William away from his Dutch allies) followed the Emperor's example, with the result that the King of Denmark asked for Sophie-Dorothea's hand on behalf of his son Prince George. This match fell through, and six years later the Danish Prince married Princess Anne, who became Queen of England in 1702.

To Ernst-August's enraged objections, George-William replied, 'I cannot help it if His Imperial Majesty's envoy addresses my wife as Duchess of Brunswick,' and again assured his brother that he would keep his promise about the succession. Whether he did so or not mattered little to the triumphant Eléanore. She was now reigning Duchess, and she and her daughter were magnificently dowered; it was therefore obvious that Sophie-Dorothea could look higher than an impoverished Prince of Brunswick-Wolfen-büttel for a husband; so her parents decided to keep that marriage in reserve until she was old enough to leave home, when more profitable alliances might be forthcoming.

Sophia's fury exploded in her letters to Liselotte. 'To think', she wrote, 'that we shall have to call that piece of filth [she used a coarser word] Duchess of Brunswick!' Loyally, Liselotte assured her husband and brother-in-law that George-William's marriage was morganatic, and when this was reported to and denied by the court of Celle, Eléanore added Liselotte to her list of enemies. Meanwhile, with less than her usual clearsightedness, Sophia refused to believe that the Danish King had asked for Sophie-Dorothea. 'I am disgusted by George-William's treachery,' she burst out to Charles-Louis. 'He is a weak vessel and has behaved like a child, and is entirely governed by Schütz.' She could not bring herself to admit that the beautiful and stately Eléanore had succeeded through her own efforts and her husband's devotion. When Liselotte told her that Eléanore had at one time been betrothed to a valet, now in her own employ, Sophia was delighted. But she could not forget that it was she herself who had helped to bring disgrace on their House by encouraging George-William's courtship of 'that creature'.

Sophia's worries were increased by the distress of her husband's subjects, the hideous details of the campaign and — worst of all — her eldest son's attitude towards herself. No doubt George-Louis was beginning to resent his mother's authority. Interested only in sport and war, he scorned her intellectual pursuits and treated her as insolently as he dared. ('And also,' she remarked, 'he is so ugly.') She consoled herself with her treasured Figuelotte, who was already an ideal companion. The second boy, 'Gussie', was her favourite son; he reminded her of his uncle Rupert — 'but', she added hastily, 'I love them all.' She was a little taken aback by the ten-year-old Maximilian's piety. 'He does not get that from his father or his mother,' she wrote to Charles-Louis, adding, 'There are so many sillinesses about Christianity — I do not know what I am.'

In fact, without realizing it, Sophia had submitted herself to another faith, better than some and no more arbitrary than most, that of dynastic power — not in the material sense, for she had a horror of war and conquest for their own sake — but on the understanding that the purity and dignity of a royal House should be sustained and unspotted. This, coupled with her care for her children's rights, became her creed, her ideal and her cause.

I I

After the marriage of George-William and Eléanore an uneasy peace was established between the courts of Osnabrück and Celle, followed by one between France and the Allies. The two Dukes continued to see each other from time to time, but their wives did not meet, and so Sophia's criticisms of Eléanore ceased until, in October 1677, she heard that a genealogical tree, showing the new Duchess's descent from the Kings of France, was being circulated. With an appropriate comment, she passed on the news to Liselotte, who replied in the same manner, enclosing another tree proving her cook's descent from Philippe le Bel. No doubt Ernst-August flinched from the acid mockery of his wife and her niece; for a while he and George-William were estranged. These disputes in no way affected the happiness of the Celle family; the elegance and culture of their court became increasingly famous, with the result that a number of foreign nobles sent their sons to serve the Duke and Duchess as part of such young men's education.

One of these was a handsome youth of thirteen, Count Philip Christopher von Königsmarck, whose mother was known to Sophia and Ernst-August, and whose elder brother, Count Carl, was already a famous soldier. Philip's uncle and Eléanore had known one another at the court of Louis XIV; it was through her patronage that the nephew's military training began at Celle.

Much has been invented and more conjectured about the early acquaintance of the twelve-year-old Sophie-Dorothea and the Swedish Count. That he admired and perhaps tried to flirt with her, is proved by their later — and fateful — correspondence.* But there is no indication that she encouraged him; he was one of many presentable and charming young men, all of whom paid her court and whose admiration was her daily incense. The atmosphere of infatuated praise in which she lived is partially accounted for by an early portrait, presumably painted for the young Prince of Brunswick-Wolfenbüttel.

This picture is of greater interest than any which succeeded it, in that the artist, apparently captivated by the sitter, has rejected the customary formal pose and court dress. In a flowing white gown, without jewels, Sophie-Dorothea is seen at three-quarter

* See p. 178.

length, her arms full of wild flowers and grasses, as if she has just run in from the meadows beyond the castle. She leans forward, smiling, expectant, hopeful. The fragile yet luscious outlines, the rounded delicacy of cheek and chin, the set of the head, the large, sleepy eyes, the nymph-like poise, the hint of wildness, combine to make her irresistible, infuriating, provocative: an innocent Morgan le Fay, a child Armida. It is not surprising that the younger Königsmarck could not get her out of his head in the ten years which elapsed between his departure for England and their next meeting.

Sophia, who had seen very little of her husband's niece, regarded her simply as the appendage to her defaulting and devious parents. She saw Sophie-Dorothea's value going up as the settlements made on her and her mother increased, and perceived that both Louis XIV and the Emperor were interested in her future, not only because she was an heiress, but because Eléanore, although a Huguenot, was guiding George-William towards a French alliance. She returned from a visit to Elizabeth, who had not been well, to hear that the marriage of Sophie-Dorothea to George-Louis had been suggested; she firmly endorsed Ernst-August's reply, which was that he could accept his niece as a daughter-in-law only if she brought with her a dowry of a hundred thousand crowns and two fortresses. This was more than George-William was prepared to give, and the negotiations came to nothing, much to George-Louis's relief. He did not want to marry sooner than he needed to and felt, as his parents did, that an alliance with his cousin would degrade him, quite apart from the fact that he did not like her.

Then the Duchess of Mecklenburg, a friend of both Ernst-August and George-William, suggested to Sophia that they should visit the French Court, with a view to finding out if there was a chance of Figuelotte being contracted to the Dauphin, whose marriage had not yet been arranged. Sophia was eager to go, not only for her daughter's sake, but also because she wanted to stay at Maubuisson with Louise, and to see for herself how Liselotte — whose eldest stepdaughter was about to be married to the King of Spain — was getting on. So she, the Duchess and the eleven-year-old Figuelotte ('Her beauty,' said that tactful friend, 'might well bring about the alliance'), set off together.

Sophia's gaiety revived during their three weeks' journey; the

occasional discomforts and setbacks amused her. She and Figuelotte went sightseeing and shopping, enjoyed some rather strange
meals and had a good laugh over the odd characters who received
them. On August 22nd, 1679, they arrived at Maubuisson, where
Sophia had arranged to stay incognito, so as to remain undisturbed with the sister she had not seen for thirty years. As their
coaches entered the courtyard of the convent, they saw another
drawn up — and Liselotte running towards them, her arms out-
stretched, tears of joy pouring down her face.

After a great deal of hugging and kissing, the Duchesse d'Orléans presented the future Queen of Spain, 'little Mademoiselle',
to her aunt, and then, clinging to her arm, led her to the main
entrance, where Louise was standing with Monsieur, whose
painted face and heavily jewelled dress contrasted oddly with the
black and white of her Abbess's habit.

Rather to her surprise and much to her relief, Sophia found the
notorious Duc d'Orléans quite charming, and soon perceived that
her dear Liselotte was happy, both in her marriage and in her
surroundings. She could not, as she had often written to Sophia,
respect or like the frivolous and time-serving French courtiers; but
she adored Louis XIV — indeed, she had fallen a little in love with
him — tolerated her husband's posse of young men, was immensely
proud of her clever, ugly, five-year-old son, the Duc de Chartres,
and revelled in the hunting, which far surpassed any in Germany.
She did not like French cooking, and longed for beer and sausages;
but she greatly enjoyed showing off the glories of her husband's
palace of St Cloud, while he treated Sophia 'as if he had known
me all his life', and insisted on her leaving Maubuisson to stay with
them in Paris, at Fontainebleau, and finally at Versailles for the
wedding celebrations.

Sophia enjoyed every moment of her visit, escaping from time to
time to Maubuisson — where she found Louise much fatter, and as
odd and amusing as in their young days — and returning to confer
with Monsieur over his stupendous collection of jewels, some of
which were destined for his daughter; the larger and better quantity he reserved for the decoration of his own small, rotund person.
There was an awkward moment when she came upon him in his
dressing-gown, without his make-up, turning his face away 'in great
embarrassment'. Tactfully Sophia asked what brooches and ribbons he was planning to wear in his hat, and the situation was saved.

Balls, banquets and theatricals led up to the wedding itself, where Sophia was much amused to see Louis XIV gazing at his latest mistress 'with more devotion than at the altar', and then falling asleep with his mouth open. Next day, she was told that His Majesty would give himself the pleasure of waiting on her. He was preceded by the Dauphin, whose conversation was confined to monosyllables. Then Louis came in, accompanied by his too assiduous brother and sister-in-law, whom he relegated with, 'It is not you, Madame, but the Duchess of Osnabrück I have come to see,' and desiring Monsieur not to whisper. He went on to say how rejoiced he was at this meeting, not only for its own sake, but because he had so much admired Duke Ernst-August's skill and courage at the Bridge of Conz, where the French troops had been beaten by the Germans. 'As we were not so fortunate as to acquire Your Majesty's goodwill,' Sophia replied, 'we could only hope to command your approval of our efforts as soldiers.' 'At that time, I dared not hope for your friendship,' said Louis smiling. 'I am very glad that time is past, and that peace is sworn,' Sophia went on. 'That will last as long as it benefits my kingdom,' Louis replied. 'I hope it will be a very long time indeed,' was the blunt answer. The King shook his head. 'I do not think the Princes of Germany will make war on me again,' he said, going on to describe France's military strength. He then complimented Sophia on her daughter's beauty, adding, 'I hear she is very clever. Should I address her as Madame, or Mademoiselle? I believe Madame is the custom in Germany.'

Sophia was then taken by Monsieur to see the Queen, a plain, stout little creature with bad teeth, whose Spanish hauteur made their discourse rather barren. When Sophia said something about the difference between French and Spanish etiquette, Her Majesty replied, 'I had no difficulty with that,' adding abruptly, 'The King loves me, and so I am grateful to him.' 'That is not surprising,' said Sophia politely, and changed the subject.

Then followed shopping in Paris and another stay at Maubuisson, after which Sophia and her daughter left for St Cloud. As their coach entered the palace courtyard, where Monsieur was awaiting them, the horses shied, and they were flung out. He ran to help them up, calling, 'Chamber-pots—bring chamber-pots!' afterwards explaining to Sophia that fright always brought about the immediate need of these articles. Reassured, he presented his court to her, and insisted on her kissing his principal favourite, the Chevalier de Lorraine. They then went to the opera, which Sophia found inferior to that of Osnabrück, and watched the parting of the new Queen of Spain from her father and step-mother, during which everyone cried bitterly—'but I think,' she says, 'that most of the courtiers did so because it was the custom,' adding, 'They were like so many slaves.'

After a last visit to Louise came the presentation of the King's farewell gift of a set of diamond buttons, 'rather bad ones,' for which Monsieur apologized. Sophia then received Monsieur de Gourville, formerly ambassador to the court of Celle, who asked her of what religion her daughter was. 'Of none, as yet,' Sophia calmly replied. 'We are waiting to see of what religion her husband will be, so that we can instruct her either way.' When he had recovered from this shock, de Gourville said, 'The Duke should become a Catholic.' 'He is too old to change his faith,' said Sophia, smiling. De Gourville long remembered the Duchess's wit and amiability. 'She teased people,' he says, 'but in such a way as never to offend, and could always make one laugh by her judg-ments of others.' So ended this delightful visit, slightly damped by the news that the Dauphin's marriage with a Bavarian Princess was already being negotiated. Liselotte was very disappointed, but Sophia took the setback philosophically. Now all her thoughts were of home; she longed for her husband and children.

A shadow was cast over her return by Ernst-August's announce-ment that he was about to leave for Italy; Sophia was saddened when he added that he had begun to reconsider the marriage of George-Louis and Sophie-Dorothea. 'It would ensure the inheri-tance,' he said, 'in the event of my dying before my brothers.' Once more, terms were discussed but not concluded, and then Duke John-Frederick, who had no sons, suggested that George-Louis should marry his eldest daughter; Sophia thought this a much better plan. As her husband was now on his way to Venice, Duke John decided to follow him there. She was then sent for by Elizabeth, who was dying. A few days after her arrival news came of John-Frederick's death. She hurried back to Osnabrück, to be joined by Ernst-August, who said with a shrug, 'Well! I am very glad that *I* am not dead.'

He had been fond of John-Frederick; but what now concerned him was that he had inherited his titles and estates, and so must seriously consider the union of Hanover and Celle; for it was certain that George-William and Eléanore would have no more children. He himself had not been well; he might predecease his brother, and was anxious finally to secure the succession. Sophia saw the sense of his reasoning, as did George-Louis, now Prince of Hanover. 'But,' she wrote to Liselotte, 'the boy has a dislike to the marriage, and we do not care for an alliance with the d'Olbreuse. He is now,' she added, 'with his mistress.'

Once more George-William was approached, and this time he replied that he would give his daughter a yearly allowance of eighty thousand crowns. 'It is a hard pill to swallow,' Sophia told her niece, 'although well gilded. For myself, I dislike the whole affair.' She also disliked reading and having to answer Eléanore's letters and messages of condolence on the death of their brother-in-law; they did not ring true. 'All is not well, not sound,' she wrote to Charles-Louis. Liselotte's protests ('Such a marriage would be a sin against the Holy Ghost') were followed by the news of Elizabeth's death after a long and terrible illness. Sophia could not get her sister's sufferings out of her mind.

As nothing could be settled while they were in mourning, Ernst-August and Sophia made a short visit to Denmark, and here her spirits revived. She went out shooting with the King and Queen, and although she had never held a gun in her life, was persuaded to take one and fire; she did so, a hare fell dead, and she received, much to her amusement, 'the undeserved praise' of the Danish court. She and Ernst-August felt more cheerful as they entered their new duchy, only to hear of the death of Charles-Louis.

Sophia was heart-broken. 'He loved and cherished me as if I had been his daughter,' she wrote; 'his letters were my greatest joy.' She was fifty; surely she would not long survive the brother and sister whose loss seemed irreparable; and she was alone, for Ernst-August had set off for Italy. Then it occurred to her to find distraction by writing her memoirs; as she concluded them she began to think that she might perhaps live on a little (she would have been horrified at the thought of doing so for thirty-three years) to enjoy her gardening, her books, her correspondence with Leibnitz and Liselotte, the redecoration of all her palaces— Osnabrück, Hanover, Iburg—and the building of a new one, Herrenhausen, which was to be her particular concern. And it was a relief to feel that the plans for the marriage of George-Louis and

Sophie-Dorothea were slowing down, which meant that the Celle family need not be invited to stay. Eventually they were, upon which Sophia told her husband that she could not, in any circumstances, give her sister-in-law precedence as the wife of the senior Duke; so the visit, and the marriage discussions, were again postponed.

Then came an approach from Charles II. He and his brother, the future James II, heir-presumptive and father of the Princess Anne, were considering an alliance between that Princess and the House of Hanover; George-Louis was invited to England. He went unwillingly. His reports of the country he came to rule, as unwillingly, thirty-four years later, were brief and denigrating. He did not care for his Stuart relations, and took against his cousin Anne, then a pretty girl of seventeen, who, he pointed out, was a far worse match than Sophie-Dorothea, for she was not much of an heiress—and the granddaughter of a lawyer. This objection was repeated to the Princess, who never forgot or forgave it.

In the spring of 1682 the negotiations for his marriage to Sophie-Dorothea were resumed, and continued throughout the summer. The bargaining was complicated by Ernst-August's suspicions of his brother's good faith and his son's reluctance. If agreement was not soon reached the heiress of Celle would be betrothed to someone else, thus destroying the union of the duchies, now urged on by the Emperor and Louis XIV.

More wrangling over details ensued. In October the contract was signed. On the evening of November 21st, 1682, George-Louis and Sophie-Dorothea were married in the chapel of the Castle of Celle. The festivities continued for over a fortnight; so the gilded pill was swallowed. On December 10th the Prince and Princess of Hanover made their state entrance into that city and took up residence in the Palace of the Leine.

FIVE

I

SHORTLY before the marriage of the cousins two events took place which indirectly but permanently affected both the fortunes and the reputation of Sophia and her family. Philip of Königsmarck's brother, Count Carl, narrowly escaped being executed for murder in London; and Duke Antony-Ulric published his first novel. These seemingly disparate incidents were later connected in such a manner as to create a legend and a mystery which in their turn became intertwined, thus producing a problem without a solution.

Philip of Königsmarck was fourteen when his elder brother was tried for the murder of Thomas Thynne, whose wife, an heiress, he had been planning to marry. The verdict of Not Guilty was so obviously the result of Charles II's intervention that an outcry ensued, and the brothers were desired to leave England. A few months later Carl, fighting for the Venetians in Greece, died of fever, and Count Philip inherited his wealth and estates. During the next few years he travelled about Europe, and by the time he reached the court of Hanover his reputation as a soldier and a *galant' uomo* of great possessions had preceded him; wherever he went, he had been professionally in demand and very popular with both sexes.

When Sophia began to read Duke Antony-Ulric's *Eramena*, a romance in the manner of Mademoiselle de Scudéry, she complained that it was extremely dull and 'longer than the Bible'. Her opinion was not shared by the novel-addicts, with the result that the author produced several more books, of which the most famous was *The Roman Octavia*, a story based on events at Celle and Hanover and first published in 1707; its principal characters were, recognizably, himself, his son, the two other ducal families and their intimates. This kind of novel was, as in the case of Madame d'Aulnoy's *Mémoires de la Cour d'Angleterre*, 'faked' history, and subsequently treated by many biographers as factual. Later on, this particular work inspired other authors of fiction to enlarge on the same theme; and so, for more than two hundred years, truth and falsehood have been inextricably confused.

Antony-Ulric's account of the last-minute rupture of the engagement of Sophie-Dorothea and his son in favour of George-Louis sprang, naturally, from furious resentment. He describes Sophia as forcing on the match, in the face of Duchess Eléanore's horror and Sophie-Dorothea's hysterical appeals against marriage with a man she loathed, together with her father's brutal sacrifice of both women's happiness. The wedding takes place in a thunderstorm, the bride swoons, the bridegroom is sullen and indifferent, his wicked mistress insults the virtuous young Princess, Sophia is coldly hostile, and Ernst-August weakly tries and fails to improve matters.

Such an account made very good reading for a public who, then as now, enjoyed *romans à clef*. The beginning of the true story may be found in Sophia's description, to Liselotte, of the attitude of her husband and son, supplemented by those of one or two other contemporaries. Having made it clear that she had been forced to accept the marriage by her husband, she goes on: 'Ernst-August always had a queer head, and how such an idea [of the alliance] could have entered it, passes all my understanding. However, one hundred thousand thalers a year is a goodly sum ... without speaking of a pretty wife, who will find a match in ... George-Louis, the most pig-headed, stubborn boy who ever lived, and who has round his brains such a thick crust that I defy any man or woman to find what is in them.'

In Sophia's account of the wedding celebrations there is no mention of a storm, or of Sophie-Dorothea behaving other than correctly. During the next few years her comments on her daughter-in-law are rare, uninterested and occasionally critical, but never spiteful. She and Sophie-Dorothea had nothing in common, and although her prejudice against this 'half-breed' addition to the family was inevitable, it might, eventually, have been overcome if the Princess had been able to share her mother-in-law's tastes or to behave *as* a princess; that she could do neither was the fault of her upbringing, and Sophia's sense of fairness helped her to overlook this, until Sophie-Dorothea broke all the rules of conduct, continuing to do so regardless of protests and warnings.

In the same way, Antony-Ulric's portrait of George-Louis was swallowed whole, and he emerged as a monster. This process was facilitated by the fact that the Prince of Hanover was, as his mother often pointed out (perhaps even to himself), an unattractive, stumpy, red-faced youth, who took no trouble to make himself agreeable. His intelligence, that of a man of action, was entirely practical, except in his taste for music, the only art Sophia did not understand. He was brave, truthful and loyal. His manners were graceless, rather those of the camp than of the court; but he maintained, in the face of great provocation, cold dignity and remarkable self-control. He was perfectly indifferent to admiration and despised flattery.

In almost every respect Sophie-Dorothea's tastes and temperament were directly opposed to her husband's. She was undisciplined, rather silly and inclined to self-dramatization. She had no sense of tradition and no intellectual interests; accustomed, all her life, to adulation, she became a public figure without any of the necessary qualifications but those of beauty and elegance. Taking the ha'pence for granted, she was amazed and infuriated by the kicks. She remained polite, dutiful and charming just so long as it suited her, no more. She did not at first expect more than George-Louis was able to give, and she got on very well with Ernst-August, who liked to indulge her. Although her daily routine was monotonous, she had many privileges and was not, on the whole, deprived of essentials. Her closest friend, Eleanora von Knesebeck, came with her to Hanover as her lady-in-waiting. She bore first a son (later George II) and then a daughter, another Sophie, thus achieving success in her *métier* and in the eyes of all her relatives. Both children were healthy, intelligent and pretty; and shortly after the birth of the younger, her husband, while attending her on most formal occasions, ceased to trouble her, so that she was spared the exhaustion of repeated confinements. Few princesses of her day could have asked for more. Sophie-Dorothea did: hence her tragedy, so ingeniously exploited by the best-selling Antony-Ulric.

Life in Hanover provided pleasures unknown in Celle, for Duke John-Frederick had made it a centre of Franco-Italian culture. When Ernst-August succeeded he built a new opera-house, in which he installed a Venetian director, and spent vast sums on tapestries, pictures and stucco-work for the Leine Palace, while employing French and Italian muralists to decorate that of

Herrenhausen. Balls and hunting expeditions enlivened the daily routine, which began early for Sophia; she liked to be out and about, superintending her gardeners or talking to her librarians as soon as she was dressed. At midday the ducal family descended for dinner in order of seniority; when bows and curtsies had been interchanged (Sophie-Dorothea was sometimes at fault in the regulation of these salutes) they sat down to a meal cooked by French chefs, and after a further interchange of courtesies retired to their rooms. In the afternoon the Duchess, her daughter-in-law and their ladies went for a drive, returning to change for supper, after which they and their husbands received foreign guests, listened to a concert or a comedy and then played ombre and quadrille for high stakes. During the summer, pastoral plays were performed in the open-air theatre at Herrenhausen, followed by fancy-dress balls and fireworks in the gardens; on these occasions the guests wore dominoes and Venetian masks. For one of these parties Sophie-Dorothea chose the peasant's dress in which she was painted; she wears a wide-brimmed straw hat and a low-cut, laced bodice with flowing white sleeves; her pouting mouth and rather set look are those of a standardized beauty; the smiling, mischievous creature of the pre-marriage portrait has been tamed.

In 1683 Ernst-August and his two eldest sons left to fight for the Emperor against the Turks, who had besieged Vienna; they were absent for some months. Sophia, ruling the duchy, felt more than usually isolated, and would have been desolate but for Figuelotte, for Rupert had died in 1682, and she and Louise — whom she never saw — were the only ones left of the thirteen Palatine Stuarts. Her principal distraction was her correspondence with Liselotte. That lady's brilliant, malicious, comical letters, some twenty to twenty-five pages long, arrived two or three times a week.

In 1684 Sophia parted with her idolized daughter, who was married to the widowed Elector of Brandenburg. A few months later her husband left, with Baroness von Platen, for Venice; as George-Louis had gone back to the war, Ernst-August sent for Sophie-Dorothea to join himself and the Baroness, and they spent some time in Venice and Rome. Naturally the Princess was admired and courted. Liselotte, whose jealousy of her may have been caused by her own resentment at being exiled from Germany and parted from her aunt, spread rumours of her having had an affair with the notorious Comte de Lassaye; these were without foundation.

When Ernst-August returned to Hanover he reorganized his inheritance according to the laws of primogeniture, thus maintaining the unity of the two duchies in favour of George-Louis. This eminently sensible arrangement enraged his second son, Frederick-August, who wanted him to revert to the former division of his estates. Angry scenes ensued, and Frederick-August was forbidden his father's Court. 'Poor Gussie', Sophia wrote to her niece, 'is altogether cast out; his father will no longer support him. I cry about it all night, for one child is as dear to me as another.' This was not quite true; after Figuelotte, Frederick-August was still her favourite; but she was less impatient, now, with George-Louis, who was no longer the lover of Catherine von Busche, and had not replaced her. He seems to have been on amicable if not very ardent terms with his wife. So Duke Antony-Ulric's picture of a persecuted heroine fades from the scene.

George-Louis secretly resented his mother's support of Frederick-August. When he realized that, while acquiescing in all her husband's decisions, she would have liked their other sons to have a larger share of the inheritance, the heir was very angry. Respect on his side and goodwill on hers were outwardly maintained; but he had no sympathy with her point of view on any subject; nor did he subscribe to her correspondence with her English cousins.

Although she had not seen James II since his seventeenth year, Sophia continued to write to him after his accession as if they had always known one another, and he responded in the same manner. It was at about this time that she began to think more of her Stuart than of her German blood, although three persons—James's elder daughter Mary, now married to William of Orange, her sister the Princess Anne and William himself—stood between Sophia and the succession. James's children by his second wife, Mary of Modena, were dead, Mary of Orange had none, and those of Anne and George of Denmark had not survived. But these three women were all young, and might well produce male heirs.

Sophia's increasing interest in English affairs may have arisen from her disappointments in Hanover. Although she was now a very great lady indeed, with a European reputation, her private life had been saddened by Ernst-August's more blatant infidelities (of which she never complained), the bitter pill of George-Louis's marriage, the departure of her daughter and the dispute which ended in Frederick-August's leaving home. Resolutely, she turned towards her hobbies, petted her grandchildren and tolerated her daughter-in-law, who now spent a great deal of time with her parents at Celle and in their country palace at Brockhausen.

There were many cracks in the surface of the situation; and in 1688, when Sophia was chiefly concerned with the upheavals in England which eventually resulted in the flight of James II, his Queen and their infant son (later known as the Old Pretender) and the joint accession of William and Mary, George-Louis took a second mistress—Melusina Ermengarda von Schülenberg.

At first, this seemed a matter of no importance. The young lady, a large blonde of nineteen, described by Sophia as 'the tall Malkin', was well bred and discreet; and it did not occur to the Duchess, who looked on such persons as part of all royal establishments, that this one's appearance could be a source of trouble. She then perceived that Sophie-Dorothea, who was as indifferent to George-Louis as he to her, was not only enraged at his infidelity, but openly assuming the part of an injured wife. To Sophia, who had put up with Ernst-August's adulteries for thirty years, this attitude was degraded, infuriating and senseless. Such faint kindness as she might have felt for her daughter-in-law withered away, and she dismissed her as an underbred little fool. So the Princess, already wearying of existence in Hanover, was more than usually isolated. Furthermore, although only in her twenty-first year, she had lost something of her beauty; the portraits show her as having put on weight; discontent and ennui have dimmed and hardened the fragile loveliness of girlhood, as her mirror may have told her. Since her marriage, the formality, the inexorable etiquette which ruled her life had precluded the courtly gallantries, the personal and flattering approach which had nourished her first sixteen years. Thus deprived, she was still under her mother's influence and its effect on her father; these had accustomed her to what Sophia would have called a bourgeois outlook, which regarded adultery as a sinful and humiliating disaster. Finally, she had inherited George-William's passionately amorous temperament, which up to now had found no outlet of any kind.

It was at this point that Philip of Königsmarck arrived in Hanover, was courteously received and took a house near the

Leine Palace. He then entered the service of Ernst-August, who presently made him colonel of a regiment of guards. He and George-Louis became close friends.

I I

Sophia's distress at parting from her daughter had been mitigated by relief; she told the Duchesse d'Orléans that Sophie-Dorothea was not a good example for Figuelotte, and that she regretted their having been thrown together. She need not have concerned herself. Although Sophie-Charlotte was two years younger than her sister-in-law, she had by far the stronger character, and was a replica of her mother. The only taste they shared was that common to most young girls, of dancing, preferably in fancy dress. After she became Electress of Brandenburg Sophie-Charlotte came often to Hanover, staying for weeks at a time. Her third pregnancy prevented her joining her family for the carnival festivities of 1688.

On an evening in February of that year Philip of Königsmarck left his house and strolled over to the huge medieval town hall to find the citizens grotesquely disguised and 'frightful to behold', according to an eye-witness—by heads of giants, imps and wild beasts. Himself masked, he watched them dancing in circles round the families of Celle, Hanover and Wolfenbüttel. Presently these personages, twenty-one in all, retired, with their courtiers, to gamble; another visitor saw 'vast heaps of ducats and new silver money piled on the tables'. The royal party then put on gold or scarlet dominoes, feathered caps and Venetian masks and entered an adjoining room, where Italian pedlars were selling sweets, lemonade, cakes and wine. After an hour or so the trumpets sounded for supper from the Leine Palace, and with their guests the ducal families left the Hall. Next day Sophia gave a great dinner, followed by a theatre party.

That after ten years of war and wild living he should have come upon the exquisite creature of his innocent fancy surrounded by jigging shapes whose monstrous heads were those of goats, apes and devils has, now, an odd significance, a prophetic aptness; not to Königsmarck himself, who seems to have been received by the Princess and her family as an especially favoured guest, in that he

155

was a wealthy and distinguished soldier. Whatever he may have felt, there is no record of any immediate result of that first meeting. With some two dozen servants, a secretary and a major-domo, he settled into his tall, gabled house on the Leine, came every day to court, gambled, danced, hunted and led his troops into battle, with the Princes under whom he served, like all the rest.

Yet the fascination which became a legend can be dimly perceived in his portrait, that of a gay, reckless young patrician; something of a dandy, a bit of a rake, a gallant comrade, an accomplished courtier, fortune's favourite; one, in fact, who has always had his own way and cannot conceive that he should be denied it. Beneath the trappings of the period — the great curled periwig, the lace cravat, the velvet coat — the magnetism is there. Few, men or women, could resist Königsmarck; and it was not in his nature to refuse their gifts. Such men are more dangerous to themselves than to those they suborn.

Within a few months of his arrival at Hanover Königsmarck left for the front. Serving under Prince Maximilian, he fought in a great battle against the French, thereafter succumbing to fever, and did not return until the spring of 1689. Some time between then and the summer of 1691 his approach to Sophie-Dorothea began; at first it was a matter of courteous gallantry on his side and mild coquetry on hers, no more. Sophia, whose nearness to the English succession had been curtailed by the birth of a son — William Henry, Duke of Gloucester — to the Princess Anne, was too preoccupied to take much notice of the change in her daughter-in-law's behaviour. She had already observed that her smiles and tears came too easily and that she lacked dignity; when Sophie-Dorothea ceased to complain of her husband's infidelity, Sophia seems to have taken her back into favour, without realizing the cause of this complaisance. So the correspondence between Königsmarck and the Princess began. His first extant letter, dated July 1691, shows that it had been going on for some time.

With 'respect as great as my love,' he signs himself her most obedient servant, and continues on the high romantic note then in vogue, describing his swoons and sobs and subjoining doggerel rhymes in German and Italian.* (Königsmarck's fluent French

* The greater part of this correspondence is preserved in the Swedish University of Lund.

had no connection with his spelling, which was phonetic; nor did he know the uses of punctuation.) Gradually, the Princess was persuaded, first, to answer his letters and later to see him alone. Then came a change. The rather stereotyped gallantry which had brought Königsmarck so many conquests yielded to a violent and tormented sincerity. Still Sophie-Dorothea held back, alarmed, perhaps, by the strength of her own feeling and torn between the scruples implanted by her upbringing and her need for love. Königsmarck was not yet irresistible. Naturally, this shrinking increased his fervour; the sufferings of a modish 'sensibility' became hideously real, himself obsessed to madness and his pursuit one of frenzied adoration. Within a few months they were lovers — and now Sophie-Dorothea was as deeply committed, as desperately passionate as he. But as she was also afraid for them both, she advised him to marry, and thus mislead those who suspected them. Königsmarck agreed to consider this 'sentence of death', only to find that he could not face it. So, between his absences at the front and her visits to her parents, they continued their secret meetings.

The complications and the danger of these trysts could not have been overcome without a go-between; this was Eleanora von Knesebeck, who sometimes wrote, at the Princess's dictation, her transparently coded letters, conveyed messages and kept watch. The lovers wrote to one another every day; and presently some of their letters were stolen, which caused misunderstanding, accusations and jealous strife. It was at this point that Baroness von Platen came into the picture.

For a short time, probably soon after Königsmarck's arrival in Hanover, she had been his mistress. She now attempted to lure him away from the Princess, partly with a view to marrying him to her daughter; such an arrangement would have staved off Ernst-August's jealousy, while enabling her to make rendezvous with the younger man. Also, she was pursuing him and spying on Sophie-Dorothea at Ernst-August's instructions. It was both her desire and her duty to break up an affair which now became the talk of Hanover, Celle, Wolfensbüttel and Brandenburg.

Two people kept their heads in the rising storm: Sophia and George-Louis. From Sophie-Dorothea's accounts of her talks with her mother-in-law it transpires that Sophia, having warned her, stood aside and refused to interfere. She may have thought that Königsmarck would eventually tire of the Princess and return to

Clara von Platen; if he did so, there was a chance that the Baroness would lose her power over Ernst-August. But Sophia did not know that Königsmarck and Sophie-Dorothea had agreed to placate his former mistress by his acceptance of her invitations to supper. One evening, this resulted in his spending the night with her and thus sinning, he told the Princess, 'against our love'. The wretched girl's jealous agony burst out in a scene he recalled in his next letter. 'Go—leave me in peace!' she exclaimed, and Königsmarck rushed away 'to seek death' in the Morea, where he and Prince Frederick-August had been summoned to fight for the Emperor against the Turks. Death came—for Sophia's 'poor Gussie', whom she had not seen since his father sent him packing. A few months later Prince Charles-Philip was killed in Albania. Sophia broke down completely, retiring for a cure to Wiesbaden, where she remained for some weeks.

George-Louis's attitude was less complicated. His wife's absorption in his best friend (whose military services seem to have been irreplaceable) saved him trouble and enabled him to see Ermengarda von Schülenberg undisturbed. But as the affair became the talk of four principalities, with himself in the role of cuckold, he began to consider making use of it in order to divorce Sophie-Dorothea. That this would involve the departure of Königsmarck was extremely inconvenient—and distasteful, for he had no personal quarrel with the young man. Nor had he any further use for Sophie-Dorothea, who had provided the necessary heir, and now detested the sight of him. But he was still working with Königsmarck, and so delayed taking action. Also, his long absences at the front and elsewhere contributed towards a *laissez faire* policy, which resulted in Königsmarck and the Princess telling one another that they would eventually be left alone; yet this was not enough. As neither of them liked, nor had any gift for, intrigue, they began to discuss an elopement.

In December 1692 the situation was further complicated by Ernst-August being granted the title and status of Elector, as a reward for his services to the Emperor. At about the same time William III informed Sophia that the little Duke of Gloucester's delicacy and the unlikelihood of Queen Mary's bearing a child had brought her one step nearer the succession. She replied courteously; but she was too broken to care for this prospect or for the title by which she is known to posterity; nor was she in a state to heed the reports on her daughter-in-law, whose reckless-ness was making her more conspicuous than ever.

Sophie-Dorothea's faltering attempts to behave as usual drove Königsmarck to despair. When she was playing cards in the Great Hall he would pass and re-pass while she tried not to look at him. He called her Frozen-Heart, and when she wept, imploring forgiveness, he would recall their early, happier days. 'I have always been yours. As God is my witness, I have wanted to be so all my life ... Will you come to my house tonight? Farewell, my sweet dark lady, I kiss your knees.' She obeyed, then stole back to the Leine Palace to pour out her longings. 'No woman ever loved as I love you ... I watched for you at the window ... I love you to madness ... till death.'

Staying with her parents at Brockhausen, she was conveniently placed in a little house of her own. Königsmarck, following her there, would walk past the back door and whistle the opening bars of *Les Folies d'Espagne*; once he did so in vain, returning two hours later to hide in a ditch from the Baroness's spies; next day he had to leave for the front without seeing the Princess. During the greater part of 1693 he was refused leave, warned by his superior officers and taunted by his comrades, who one evening asked him to propose a toast. By this time he had drunk deep, of misery and wine. He took out a fragment of ribbon, dipped it into his glass and gave them 'Léonisse', his private name for the Princess. What did it matter? George-Louis, 'the little man', had done nothing; somehow, he and his dark lady would find happiness together. Then came a disaster in which she was involved.

Prince Maximilian and his friend Count von Moltke had formed a plot by which Ernst-August was to be forced to change the succession in the Prince's favour. It was discovered, von Moltke was executed and Maximilian imprisoned. He and Sophie-Dorothea had been on friendly terms (he had made advances to her) and so she was suspected of conspiring against her father-in-law, the one person who had always been kind. Now she was friendless, for her own parents were angry and hostile. They lectured, scolded and sent her back to Hanover in disgrace. 'Devil take your fool of a mother,' wrote Königsmarck. 'Why is she always preaching?' This letter, and another containing Sophie-Dorothea's suggestion that she should ask for an allowance and a separation from her husband, were stolen and presently shown to the Duke and Duchess of Celle, with the result that she was more closely watched—and warned, over and over again, by Sophia and Ernst-August, by her husband, and finally by the Baroness von Platen. Shortly after she and George-Louis became known as Their Electoral Highnesses, he grimly renewed their relationship —so Königsmarck, now in camp, was told. He decided to get himself wounded in order to return, and upbraided Sophie-Dorothea in a long and furious letter. Eventually he did return, unwounded and without leave. She came upon him in the Great Hall of the Leine Palace, building card-castles for her little boy and girl—a characteristic gesture. She managed to prevent herself fainting, and withdrew. Once more they made an assignation, only to part again.

Königsmarck, gambling, drinking, desperate, was now heavily in debt; he realized that even if they did succeed in running away, he would not be able to support the Princess. Then his sister, the beautiful Aurora, mistress of the Elector of Saxony, came to the rescue. She summoned Königsmarck to Dresden and told him that she had persuaded her lover to give him a generalship in the Saxon army.

During Königsmarck's absence, which lasted three months, Sophia changed her tactics, and was very kind to her daughter-in-law. She took her for walks and drives and talked incessantly of Königsmarck, praising his looks and his courage. Sophie-Dorothea, attempting indifference, knew that she had failed. 'When people speak of you,' she wrote, 'I feel my whole face change.' She begged Königsmarck to give up his profession and live with her—somewhere, anywhere. Duke Antony-Ulric, who had supported the von Moltke plot, might receive them—why should they not leave for Wolfensbüttel? But Königsmarck, once more in funds, had a better plan. With his sister's and Augustus of Saxony's support, he and Sophie-Dorothea might live near Dresden, unmolested.

Quem deus vult perdere ... In wild spirits and very drunk, he gave a dinner-party at which he boasted of his hold over the Baroness von Platen, and hinted at another, more glorious conquest. The news of this final indiscretion preceded him to Hanover, where he arrived in June 1694. By this time, George-Louis and his father had made up their minds.

Königsmarck was not only a fornicator, but a cheat; in accept-

THE ELECTRESS SOPHIA IN OLD AGE

ing the Saxon generalship he had betrayed them professionally. The time had come for him to be used and cast aside.

Yet his dismissal from Hanover was not so much the main object of their plan as the divorce of Sophie-Dorothea; nor was adultery her only crime. For some years she had shown that she was not interested in the English succession, and that her policy — in so far as she had one — was pro-French; in fact, she had declared that she would rather be a marquise in France than a princess in Germany. Thus she had become, in every sense, a traitress — and also a liability. The scandal caused by a divorce would be as nothing compared with that which she and Königsmarck had already created. So it was agreed that George-Louis should leave Hanover while the evidence of her guilt was collected. Königsmarck would then be cashiered and dismissed and the Princess sent to live in retirement; her children would be brought up as if she no longer existed.

Knowing that his departure would be the signal for the reunion of his wife and her lover, George-Louis instructed three of his officers, one Italian and two Germans, to wait in the Leine Palace till the time came for them to break into the Princess's apartments and find her and Königsmarck *in flagrante delicto*. They were then to arrest him, while she would be confined to her rooms until the arrangements for the divorce were completed and Königsmarck's house searched for further evidence.

In this carefully worked out scheme no provision seems to have been made for the fact that Königsmarck was a skilled and fearless swordsman, presumably because the witnesses expected to come upon him in bed and unarmed, and would not enter until they were sure of finding him defenceless, so that he could be hustled away without much difficulty. Their attack was put off until after the departure of George-Louis, in order that the lovers might feel themselves secure.

On the night of July 1st, 1694, Königsmarck's steward watched him leave his house and make his way towards the Leine Palace. He was never seen again.

Within a few days, his disappearance and the incarceration of the Princess began to form the basis of the legend epitomized, thirteen years later, by Duke Antony-Ulric in his *Roman Octavia*. For two and a half centuries this version of the tragedy — in which there was an element of truth — passed as authentic.

Those who knew what had really happened never contradicted it. The Duke's story centres round Clara von Platen, whom he describes as a jealous fiend, determined to revenge herself on Königsmarck and the Princess. With Ernst-August's permission, she employs four men-at-arms to set upon Königsmarck as he passes through the Hall of the Knights after leaving the Princess's rooms. She guides them there. He enters, humming a tune. After a brief struggle he is struck down, crying out, 'The Princess is innocent! Save the Princess!', upon which the Baroness grinds her heel into his mouth. According to a later version of the romance, he expires 'with his mistress's name upon his lips'. His body is walled up (to be discovered a hundred years later) and all traces of the murder are removed, while the Princess, who is on the point of elopement, is imprisoned and left in suspense for a fortnight. Baron von Platen then tells her what has happened, and a dramatic scene ensues. A contemporary print shows Königs-marck in his nightshirt, being stabbed by three men, one of whom is holding a torch; a half-seen female figure watches from behind a door. This picture may have been designed as an illustration for Duke Antony-Ulric's novel. It was impossible to refute his account unless by word of mouth, for all the written evidence and all comments on the murder had been destroyed—or so it seemed.

In 1958 the real story came to light through further research into the Hanoverian archives. Königsmarck and the Princess were discovered, according to plan. But by the time the three officers broke in he had sprung out of bed, seized his sword and was ready to defend himself. In the ensuing struggle the two Germans kept their heads in order to overpower and remove him, as instructed. The Italian killed him.*

So an extremely awkward situation was created. The very last thing the Elector and George-Louis wanted was to have a murder on their hands, least of all that of a well-known and distinguished man whom they had employed for six years. They may have considered trying and imprisoning him; as he was a foreigner and the subject of an ally, the question of his being executed would not have arisen. A report from the Danish ambassador implicates Clara von Platen as having bribed the Italian to kill her former

* It is possible that Königsmarck had already left the Princess's apartments, and that the struggle took place in the Hall of the Knights, as in Duke Antony-Ulric's version.

lover; if she did so, it would have been without Ernst-August's knowledge or consent. Her share in the murder cannot be proved.

It is not known, and probably never will be, whether Königsmarck was killed under the eyes of the Princess; nor has it transpired what was done with the body. One assumption is that he was thrown into the Leine, then a fast-flowing river; and as the three officers must have been appalled at the miscarriage of their instructions, this is what they might have done.

As soon as Ernst-August and Sophia were told what had happened, they and their ministers decided that secrecy must be ensured by settling annual allowances on the officers, who were told to leave Hanover, and warned that if they revealed themselves as the murderers, they would be seized and executed. Naturally, they obeyed orders. A guard was set upon the Princess's apartments, and she was informed that she would not be allowed to communicate with anyone. The Elector and his Council then drew up plans for the divorce.

SIX

I

WITHIN a few days of the murder of Königsmarck Ernst-August and his ministers decided that George-Louis must divorce his wife on the grounds of desertion and not, as originally planned, of adultery, thus creating the impression that her lover had simply disappeared. For this they needed the Princess's co-operation; all she had to say was that in no circumstances would she continue to live with her husband.

Nothing is known of Sophie-Dorothea's state at this time. Eleanora von Knesebeck was arrested, presumably within a few hours of the murder, and imprisoned in a fortress in the Harz mountains. Whether struck into shocked passivity or not, the Princess agreed with her judges and advisers on the main point: she wished never to see her husband again, and was perfectly indifferent as to the means of their separation, so long as it was accomplished. She may have thought, when she was once more able to do so, that after a period of retirement she would be able to go home, and presently see the children she had been ready to abandon without scruple or hesitation.

Sophia's attitude towards the affair had been calculated but not disingenuous. She had tried to gain her daughter-in-law's confidence by showing that she herself had no animosity towards Königsmarck—that she was in fact very much taken with him—but that, if he and Sophie-Dorothea persisted in advertising their relationship, he would be dismissed and she would never see him again. Here her intuition failed; she could not grasp the nature or the violence of the Princess's passion; nor did she understand that both she and Königsmarck were incapable of the most elementary discretion.

Ernst-August's first step was to consult the Duke and Duchess of Celle and to obtain their agreement about the grounds of divorce. Having searched Königsmarck's rooms, he was able to show them a number of Sophie-Dorothea's letters, which not only convinced them of her guilt, but caused her father to declare that he would have nothing more to do with her. A few weeks later, Aurora von Königsmarck and her sister, the Countess von Lewenhaupt (whom Sophia describes as 'the witches from Dresden'), began to make inquiries about their brother. As Aurora had been entrusted with his and Sophie-Dorothea's correspondence (they had not dared keep, but could not bear to destroy, each other's letters), she knew that they were on the point of eloping. She came to the conclusion that he had been imprisoned, and when it was hinted that he might have been killed, refused to be put off by what she considered an excuse to prevent further inquiries. As she had in her possession one of Sophie-Dorothea's letters warning Königsmarck against Clara von Platen, she accused that lady of engineering his arrest. Sophia replied defending the Baroness and desiring Aurora not to insult one of her most valuable servants. Aurora then persuaded the Elector of Saxony to send a representative to Hanover with the demand that Königsmarck should be produced and given up to his master. To this Ernst-August truthfully answered that he did not know where the Count was; he then forbade the sisters to enter his territory.

At the same time, Sophia instructed her intimate correspondents — Liselotte, Leibnitz and her daughter — to destroy all letters mentioning Königsmarck's and Sophie-Dorothea's relationship. With the systematic destruction of other documents referring to Königsmarck's movements and behaviour, conjecture was partially stifled, except at Versailles, where it was asserted that he had been stabbed and thrust into a furnace — which might have been the case if the murder had not taken place in the height of summer.

On December 28th, 1694, the marriage of Their Electoral Highnesses was formally dissolved (and all the evidence destroyed) on the grounds of Sophie-Dorothea's desertion. By this time, she had been removed to the castle of Ahlden, some twenty miles from Hanover. She was then twenty-eight. She remained there, in 'honourable', indeed luxurious, confinement, having been forbidden to receive any visitors, for thirty-three years.

The village and castle of Ahlden have changed hardly at all since Sophie-Dorothea — henceforth known as the Duchess of Ahlden — was taken to the sixteenth-century red-brick mansion which had once been a moated fortress. The Aller ran beneath one side of the castle; on the other stood, and still stand, a minute church and a cluster of cottages. These were encircled by marshy plains, with occasional patches of heather and a few stunted copses. The Princess was established in her own Court—of spies and guards—and visited twice daily by the Intendant of the castle. She had her coach and six, in which, escorted by a troop of cavalry with drawn swords, she was allowed to drive for six miles along the only road from the village. She was not permitted to walk beyond the castle grounds, nor to speak to the peasants who sold their produce to her jailers. Entering this prison in the fullness of youth and strength, her health was carefully watched, and her slightest ailment reported and dealt with; she had nothing to do but survive. Her son and daughter, aged eleven and seven respectively, were forbidden to mention her; she was never spoken of by the families of Hanover and Celle. No foreign envoy inquired for her. She sank, with her memories, into total oblivion.

There was, as we say now, no harm in Sophie-Dorothea; indeed she was probably more innocent of evil intentions than most young women. But there had been, until the advent of Königsmarck, an emptiness in her character, which lay ready to receive and so to foster the passion that resulted in a far more dreadful fate than her lover's. She accepted it; she made no attempt to escape. She endured her living death as if she had already been laid in her coffin.

On the day that George-Louis obtained the divorce which enabled him, but not Sophie-Dorothea, to marry again, Queen Mary II died of smallpox at Kensington Palace. At first, it was believed that William III would re-marry in order to ensure the Protestant succession; for the little Duke of Gloucester was still very delicate, while his mother's yearly pregnancies continued to end in miscarriages or still-born children. Then the reports showed that William's grief had so affected his health that he might not survive; nor had he any intention of taking another wife. The Catholicism of the rightful inheritor, the seven-year-old *de jure* Prince of Wales, put him out of court with the majority of the English people; this did not prevent another Catholic grandchild of Charles I, the Duchess of Savoy, pressing her claim, in the event of the Princess Anne predeceasing William III.

Sophia, now nearer still to the succession, was unconcerned. She did not expect to outlive the Princess Anne; and she had so much to think about within her own family circle that brooding over the far-off possibility of becoming Queen of England would be a sad waste of time. There were, for example, her two eldest grand-children, George-Augustus and the younger Sophie-Dorothea, now her sole responsibility. Sophia asked her daughter to bring her boy, Frederick-William, for a visit, so that the cousins should become friends — with disastrous results. From the moment of their meeting the little Princes conceived a violent hatred for one another, which was to last all their lives. George-Augustus was a good-tempered child; but Frederick-William, a savagely belli-gerent character, never ceased to torment his cousin, who was well able to defend himself. They fought every day, and were regularly torn apart by their attendants.

Then Frederick-William, rampaging round the peaceful soli-tudes of Herrenhausen, was seen swallowing a silver buckle. As he had now been left in Sophia's charge, her agitation was extreme. Doctors were called in and the usual hideous remedies applied, with no effect but that of a certain smug complacency on the face of Frederick-William, who seemed to be enjoying his grandmother's alarm. A few days later, watching the naughty boy stuff down an enormous meal, Sophia burst out laughing. 'He must be convalescent!' she said, and sent him back to Brandenburg, declaring that he had been more trouble than he was worth.

She returned to her usual pursuits in excellent spirits. No doubt the removal of Sophie-Dorothea and George-Louis's long absences were a relief after the turmoil of the last few years. She became more than ever absorbed in her plans for Herrenhausen, listening to the nightingales on summer evenings, adding to her collection of rare birds and reading a number of theological works. On the whole, she told Leibnitz, she found *Don Quixote* a more amusing book than that he had just sent her, on the Real Presence, or another about vampires and giants. At dinner, Ernst-August and his court were in fits of laughter at her satirical comments on precognition stories, cold-cures and miracle-working images. Yet her mockery was seldom spiteful and never inept.

At this time Sophia's life was so full that she could afford to disregard the continued enmity of Duke Antony-Ulric and the conversion to Catholicism of Prince Maximilian (she had always mistrusted his religiosity), but she was worried about Ernst-

August, whose health, with his eyesight, was beginning to fail; now he spent more time with her than with Baroness von Platen. Sophia, endlessly patient and affectionate, played simple games with her husband and read aloud to him. In 1697 she and her daughter were asked to receive Peter the Great, who was touring northern Germany. As Ernst-August was not equal to what promised—in view of the Tsar's reputation—to be something of an ordeal, the two Electresses set off for Coppenbrück, near Celle, to help George-William entertain him.

With his Swiss favourite Le Fort, three ambassadors and a vast entourage, the twenty-five-year-old potentate consented to receive Sophia and her daughter on condition that the public did not see him. Sophia arranged with Duke George-William that their guest should arrive as a member of his own suite. When he saw the Electresses, the Duke and Duchess, Prince Christian, Prince Ernst-August and Sophia's two eldest grandchildren drawn up in line, he put his hands over his face exclaiming, 'I cannot speak!' and called to Le Fort to do so for him. Sophia and her daughter coaxed him into supper, placing him between them. He then regained his poise: but his grimaces (he had a nervous tic) were frightful, his table manners shocking, and he was very dirty. Undeterred, Sophia began to ask him about his travels, regardless of Russian etiquette which forbade the questioning of royalty, and he answered in rather halting German. At last she persuaded him to allow her courtiers to be presented, and he received them with much twitching and jerking. Suddenly he shouted to Le Fort to shut all the doors, and filling up the glasses, himself carried them round. He produced diamond snuff-boxes for the Electresses; as the orchestra began to play, Sophia asked him if he liked music. 'No,' was the rather strange answer, 'but I like fireworks and navigation.' He then thrust his filthy hands into her lap, so that she might feel how calloused they were. Sophia admired his height and strength; indeed, she was beginning to think him quite handsome. He remained sober, and increasingly talkative; his nobles became so drunk that they fell forward over the tables and had to be carried off, 'smiling and amiable in the depths of intoxication.'

The Tsar then danced with the Electresses. Amazed by their corseted bodices, he exclaimed, 'I did not know German women had such hard bones!' During a pause he picked up little Sophie-

Dorothea, whom he kissed so violently that her hair tumbled down; she screamed, and he turned to her brother, who took his embrace more courageously. 'I would not have missed seeing him for a great deal,' Sophia concluded. 'He is most amusing' — but she was somewhat disappointed by his parting gift of sables and damask. The furs, when cleaned of lice, were very fine; the damask had been cut into small squares, and was unusable.

Shortly after returning to Hanover Sophia received Bishop Burnet, who visited her and Ernst-August as the private envoy of William III. She sent a coach every day so that he might drive out to dine at Herrenhausen. 'I remember your grandfather,' she told him, and went on to speak of her Stuart cousins. 'King James is weak; Queen Mary was a good woman. But I am piqued at the Princess Anne, who has not spoken well of me. Their Majesties', she continued, 'once asked me to stay in England, but I am grown old, and I cannot leave the Elector and my family.' When she added, 'I should be glad to see my own country before I die, and would willingly lay my bones by my mother's, in Westminster Abbey,' the Bishop was puzzled by this sudden affiliation with the kingdom she had never entered. She then referred rather sharply to King William's bestowal of the Garter on Duke George-William. 'The Elector might have expected it on my account.' Recalling her youth, she spoke with less than her usual accuracy. 'I was once like to have been married to King Charles,' she said, 'which would not have been worse for the nation, considering how many children I have brought.' She then told Burnet that she corresponded as warmly with the exiled King James as with his successor. 'The Prince of Wales is not a bastard,' she began, but reverted to her satirical tone when discussing James II's refusal of the crown of Poland. 'He may well pass for a saint,' she remarked, 'since we are told to become as little children in order to enter the kingdom of heaven.'

Soon after Burnet's departure Ernst-August became very ill. Sophia nursed him devotedly; her differences with the Duke and Duchess of Celle were made up as George-William shared her grief; Ernst-August died in his arms in January 1698. 'As I have now little left,' she wrote to an old friend, 'it is to be hoped that the Creator will soon summon me to join my dear Elector.' When George-Louis took over the government he and Sophia received cringing letters of condolence from Sophie-Dorothea. 'My sorrow for my faults', she informed the new Elector, 'is keen and bitter ... Allow me to see and embrace our children ... I should be content to die, afterwards.'

These appeals were ignored—not unjustly, according to the rules of that day. A century earlier, Sophie-Dorothea would have been executed for high treason; that she was allowed to live as became the rank she had dishonoured (she had an entourage of some three dozen persons) surprised many of her contemporaries. By now, she had renewed her interest in fashions; she drove out magnificently dressed, with diamonds in her hair, her guards about her, a lady-in-waiting at her side. Although much fatter, she was still beautiful; the villagers were rather proud of their mysterious great lady, whose charity they received, but who never entered their cottages, nor was allowed to speak to the women who came in to clean her rooms.

In 1698 Eleanora von Knesebeck escaped, and was sheltered by Duke Antony-Ulric. She maintained her defence of Sophie-Dorothea's innocence, swearing on the Sacrament that she and Königsmarck had never been lovers. His sisters' concealment of their letters, which reveal their relationship in all its passion and despair, was maintained till the end of the eighteenth century.

At her son's accession Sophia retired to Herrenhausen, only visiting the Leine Palace on formal occasions, when the people, who adored her, would rush out and surround her coach. She and George-Louis were not on good terms; he spoke of her contemptuously (as he did of most people), while she ignored his rudeness and did what she could for Maximilian and Christian, who were bitterly resentful of his inheritance; the youngest brother, Prince Ernst-August, was devoted to him, and they were always together.

In middle life Sophia would have been tormented by these dissensions; her seventieth year found her contemplating them as serenely as she did the prospect of the next world. 'I trust in God,' she told Leibnitz. 'Why should He have created me in order to hurt me?'—going on to express her horror of bigotry and her dismay at Burnet's presentation of his book on the Thirty-Nine Articles, which was, she concluded, 'better to skip than to read'.

Gradually, in the quiet of Herrenhausen, her spirits revived; she no longer wished to leave a world in which she had time to renew her old hobbies—needlework, sketching, botany; she would walk there for two and three hours at a stretch, settling the installation of temples, statues and her box-hedged, 'English' garden.

She was still very handsome. The portraits show a magnificent, cynically smiling old lady, whose piled grey hair is set off by a discreet *fontange* and a transparent black lace veil; indeed, she wore her mourning very lightly. Her informal manners and lively questions disarmed the reticent and put shy guests at their ease. One English visitor was amazed at the freedom with which she was approached and at her ability to switch from German to French, or from Dutch to Italian, and thence to English, although he was slightly pained by her 'sitting very loose in her religious opinions'. At this time she inaugurated theological debate by setting a Catholic priest to argue with one of her chaplains; the resultant absurdities fascinated her; her interventions, although good-humoured and tactful, were sometimes disconcerting. Yet she was so 'merry and debonair', according to another visitor, that these duels always ended amicably.

In July 1700 the twelve-year-old Duke of Gloucester died of meningitis, and Sophia and her daughter set off to visit King William at Loo, in order to discuss the question of her son-in-law becoming King of Prussia. Passing through Rotterdam, the two ladies sent for Bayle, then at the height of his philosophic fame as a free-thinker. After some difficulty, that rather bearish sage was induced to wait on them, but complained bitterly of Sophia's persistence; in fact, he was unable to answer all her questions. 'She wants to know the *pourquoi de pourquoi*,' he said, and refused to accompany her and the younger Electress to Delft.

After a satisfactory interview with William, mother and daughter parted, and once more Sophia had to emphasize that, although she thought of England as her own country, she desired the throne for her descendants rather than for herself. 'If I were younger,' she told Leibnitz, 'I might flatter myself with the thought.' The fortunes of 'the poor Prince of Wales' still so concerned her that she wrote to an English envoy urging his claim. 'He has learned and suffered so much for his father's errors that he may make a good King of England,' she insisted. She went on to admit that George-Louis might not be popular in that country, adding that if she herself thought of a crown, 'it must be a heavenly one.'

Meanwhile, she rightly gauged the capriciousness of the English politicians. 'I don't dislike *hearing* of a crown,' she confessed, 'but one can be sure of nothing.' So it was that the Act of Settlement on herself and her heirs left her unmoved, and the death of William III in the following year affected her less than Prince Maximilian's debts. Sorrow was renewed with the death of Madame von Harling, who had been her lady-in-waiting and constant companion for half a century. That loss and the memory of those preceding it made the assiduities of the English statesmen a subject of harsh mockery. When they arrived in bulk she told Leibnitz, 'They are very kind to me, which is a pity, for I cannot outlive Queen Anne to please them … She must hurry up and die, if I am to be Queen.' And these gentlemen were not impressive. There was Mr Ding, 'whose eyes please Mademoiselle Kilman-segge [Baroness von Platen's daughter] and whose teeth please nobody,' Mr Griffin, who, 'finding no good tobacco in Hanover, has gone to Holland,' and 'my lord Winchelsea,' a foolish, 'good little man'. When it came to Mr Windle, words failed her. She scribbled four large noughts after his name, and so left him.

II

When the war between France and the Allies seemed about to encroach on his territory, Duke George-William sent for Sophie-Dorothea and established her in the castle of Celle, where she remained, as much a prisoner as at Ahlden, for several months. During that time he refused to see her, although he let her mother do so. After her return she was allowed to hold receptions for the local dignitaries once a month, and a little later Duchess Eléanore came to visit her. These were her only contacts with the outside world until her death; she made her last journey—to the chapel of Celle—in 1726.

This war, that of the Spanish Succession, brought Hanover and Celle into line with Marlborough's armies, and once more Sophia ruled while the Elector and his brothers fought in the Low Countries and in Central Europe. In 1703 Prince Christian was drowned during a retreat across the Danube, and in the following year Sophia's grief gave way to anxiety as the French seized Antwerp,

Luxemburg, Namur and Mons. Then came the victory of Blenheim, the return of her three remaining sons, and a visit from the great Duke himself.

Sophia was entranced. 'I never met anyone pleasanter, nor more courteous and obliging,' she told Leibnitz. 'He is as good a courtier as he is a brave captain.' On one occasion Sophia and Marlborough sat down to cards with Lady Bellmont, formerly the mistress of Prince Rupert, to whom the Duke made himself equally agreeable, although he knew that she was one of many Jacobite spies frequenting the German courts at that time. This, and his success with Sophia, enraged Sarah Marlborough, who thereafter referred to the Electress-Dowager as 'that ridiculous creature', and did her best to increase the nervous jealousy of Queen Anne, with the result that that unhappy lady began to favour the Old Pretender's claims, although she did not attempt to alter the succession or to prevent the visits to Hanover of the Whig politicians.

Sophia then began to attend the services of the Church of England. 'I do not wish it said', she told an English visitor, 'that my religion is different from yours,' adding with a smile, 'I hope the country will not be sorry for having chosen an old woman, and that none of their descendants will tire of the House of Hanover.' With Leibnitz, she was more outspoken. 'I am much older than Queen Anne,' she told him, 'and my flesh, unlike the Catholics' wafer, is incapable of miracles.'

With the prospect of her daughter's visit for the carnival of 1705 and the arrangements for the marriage of her grandson George-Augustus to Caroline of Ansbach, Sophia's spirits rose. She fell ill while Sophia-Charlotte, now Queen of Prussia, was on her way, and was still in bed when the Queen developed typhoid and died before her mother could reach her.

This loss was the most terrible of Sophia's life. She would not leave the Leine Palace, where the body of the dearest of all her children lay in state; she could not eat, or weep, or speak. Liselotte wrote in an agony—could not her aunt be persuaded to move out to Herrenhausen? At last she did so, and in the autumn of that year was able to play her part in the privately celebrated wedding of her grandson. For the next nine years the young couple remained with her; gradually, the brilliance and charm of her granddaughter-in-law (whom the Elector described as '*cette diablesse de Madame Caroline'*) helped Sophia to recover. The new Electoral Princess was very like Sophia-Charlotte; she studied philosophy and theology, and read the same books. With the birth of Sophia's great-grandson in 1706 ('poor Fred,' the Prince of Wales who was to predecease his father), she regained her usual vigour. In the following year Lord Halifax arrived to celebrate with her and the Elector the union of Scotland and England, and to name her first subject and heiress of Great Britain. On this occasion Sophia behaved very strangely. Halifax never forgot the incident, and recounted it many times.

The Court had assembled in the great hall of the Leine Palace, and Halifax was waiting for Sophia to reply to his speech, when suddenly the old lady of seventy-seven sprang up from the dais and ran, as lightly as a girl, to the other side of the room; there she remained, while the ambassador invested George-Louis with the Garter.

Completely bewildered, Halifax asked her courtiers to account for this freak—which was, in fact, a gesture. Sophia had been facing a portrait of the cousin she had never seen, the Pretender who, as 'James III', was to survive her for half a century. She accepted her inheritance by the will of the English Parliament and the law prohibiting the rule of a Catholic monarch; but she wanted, if only symbolically, to protect (and perhaps also to hide) the shadowy reminder of the rival whose claim she had tried to put before her own and that of her descendants. She could not deny the instincts of her blood; the Hanoverian heiress was a Jacobite at heart.

Halifax was rather amused than impressed. What chiefly struck him was the Electress-Dowager's vigour and gaiety; she carried herself like a young woman, read without spectacles, was unwrinkled and had all her teeth. Another visitor, equally fascinated by her animation, found little to say for the Elector, who neglected to bow, seldom spoke and snubbed those approaching him. Sophia ignored these glum withdrawals; and she reserved the expression of her private griefs and hopes for Leibnitz and Liselotte. When Louise, the last but one of the Palatine Stuarts, died at the age of seventy-seven, she mourned her briefly; but then they had not met for thirty years.

After Halifax's departure it was suggested that Sophia should come to England to receive the title of Princess of Wales and the homage of her future subjects. She was too wise to accept out of hand, and may indeed have known that in certain squibs and pasquils she was described as 'the Lutheran Dame' and 'old Sophy'. Nor would she affiliate herself with any political party. 'I refuse to distinguish individuals under the names of Whig and Tory,' she told the Hanoverian envoy at St James's, and reverted to the pleasant routine of Herrenhausen. 'I love the sound of birds and frogs,' she wrote to Leibnitz. 'I would rather go on living here than be Queen of England. I hope to die', she went on, 'without knowing it, and with neither priest nor physician near me.' As to the book he had sent her on free-thinking, 'One can do that without an author's help,' she remarked, and pursued her inquiries about new inventions, adding that these endless wrangles over the succession were becoming tedious. To Liselotte she wrote satirically of the Elector's latest hunting expedition, in which he had killed fifty boars and wounded one forester.

Although she had begun to work out a scheme for the union of the Church of England with that of the old faith, she was more frivolous than in her middle age, dancing, reading novels—and disregarding her doctors' orders, with the result that in 1713 she went to bed with a rash and a temperature. Sourly, the Elector told her that she should not eat so much fruit. 'How do you find it odd that a woman of eighty-three should fall ill?' his mother inquired. 'You ought to find it odder still to see me alive. I think I shall not give up yet,' she rather maliciously added. Then she became strangely sad. 'I want to go home—I must go home,' she kept on saying; and it dawned on her attendants that she was speaking of England. This mood vanished with her recovery and the preparations for Peter the Great's second visit.

Seventeen years of absolutist administration had accustomed the Tsar to public appearances. Escorted by the Elector, he arrived in a litter, was greeted by a salute of a hundred cannon and supped privately with Sophia. He behaved perfectly until conducted to his suite, when he refused to sleep in the bed of state. 'I might spoil it,' he said, and sent for a camp-mattress, which was laid on the floor. In the morning he called for tea (this caused some agitation) and presently came down to eat a large breakfast. He and Sophia met for dinner, and she took him to the opera; they then drove out to Herrenhausen for a masked ball. The climax of the evening came with the grand polonaise or taper-dance, headed by the Tsar and Sophia, who were followed by three generations of the Electoral family and the whole Court, in order of precedence.

Hand in hand and holding lighted candles, the couples danced round the ballroom, thence proceeding through the state apartments and so back to the starting-place. On this occasion the Tsar's dwarfs brought up the rear of a cortège of some three hundred couples. The skill and poise required of the ladies, whose muslin *fontanges* were highly inflammable and whose trains were carried by pages, while they held a taper in one hand and their partner's wrist in the other, must have been considerable.

Sophia carried herself superbly; at eighty-three, she was perhaps more stately than the little princess of seventy years ago whose favourite teacher had been her dancing-master. Passing through torch-lit passages and mirrored ante-rooms, the glittering tail of her family, her courtiers and her huge partner's squat imps winding along behind her—jewelled, magnificent, serene—she seems then to have reached her apotheosis. When the last candle guttered to its socket, and the last torch sank into blackness, and the last note died away, she smilingly vanished—reappearing the next morning at six o'clock to see the Tsar drive off, and then resuming her routine of walks, reading, correspondence and needlework, as if indestructible.

The changing seasons, the endless visits, the long audiences found her, as ever, gay, amusing, acute in observation, sympathetic in response. An acrimonious correspondence with Queen Anne about George-Louis going to England left her unmoved. But in the early summer of 1714 the royal veto forbidding any member of the Electoral family to appear in London, for fear of creating 'dangerous consequences to the succession', arrived—and then Sophia, struck at through her racial pride and dynastic feeling, was deeply wounded. All her life she had subscribed to orderliness, respect for law and custom, hierarchical loyalty and the rightful claims of her descendants; that she, with them, should be suspected of wishing to inculcate dispute and confusion was monstrously unjust. She concluded that Queen Anne was going to defy Parliament, break her word and instal the Pretender. 'This', she burst out, 'will kill me! I shall publish the letter, to show that it is not my fault if my children lose three crowns.'

No more was said. The sick Queen's murmured regrets for 'my poor brother' were reported to, and ignored by, Sophia and the

Elector — and still the dying woman lingered on. On a fine evening in June, Sophia was walking with the Countess of Bückeburg and her other ladies in the alley of the English garden. In the distance she saw her dear Caroline and Madame von Busche. Pausing to watch them, she said, 'Is she not beautiful?' and then resumed her walk and her conversation with more than her usual vigour.

It began to rain. Sophia picked up her skirts and hurried towards the nearest shelter. A change came over her face. 'I think Your Highness is walking too fast,' ventured Madame de Bückeburg. 'I believe I am,' said Sophia, and stopped; then she gasped out, 'Give me your hand, I am not well —' and sank down. Madame de Bückeburg caught her, supported her and called for help. Servants and courtiers dashed forward; someone ran for a doctor. Madame de Bückeburg bent over her mistress. 'Madame — Highness — !'

Sophia was dead: with neither priest nor physician to attend her — as she had wished.

Seven weeks later Queen Anne died; and six weeks after that George-Louis left Hanover and impassively accepted the homage of his English subjects. Meanwhile, Sophia had been laid beside her husband in the chapel of the Leine Palace, with great pomp, but with no religious ceremony of any kind. There they remained for two and a half centuries. In 1960 they were brought back to Herrenhausen. Their palace had been destroyed, twenty years before, by English and American bombs; so their coffins were placed in the eighteenth-century mausoleum of their House.

Sophia's statue is her most fitting memorial. Seated in a high-backed chair, stately, splendid, formidable, she looks out over the gardens she made and loved. Her expression is dreamy rather than cynical; liveliness has yielded to speculation. As in life, when no one quite knew what she was going to do or say, so here; she keeps her secret.

PRINCIPAL SOURCES OF INFORMATION

with dates of the most recent editions

Beaucaire, H. de,   *Eléanore d'Olbreuse* (Paris, 1884)

Burnet, G.   *History of My Own Time*, vol. VI (Edinburgh, 1753)

Elizabeth-Charlotte,
Duchesse d'Orléans,   *Correspondance* (Paris, 1857)

Everett Green, M.,   *Elizabeth of Bohemia* (London, 1909)

Godfrey, E.,   *A Sister of Prince Rupert* (London, 1909)

Gourville, J. H. de,   *Mémoires* (Paris, 1724)

Greenwood, A.,   *Hanoverian Queens of England*, vol. I (London, 1909)

Knoop, M.,   *Die Kurfürstin Sophie von Hannover* (Hanover, 1964)

Oman, C.,   *Elizabeth of Bohemia* (London, 1938)

Plumb, J. H.,   *The First Four Georges* (London, 1956)

Rait, R.,   *Five Stuart Princesses* (London, 1902)

Saint-Simon, Duc de,   *Mémoires* (Paris, 1951)

Schnath, G.,   *Der Königsmarckbriefwechsel* (Hildesheim, 1930)

Sophia, Electress of
Hanover,   *Memoirs and Correspondence* (London, 1888)

Spence, J.,   *Observations, Anecdotes and Characters ...* (London, 1820)

Strickland, A.,   *Queens of Scotland and English Princesses*, vol. VIII (London, 1888)

Toland, J.,   *Courts of Hanover and Prussia* (London, 1705)

Ward, A. W.,   *The Electress Sophia and the Hanoverian Succession* (London, 1909)

Wendland, A.,   *Letters of Elizabeth of Bohemia* (London, 1953)

Wilkins, W. H.,   *The Love of an Uncrowned Queen** (London, 1900)

* This book, which follows the semi-fictional version of the relationship between Königsmarck and Sophie-Dorothea, contains a large portion of their correspondence.

HORTENSE MANCINI, DUCHESS MAZARIN

(1647 — JUNE 1699)

'And there appeared a great wonder ... a woman clothed with the sun, and the moon under her feet, and upon her head a crown of twelve stars ...

'And to the woman were given two wings of a great eagle that she might fly into the wilderness ... for a time, and times, and half a time, from the face of the serpent ... '

THE REVELATION OF ST JOHN THE DIVINE

ONE

I

THOSE who had suffered under Cardinal Richelieu in the latter half of the reign of Louis XIII soon came to the conclusion that Cardinal Mazarin, his successor and protégé, was even more detestable and dangerous. When their revolt resulted in the wars of the Fronde, and the eleven-year-old Louis XIV, with his mother and brother, left Paris, while Mazarin fled abroad, it was hoped that the odious Minister would not return. By the time he did so the Frondeurs were being defeated, and the young King had reached his majority. As Louis had always been jealous of his mother's devotion to Mazarin, the anticipation of the Cardinal's downfall was renewed, with the same indignant questions. What were his origins? Why should a jumped-up Italian, who was still in deacon's orders and therefore free to marry the besotted Anne of Austria, rule France? Was he already her husband? Could nothing be done to defeat him?

Rumour replied with a series of contradictions. Mazarin might have come from Mazara, in Sicily; some said he was the son of a hatter; others had heard of him as a nobleman's bastard, born in Castello Mazarino and educated in Rome; there, in fact, he had studied civil law, presently obtaining a post at the Vatican and the favour of Cardinal Richelieu, who bequeathed him his powers, with the approval of the Queen-Regent. On one point all were agreed: that although Mazarin's foreign policy, and his wars, had been successful, his interior administration was even more pervasively tyrannical than that of his predecessor. Yet he remained supreme and was amassing a vast fortune. His collections of pictures, statues, tapestries and jewels were the finest in Europe. The young King, swallowing his resentment, consulted and obeyed him. His activity was prodigious, his brilliance undeniable and his efforts for the greatness of France had consolidated his own powers.

To rebel against such a man as this had already proved pointless and fatal. As his manners and appearance were impressive, and his hospitality was worthy of them—the parties at the Palais Mazarin resembled those of an oriental potentate—his greed, his intrigues and his deceit were accepted. It was thought that he might, after all, achieve permanent peace with Spain, and thus partially justify his dictatorship. Also, for many years he stood alone, without favourites, making no attempt to import, establish or dower his family. 'These', he had said, smilingly indicating his Roman statues, 'are the only relatives I am bringing to France.'

Mazarin had two sisters younger than himself, Margharita Martinozzi and Hieronyma Mancini. Both had married into the Roman nobility and were now widowed. Margharita had two daughters, Anna-Maria and Laura; Hieronyma had five daughters —a second Laura, Marie, Olympe, Hortense and Marianne—and three sons, Paul, Alphonse and Philippe. No one at the French Court had heard of any of them until 1647, when the first batch, that of Anna-Maria Martinozzi, and Laura, Paul and Olympe Mancini, arrived. Mazarin at once presented the four young people to the Queen, who petted them and praised their looks. When they left the Louvre for the Palais Mazarin he received them rather coldly, and for the next few months appeared to take no interest in their progress; indeed, he made fun of those who paid court to them. 'But', observed the astute Madame de Motteville, 'his indifference was feigned ... It is not always in the theatre that the best comedies are played.' During their second visit to the Louvre Madame de Villeroy whispered to Gaston, Duc d'Orléans, Louis XIV's uncle, 'Those little girls are not yet rich, but soon they will acquire castles, wealth, jewels and perhaps rank and dignity.' This foreboding was followed by general protests and a number of squibs and ballads about the 'Mazarinettes', which the Cardinal confiscated; after a judicious interval he sold them again on his private black market, thus adding large sums to his income.

During the wars of the Fronde Mazarin's elder nieces and nephew had remained in France. Laura Mancini was then married to the Duc de Mercœur, and Anna-Maria Martinozzi to the Prince de Conti; Olympe Mancini was too young to be given a husband; Laura Martinozzi outdid them all by marrying the Duke of Modena.

In 1653 the second batch appeared, that of Marie, Hortense and Philippe Mancini, with their mother. The thirteen-year-old Marie, and Hortense, aged eight, were placed in a convent, while Philippe was put in the charge of Jesuit tutors. A few months later the two girls and Madame Mancini were given apartments at the Louvre, where they were joined by the eleven-year-old Olympe.

They were a strikingly handsome family; but Hortense's beauty far outshone that of her sisters and cousins; she had always been her mother's darling. As soon as she arrived the thirteen-year-old Duc d'Anjou, Louis XIV's younger brother (who later succeeded Gaston as Duc d'Orléans, or 'Monsieur'), became passionately attached to her; he would not let her out of his sight, with the result that she was sent back to the convent, where she remained for the next two years. By that time Anjou's homosexual tendencies had prevailed and when, at the age of ten, Hortense returned to Court, all danger of his pursuing her was removed. She was admired by everyone but Louis XIV. 'I do not like little girls,' he said, and chose Marie for his companion. This did not make up to Marie for her mother's dislike; Madame Mancini detested her eldest daughter and was very unkind to her. Marie and Hortense therefore made an alliance against her and Olympe, a disagreeable, selfish girl, and combined in flattering and cajoling the Cardinal. Marie, aware that Hortense was his favourite niece, was sensible enough to play second fiddle to her sister, whose portrait she painted and sent to their uncle.

The contemporary descriptions of Marie and Hortense seem to show that if they had lived in the twentieth century, Marie, a *jolie laide*, would have made a greater sensation than her sisters. She was rather thin (this worried Mazarin, who put her on a fattening diet), with the dark complexion then described as sallow, rounded features and almond-shaped eyes. Hortense's beauty was at the same time classic and voluptuous, and might now be considered heavy. As she reached adolescence her proportions became those of a goddess, and her curling masses of blue-black hair framed a face of glowing loveliness, sombre yet wild; there was a hint of savagery in those huge eyes, whose colour, between blue and grey, seemed to change with her moods; admirers compared her sculptured mouth and delicate profile to those of a Greek nymph or a Roman Bacchante.

All three sisters were lively and amusing; but at this time it was Marie who dominated by her wit, her knowledge of the arts and her skill as an actress. Hortense was then a little scatterbrain,

Olympe a would-be mischief-maker ('wilful and obstinate,' was the Cardinal's verdict on them both), while spiteful courtiers described Marie as a *précieuse*. It was this aspect which first attracted Louis XIV. He would listen, fascinated and a little envious, while she talked of plays, novels and poetry he had never read, every now and then bursting into recitations from *Polyeucte* or *Le Cid*, while Hortense and Olympe practised the new dances or teased the beribboned and scented Duc d'Anjou, whose favourite companion was Monsieur de Choisy; this youth, destined for the Church, preferred to dress, as he himself did, in girl's clothes.

At about this time Olympe, more of a rebel than her sisters and slightly less alluring, began to dress as a man. Queen Christina of Sweden had introduced that fashion, which became more popular in Italy than in France, while the eccentric lady's attitude towards her own sex set an example in both countries. But after all, if young men chose to dress as women, why should not girls dress as boys? Segregation of the sexes made such metamorphoses natural and convenient. Olympe's particular friend, Sidonie de Lénancourt, wore a coat and breeches on most informal occasions — and behaved as became her costume.

At nine years old, Hortense cared little how she dressed, so long as she was free to enjoy herself and escape from Madame de Venel, the governess chosen for the Mancini sisters by the Cardinal, who now began to plan marriages for Marie and Olympe. His first candidate was Armand-Charles de la Porte de la Meilleraye, only son of the wealthy Duc de la Meilleraye, whom he selected for Marie.

At the age of twenty-five, de la Meilleraye, heir to twenty-six million livres, although far from handsome (the fastidious Madame de Sévigné found him grotesque), was a tall, strong young man, with a ruddy complexion and distinguished manners; those meeting him for the first time described him as gracious, affable and polished. These assets may have helped them to overlook his loose mouth, haggard eyes and haunted, melancholy expression. He had already taken on some of his father's honours, specifically those of Grand Master of the Artillery, Marshal of France, and Governor of Alsace, de la Fère, Bourbon, Brittany and Vincennes. He carried out his duties efficiently, and his reputation was that of a pious and respectable servant of the state. In fact, a more desirable husband could not be imagined, and everyone assumed that his marriage to Marie Mancini would soon take place.

De la Meilleraye first saw the three sisters in October 1655, when the Court had moved to Picardy. One look at Marie sufficed. He refused her hand, and Cardinal Mazarin put forward Olympe, whom he also rejected. De la Meilleraye then asked for Hortense, adding, 'If I might marry *her*, I would not care if I died three months later.'

The Cardinal was very angry. Quite apart from the fact that Hortense had only just entered her tenth year, he had other plans for this niece, whom he destined for royalty. 'I would rather marry her to a lackey,' he said, and sent the dangerous young lady back to her convent. De la Meilleraye, now desperately in love, continued to think of her as his future wife.

In the following year Madame Mancini died, and in 1657 Olympe was married to Prince Eugène de Savoie-Carignan, Comte de Soissons. This magnificent alliance was forced on her by the Cardinal in order to remove her from the King, who had taken a momentary fancy for her. Olympe, who had begun to picture herself as Queen of France, was recalcitrant and sulky; but Mazarin was far too acute to undermine his own prestige by allowing a relative such promotion; already he was planning a marriage between his master and the Spanish Infanta.

He then sent for the youngest of the Mancini sisters, the six-year-old Marianne, who, with Hortense, joined the Court in Picardy, and at once became the pet of the Queen Mother. Mazarin delighted in her lively, natural manners, and the aplomb with which she answered the courtiers' teasing. Nothing seemed to daunt Marianne: and long afterwards Hortense, who found her rather trying, recalled the elaborate jokes played by her uncle on this self-possessed little creature. He would rally her about her conquests, going on to declare that she must surely be pregnant. Marianne denied it, 'with some heat,' says Hortense; but Mazarin persisted, telling her attendants to loosen her clothes and persuade her that she was getting very big. Marianne, now slightly bewildered, was horrified when she woke up one morning to find a newly-born child, hired for the purpose, in her bed. She burst into tears, exclaiming, 'Such a thing never happened but to Our Lady and myself—for I never felt any kind of pain!' Still the teasing went on; Anne of Austria offered to stand godmother: the courtiers urged Marianne to reveal the father's identity. 'It could be none but the King or the Comte de Guiche,' the child stoutly declared, 'for no man but those two ever kissed me—' and at last, amid peals of laughter, the explanation was given. Hortense was rather jealous; she concealed her resentment by laughing louder than anybody else, 'to make people take notice that I knew the trick.'

She then returned to her secret hobby, that of shutting herself up to write 'whatever came into my head ... doubts, questions upon all things which I could not understand.' Presently she incorporated these searchings for knowledge into letters, most of which were sent to a convent friend for whom she had a passion. 'Then,' she says, 'I grew weary of writing so often "I love you" in one and the same letter, and gave her to understand that I would only make a cross to signify these three words. According to this pretty invention, it happened sometimes that I wrote ... letters wherein ... there was nothing but whole lines of crosses.' Meanwhile, she herself was receiving ardent love-letters from de la Meilleraye, in which she took not the slightest interest. 'Our little play-games', she goes on, reverting to the theatricals organized by Marie, 'then took up all my time and thought, though they were often interrupted by the King's presence; he seldom stirred from our house.'

When Madame Mancini was ill Louis had visited her regularly, and as he continued to call on her daughters, it dawned on him that Marie had been set apart from her sisters. While Olympe and Hortense appeared at balls and parties Marie was shut up in her rooms; and Madame Mancini's last request to Cardinal Mazarin had been that she should be forced to take the vows. 'She has an evil nature,' said the dying woman. 'My husband, who was a famous astrologer, said that she would cause great misfortune.'

With her freedom, Marie's ascendancy over her sisters became complete. Every day Louis sought her out, either at the Louvre or the Hôtel Soissons; and although he behaved with his usual courtesy to Olympe and was kind to Hortense, he looked towards Marie for entertainment and gaiety. They resumed their reading of plays and novels, seeing themselves, now, as the hero and heroine of such romances as *Clélie* and *Le Grand Cyrus*. When Louis addressed the younger girls his regality produced 'an awestruck respect', according to Hortense, and they were glad to see him go; then they would tease Marie about her love for him. Later on, Hortense realized how unsympathetic she had been. 'The things which passion makes us do', she recalled, 'seem ridiculous to those who have never known what passion is.' When Marie mistook one of his gentlemen for Louis and rushed towards him, exclaiming, 'Ah, my poor Sire!' her sisters burst out laughing.

The Cardinal and the Queen Mother watched the King's pursuit of Marie with increasing alarm. Mazarin now realized that in helping to consolidate Louis's absolutism, he had forged a weapon which might lessen the greatness of France and diminish his own powers; for he could not forbid the King to marry his niece, whose strength of character he had underrated. Louis not only called Marie 'my Queen', but treated her with the respectful gallantry of a fiancé. There was no question of his making her his mistress: and her behaviour was equally restrained, although she was now desperately in love with him. So it seemed that her father's prophecy must be true, and that she was about to bring disaster upon France. Intensified war with Spain and a recurrence of the Fronde would almost certainly follow the mésalliance upon which Louis had set his will. What was to be done?

Mazarin then turned from the major problem to that of Hortense's future. She had just passed her twelfth birthday when the exiled and penniless Charles II asked him for her hand. Such an alliance could not be considered: but the courtesies must be observed; and Mazarin refused Charles's offer on the grounds that his niece must not take precedence of La Grande Mademoiselle, Louis's first cousin, who was still unmarried. Hortense knew nothing of this proposal until after the Restoration; it then became a further cause of resentment against the uncle she had always feared and disliked. She shrank from his smooth, oblique approach; her frank, unselfconscious temperament was violently opposed to his devious subtlety; his care for her future was discounted, because she could not believe in his integrity; she felt herself being used, and as she reached her teens became increasingly rebellious.

When the King returned from the victorious siege of Montmédy, he found Marie with her sisters at Fontainebleau, and their loves were renewed. During an expedition to Bois-le-Vicomte they were strolling by the river, hand in hand, when his sword-hilt bruised her wrist, upon which he drew his weapon and flung it from him — a gesture characteristic of the *amour courtois* celebrated in their favourite novels. On his return to the front he fell ill; and it was then, watching her sister's misery, that Hortense began to grasp the nature of her love. Olympe and her circle said that Marie wept because she feared the destruction of her hopes of becoming Queen; Hortense thought otherwise. As soon as he recovered, Louis told his mother and the Cardinal that he was going to marry the only woman he could ever love. The King of Spain, hearing of Louis's intentions, withdrew his approval of the alliance with the Infanta, upon which Mazarin and the Queen Mother began their attack on Louis, appealing to his patriotism and his sense of duty. The proud young man knelt and begged, with tears, for their support of his marriage to Marie. Then the Cardinal played his ace. If His Most Christian Majesty married out of his sphere, he would become the laughing-stock of Europe. Not only so: the Spanish war would go on indefinitely; and jealousy of Marie's eminence might re-create the civil disturbances which had so nearly cost Louis his throne. Was he prepared to face these disasters?

Long afterwards, in his first book, *Réfléxions sur le Métier de Roi*, Louis described the powers and position of a king as 'great, noble and delightful'. He would have rejected the final adjective when he made his way to the Spanish frontier, after a last, long, agonizing interview with Marie. In May 1659 the armistice was signed, followed, in November, by the Peace of the Pyrenees.

Olympe commented on Marie's despair with cynical harshness. Hortense was kind but bewildered. When Marie sobbed out, 'Tell me all the evil of him that you can!' she could think of nothing to say. She had done her best to help Marie by playing cards with Louis's courtiers so that he and she could talk alone. Now it was all over.

In June 1660 Louis became the husband of the Infanta, a short, stout blonde, interested only in food and Court etiquette. It was now necessary to eliminate Marie, and Mazarin began to arrange her marriage with Lorenzo Onofrio, Prince Colonna and High Constable of Naples. Then the weary Cardinal, who knew that he had not much longer to live, began to reconsider the future of the niece to whom he had decided to leave his whole fortune and all his possessions. Her brother, Alphonse, who was to have shared the estate, had just died; Paul Mancini had become a monk; and Cardinal Mazarin detested his youngest nephew, Philippe, a dissipated and idle youth, who was always in trouble.

That Hortense should become Queen of England was his first

thought, and the preliminary steps were taken. With the utmost courtesy, the ministers of the newly restored King replied that it would not become His Majesty to marry a lady whose hand had been refused him in his days of misfortune. Mazarin was hesitating between Dom Pedro, the King of Portugal's heir, and Monsieur, who had just succeeded his uncle as Duc d'Orléans, when he was approached by the Duke of Savoy; this prince, having seen Hortense during a visit to Lyons, had fallen in love with her. While Mazarin paused, Charles II's 'dear, dearest Minette' was betrothed to Monsieur; and he feared that the marriage to Dom Pedro would infuriate the Spaniards, who were still at war with Portugal. The Cardinal was then asked for Hortense by the Prince de Courtenay, a descendant of Louis XI and the greatest nobleman in France; but he was very poor ('He has nothing but his cloak and his sword,' said Mazarin) and suspected of homosexuality. It must be Savoy, then. The negotiations began and prospered, until the Duke claimed the fortress of Pignerol, a key position won back from the Spaniards at fearful cost by Louis XIII, as part of Hortense's dowry. It was an impossible concession; and the Cardinal had to think again.

I I

During the four years which elapsed between her mother's death and the King's marriage Hortense, although often concerned for Marie's sufferings, had been enjoying herself immensely. With the Court, she and her sisters travelled to Poitiers, Lyons, La Rochelle, and finally to Brouages, a dreary little seaport, where she fell ill. When they returned to Paris in January 1660, Madame de Venel told the Cardinal that Hortense was getting out of hand and had been very unkind to the ten-year-old Marianne, whom Olympe was using to spy on the unfortunate Marie. The child was caught by Hortense listening behind doors whenever the King called and reporting what she heard to Olympe, who passed it on to Mazarin and the Queen Mother. This enraged Hortense: why should not Marie have become Queen of France?

Hortense had been further encouraged in her support of her sister by Queen Christina, who, seeing Louis and Marie together, said in her deep, hoarse voice, 'You should marry her.' The opinion of a middle-aged Lesbian, with homicidal tendencies (the murder of Monaldeschi took place at Fontainebleau in 1657), was discounted by older and more conventionally-minded people; but Hortense, impressed by the ex-Queen's learning, her freedom of speech and her bold pursuit of pretty young women, was one of her admirers. At fourteen, she would have liked to be a rebel—if there had been anything or anyone to rebel against ... As it was, she confined herself to protecting Marie against Marianne and Olympe, and encouraging Marianne to tease and defy Madame de Venel.

That lady had become so nervous about her charges that she not only dogged them by day, but stole into their rooms at night. On one occasion, feeling her way towards Marianne's bed, she was bitten by her; on another, she was given a casket of sweetmeats which also contained a quantity of mice; as she opened it and the terrified creatures ran all over the room, Madame de Venel shrieked and fainted. Meanwhile, the Cardinal pursued her with instructions about her supervision of his nieces. That of Hortense most concerned him; he believed that her attractions were partly caused by her own susceptibility, and desired Madame de Venel and Olympe to find out who had taken her fancy. Cross-questioned, Hortense replied that she had no inclination towards anyone in particular; when pressed by Olympe, she tried to stop this teasing by naming an Italian musician. 'But', she said, 'I should be very sorry if he were half so pleasing in my eyes as the King is in yours,' adding that she did not even know his name.

When Mazarin scolded her she remained silent; he then lectured her on her religious duties—why did she not hear Mass every day? 'You have neither piety nor honour!' he exclaimed. As Hortense did not attempt to defend herself, he went on, 'At least, if you do not hear it for God's sake, hear it for the world's.'

To explain that she was both irreligious and unawakened was beyond Hortense; she was not precocious; and she only knew that her uncle was making a to-do about nothing. The young Italian, hearing of this dispute, then began to court her, and was rejected. What Madame de La Fayette describes as 'her languishing airs and her indifference' gave people the impression that she was stupid, when she was merely bored; and at this time she was chiefly concerned with comforting Marie, planning what dresses and jewels they would wear for the King's marriage festivities, and reading plays and novels. When de la Meilleraye followed her to Paris and renewed his advances, she treated him as she had the penniless Italian. She knew that she must soon marry: but that was her uncle's affair. Her memoirs, and those of her contemporaries, show that she was so used to young men falling in love with her that she absorbed their admiration without the faintest notion of the havoc she was causing; and her casual geniality baffled all who approached her. Floating on the surface of life, she remained unworldly, hopelessly improvident, and nearly always good-tempered.

During the last months of his life the Cardinal's failing energies were taxed to their limits by the divagations of the Mancini. Marie was planning to disrupt the King's marriage by remaining in France; she refused to accept Colonna and, defying protocol, urged her uncle to arrange an alliance with Prince Charles of Lorraine. Marianne had become so unmanageable that a tutor was engaged for her; this was the Abbé Chaulieu, later known as 'the man of a thousand mistresses'. Olympe was attempting to lure the King from Marie by telling him that she was already the mistress of Prince Charles. Philippe had caused a fearful scandal by taking part in an escapade with the Comte de Bussy-Rabutin and the Abbé Camus in the country house of a friend. After drinking heavily they undressed, killed a pig and said Mass over it—'for which', Bussy-Rabutin complacently records, 'we were banished the Court.' This incident did not prevent Camus becoming the Bishop of Grenoble and, eventually, a Cardinal.

And there was Hortense, supporting Marie, carelessly accepting the attentions of any man or woman who approached her, and apparently unimpressed by the prospect of a heritage which would make her and her future husband the richest couple in Europe. She disfigured herself by weeping with Marie, who could not contemplate the dresses she had worn in the King's company without bursting into tears. Hortense then encouraged Philippe's excesses; he was her favourite brother; and in any case, why should not he and his friends enjoy themselves in their own way? Finally, she drove the Cardinal into a frenzy of irritation by refusing to interest herself in his plans for her marriage.

Mazarin was still undecided on this point when he gave his last evening party, which was attended by the whole Court and all his nieces and nephews. As ever, the wonderful rooms were scented with jasmine pastilles burning in alabaster *torchères*; so the works of the great masters—Bernini, Michelangelo, Raphael, Rubens, Van Dyck, da Vinci, Claude—were seen through clouds of fragrance, as were the tapestries, the tables set with precious stones, the ebony cabinets and the Venetian mirrors. In addition to the finest wines of France, Germany and Italy, soft iced drinks and sorbets were served. Concealed orchestras poured forth the music of Monteverdi and Sigismondo d'India; at intervals actors and dancers appeared from the shadows to entertain the guests. Just as all this magnificence was beginning to verge on the oppressive, the host, scented even to his embroidered gloves and the pet monkey on his shoulder, led the glittering throng into the great library, where some hundreds of his most valuable possessions were laid out on tables, and his servants distributed tickets for a lottery in which everyone received a prize. Madame de Montespan, then a young woman, heard him murmur, 'To think that I must leave this!' as she was inspecting the greatest luxury of all—a chair-lift, which carried the dying man from one floor to another.

With this farewell gesture came the realization that Hortense's husband must be chosen without delay. In January 1661 Mazarin was approached by the Bishop of Fréjus, to whom de la Meilleraye had promised fifty thousand crowns in the event of his persuading the Cardinal to give him her hand. No one else of sufficient wealth and status had offered for her; and although de la Meilleraye was not of the old nobility—his great-grandfather had been a lawyer—his standing and character appeared impeccable. Also, he was the great-nephew of Cardinal Richelieu, the only person for whom Mazarin had sentimental feelings.

So the young man was told that the exquisite being he had pursued for five years was to be his wife. In addition, he would share her fortune of twenty-eight million livres and inherit the Palais Mazarin, with all it contained; he was then invested with the title of Duc Mazarin, so that the Cardinal's name might endure for ever. In view of his benefactor's humble origin, the *de* was omitted.

Hortense was quite contented. She could not take much interest in her fiancé: but he seemed unobjectionable; and she looked forward to gay times at Court, the possession of a fairy-tale palace,

THE DUCHESS MAZARIN

and as much money as even she and her family—with whom she intended to share everything—could spend.

A few days before the wedding Cardinal Mazarin received a letter from the old Duc de la Meilleraye, suggesting, in guarded terms, that it was not advisable—not even safe—to leave his son this vast inheritance. No reasons were given; but the warning was unmistakable.

The Cardinal ignored it; he may have thought that the elder de la Meilleraye was becoming senile. Long afterwards, Hortense and her supporters remembered and recorded it. Meanwhile, as it was obvious that her uncle could not live more than a few days longer, the marriage preparations were hurried forward. On February 28th, 1661, Hortense and Armand-Charles de la Porte became husband and wife in the Cardinal's private chapel. Ten days later he was dead. 'Thank God he is no more!' Philippe exclaimed, and Marie agreed.

By this time, Louis XIV had come to the conclusion that Marie had better leave France, and, ignoring her tears and prayers, forced on her marriage to Colonna, whom she had never seen, and who was waiting for her in Rome. Just before the wedding, she called on the Mazarins, and her furious resentment burst forth. She and Hortense usually conversed in French. On this occasion the elder sister reverted to Italian—not the Italian of Petrarch and Tasso, but the terse, colloquial phraseology of the slum and the gutter. She glanced at the strange, haggard face of her brother-in-law. Then, shaking her fist at the bewildered bride, she shouted, 'Crepa! Crepa! Tu sarai più infelice di me!'—and marched out of the palace.

A few weeks later it was borne in upon Hortense that Marie had inherited their father's gift of prophecy.

TWO

AT the time of Hortense's marriage the wealth and status of the aristocracy equalled those of petty kings. They had absolute power over their dependants, received special treatment from the monarchy and assumed that in the next world their place would be on the right hand of the Almighty. When Duc Mazarin's mother, a deeply religious lady, heard that a connection of hers had died in a sinful and unrepentant state, she was unperturbed. 'I am sure', she said, 'that God will think twice before damning a man of that quality,' thus expressing the current views of society.

Of that society her son was one of the most eminent and respected members before his marriage, and after it the most envied. His vast wealth, high position and his responsibilities as Governor of a quarter of the kingdom did not affect his judgment; he carried out his duties as usual, and was still noted for his agreeable manners and intelligent conversation. Hortense appreciated his gifts, and in the first weeks of their marriage achieved a contentment she had never known in the days of Madame de Venel's chaperonage and the Cardinal's lectures. Her talents as a hostess began to emerge, and she delighted in providing entertainments which far outshone those of her contemporaries, or of the King himself.

Very soon Louis found that he preferred the parties at the Palais Mazarin to any other; he often went there informally, as well as with the two Queens and his courtiers. Although he had again succumbed to Olympe de Soissons's charms and had made her superintendent of his wife's household, he found himself increasingly drawn towards Hortense, but rather as a friend than as a lover.

When the King's liking for Hortense became apparent to her husband, the situation changed, and the tragic metamorphosis of that unfortunate young man's character began. She herself was not at once aware of what was happening. She had become fond of him; but marriage had no effect on her temperament or on her conduct; both remained undisciplined and capricious. Within seven weeks of her wedding day she was approached by the Chevalier de Rohan, who, having long desired her, became a constant visitor at the Palais Mazarin. It did not occur to Hortense to reject him out of hand; she received his attentions with the carefree amiability which characterized her acceptance of her husband's violent and possessive passion. How far her relationship with de Rohan went is not clear. Although it was brief and trivial, the resultant gossip reached Louis XIV, who remonstrated with Hortense. 'I ought', he wrote to one of his informants, 'to be very displeased at what has occurred; but I prefer to hope that the person of whom you speak will conduct herself better in the future ... What causes me the most pain is the thought that a person who bears the name of so great a man should give everyone occasion to laugh.'

So the Chevalier de Rohan was sent away without the least concern on Hortense's part. Yet his advances, however received, combined with Louis's admiration to raise the lid from the cauldron of Mazarin's deeper nature, and the boiling, envenomed contents were partially revealed, thus justifying his father's warning. Hortense was at first incredulous, then indulgent, then distressed and, finally, horrified. She did not know what to do. At fifteen, her judgment was still naïve, and her experience of what would now be described as psychotic disturbance nonexistent. She did her best by complying with all Mazarin's wishes, however odd or taxing; the result was the reverse of what she had anticipated. Her alarm became panic, in spite of the fact that in company her husband was still as courteous and serene as in the days before their marriage.

In the case-history of Mazarin's recurrent break-downs there are many *lacunae*; indeed, their number is so great as to invalidate that rather formidable term; and to bring up the heavy guns of conjectural analysis would be tedious. But although the subject is too far away in time and his symptoms are too inadequately recorded to be definitively diagnosed, he might, according to present-day opinion, be described as a victim of paranoia. His form of the disease was intermittent and seems to have been confined to a certain zone of which the nature and limits can only be surmised; they appear to have been connected with his obsession about his wife. Within a short time of the consummation of his marriage with the wonderful creature he had adored in vain, the dormant mania perceived by his father began to declare itself.

It may be suggested that of all young women in the world Hortense was the last whom such a person as Mazarin should have married. Her beauty and the fascination she exercised over both sexes combined with what would now be called her a-morality to drive him into a frenzy. Her own account of their marriage, although in some respects unreliable (she represents herself as blameless and persecuted throughout) shows that her good temper was the final and fatal irritant. If she had screamed and struggled and tried to murder poor Mazarin in the approved Italian style, he might have achieved the response he needed and calmed down, if only for a time. She objected, of course, to his behaviour, with all the force of an equally—but differently—violent nature. Youth, a superb physique and an instinctive and perdurable optimism made her undefeatable. She never broke down: she never attempted suicide. This may well have thrown Mazarin into greater despair, and thence into further excesses. How could he subjugate her? Privilege, wealth, royal favour, authority, availed him nothing, made his existence a mockery in his own eyes and increased the horror of his situation. His predicament was that of a man who, dying of thirst, is yet nauseated by the sight and taste of drink. And in Mazarin's day there was no remedy for the disease which tortured him for sixty years.

That disease first became apparent to Hortense through her husband's insomnia. It seems that he was too frightened—and too much in love—to sleep alone, apart from the fact that he may have associated their union with the 'visions and ghosts' he saw round his bed. Every night, just after she fell asleep, he would spring up, light the candles, ring for his valets and search the room for evil spirits. When none were found he became even more suspicious; obviously, his wife and their servants had combined against him to hide them. The current belief in such phenomena encouraged Hortense to be patient; at that time she had her full share of superstition. Rather than make a scene—and thus provide what might be described as moderate shock treatment—she submitted, while protesting, to this ordeal. So she unwittingly fostered her husband's symptoms until they reached monstrous proportions.

Naturally most of Mazarin's household took his wife's side. One of these was an Italian eunuch, who had left Marie's service for hers; to him Mazarin confided his plans for keeping an eye on Hortense. 'I intend', he said, 'to watch her whenever the King may be there,' adding confusedly that he was going to banish all Italians from Paris. Reporting this conversation to the King, the young man said, 'He is jealous of all the world, and especially of Your Majesty.' Louis, who had borrowed large sums from Mazarin, replied, 'If what you say is true, then he is mad—but although he has inherited Cardinal Mazarin's wealth, he has not his power.' Mazarin subsequently replaced the Italian by a Provençal lady, Madame de Ruz, whom he engaged to spy upon Hortense. By this time Madame de Venel had joined the household, and was similarly employed. Hortense suggested to Madame de Ruz that they should together stage a scene which would frighten away Madame de Venel. This succeeded so well— 'Madame de Ruz rolling her eyes, screaming and weeping,' says Hortense—that Madame de Venel ran down the passage calling for help.

Hortense, who was now pregnant, resorted to 'innocent recreations', those of playing Blind Man's Buff with her servants, driving out to Cours-la-Reine at the fashionable hour, playing cards and going to the theatre. Mazarin at once forbade all these pursuits. 'It is a sin to sit up late, and a heinous crime to drive out or to gamble,' he said, adding that Hortense spent far too little time at her prayers. 'How would you have me live, then?' she asked, and got no answer. A little later he rather pathetically explained, 'Knowing how dear you are to me, I cannot be too careful. Whatever sport may be made of me, I shall try to hinder your being maligned, because I love you more than my own reputation.'

Hortense seems to have accepted these restrictions, falling back on the company of Philippe and Marianne, with whom she spent most of her time. She had already given them half her husband's wedding present of ten thousand *pistoles*, the remainder of which was kept in a cabinet; from this the brother and sister helped themselves whenever they were in need of money. One day, 'wanting *divertissement*,' says Hortense, the young people collected three hundred *pistoles* and threw them out of the window into the courtyard, 'to have the pleasure of seeing the servants scramble and fight for them.'

This gesture, which became the talk of Paris, threw Mazarin into wild agitation and, not unreasonably, he forbade Philippe and Marianne the palace. He then issued a further series of taboos. Hortense must not sit down to a meal with a man, or play cards for money; she was forbidden to receive foreigners and Huguenots of either sex. He added that his worst adversaries were the English milords, who had designs on the sanctity of his home, and instructed the porters to turn away all such visitors.

He then announced his departure from Paris. Although Hortense was in an advanced state of pregnancy, and travelling conditions might well endanger the lives of herself and her child, he forced her to come with him as far as Alsace, where they stayed for some months. In 1662 a daughter, Marie-Charlotte, was born, and they returned to Paris.

Hortense, now in radiant health, assumed that she would be allowed to go to Court and entertain her family and friends. For a short time she did so. But fatherhood, together with the knowledge of her second pregnancy, had further disturbed her husband, who began to suffer from religious mania. The spirits who visited him were no longer evil, but angelic, and their commands were definite. He was required to put an end to immorality throughout the kingdom, beginning at the top. He therefore obtained a private audience with Louis, and began, 'The angel Gabriel has desired me to tell Your Majesty that you must immediately break off your relations with Mademoiselle de la Vallière.' Louis replied, 'The angel Gabriel has told me that you are mad'—and dismissed him, It did not occur to the King to deprive Mazarin of his governorships; he was too useful, and too rich, to be treated as an irresponsible person. He and Hortense then set out on another tour which lasted some months. A second daughter, Marie-Anne, was born in 1663.

I I

When Hortense, with the help of an amanuensis, wrote her memoirs, she did so in order to make some money and restore her much damaged reputation. Yet although the worst aspects of her husband's behaviour are thereby emphasized, her innate frankness pierces the clouds of complaint and protestation to reveal the easy-going attitude which enabled her to put up with many of his vagaries. Naturally, she preferred Paris to the provinces; but she also enjoyed travelling, even when the combination of a springless coach and rutted byways made miscarriage a recurrent possibility. After each confinement—her third daughter, Marie-Olympe, was born in 1665 and her son, Paul-Jules, a year later—she emerged in greater loveliness and renewed vitality; and each return to Paris was another triumph. After the first three years of marriage she adapted herself to Mazarin's outbursts and disregarded his orders. If she spoke more than once to a valet or a footman, he was dismissed; but there were plenty of others. Any maid to whom she took a fancy was sent away; but she did not mind being surrounded by strange faces. When she ordered her coach it was immediately countermanded; then she simply waited till her husband had gone out to order it again. Marianne, now Duchesse de Bouillon, was ready to shelter and entertain her; and the King's kindness never failed, although he was sometimes embarrassed by the outspokenness which further tormented her husband. 'I should have died if she had said that to me,' Louis observed, after listening to one of her conversations with an old admirer, adding to Mademoiselle de la Vallière, 'Take care that you do not talk so.' Yet he sent for Hortense again and again, because she always made him laugh; and he preferred to ignore Mazarin's excesses.

These now became slightly sinister. Convinced that everything concerning him was divinely ordained, Mazarin forbade his servants to extinguish a fire which broke out in one of his country houses. 'It is the will of God,' he said, and beat the valets who were trying to save his property. His tortured reasoning then accused him of interfering with God's ordinance by allowing his servants to carry out the duties for which they had been trained. So he called up the greater number and wrote down their respective employments on slips of paper which he jumbled together, telling each man to draw his instructions from the heap. Thus the gardeners were put in charge of the cellars, the butler sent to the dairy, the indoor valets dispatched to the stables and the major-domo relegated to the kitchen, while the coachmen ushered in the guests. Hortense seems to have accepted this revolution without much protest, perhaps because Mazarin had so many schemes that they eliminated one another.

The next phase was that of hypochondria, and she accompanied him to Bourbon, where he took the waters. This entailed their being parted during the day, so he sent her to stay with his father in Brittany. Hearing that she was as gay as ever and hobnobbing with the local dignitaries he had refused to receive, he made her rejoin him. She was preceded by a letter from the old Duc de la Meilleraye, warning him that it was inadvisable to sleep with his wife while undergoing medical treatment, upon which Mazarin fainted away. As soon as Hortense arrived he shut her up with him when the effects of the waters confined him to his room; there she sat, while his servants emptied one chamber-pot after another. When she complained he said, 'I do not wish you to be contaminated by the world,' adding bitterly, 'You would rather enjoy yourself in Brittany than solace me in my sickness.'

He was sent for to Marseilles by the King. When they all returned to Paris he seemed no worse, and Hortense still managed to enjoy herself, chiefly in the salon of the Hôtel Bouillon, where she subjugated Jean de la Fontaine, who wrote a number of poems about her.

Then, at last, Mazarin succeeded in really alarming everybody. Both the de la Meillerayes and the Mancini agreed that his wife and the children were in danger—for it seemed that his next phase might be homicidal.

He and Hortense had just returned from a six months' stay in Brittany, where, she says, they lived in 'a miserable cottage, because [thus] I should see no company.' This had not prevented her forming a friendship with a neighbour, Madame de Coaquin, which Mazarin declared to be Sapphic. The accusation left Hortense unmoved; such relationships were common in her circle. 'I diverted myself pleasantly with Madame de Coaquin,' she recalls, 'and few days passed but we took the air, either by land or sea.' What she had disliked was leaving Paris only three weeks after the birth of her child ('Few women of my quality would have done the like') and the realization that Mazarin was dissipating her uncle's fortune on lawsuits (their total eventually came to three hundred, all of which he lost) and she began to fear that her children would inherit little or nothing.

One Saturday evening, shortly after their return to Paris, Mazarin, walking through the great gallery, became aware, apparently for the first time, of the nature of its contents. Many of the statues were naked; so were some of the figures in the tapestries and pictures. That he had housed these obscenities for nearly six years was an appalling thought. He sent for a hammer and set to work on the indecent portions of the statues, hacking and scraping away, until his curator, Monsieur Tourolles, hearing the noise, entered the gallery.

Mazarin ignored his horrified protests and continued the work of destruction. Tourolles, bursting into tears, fell on his knees and implored his master to desist. There was a pause; then Mazarin turned to the pictures, sent for scissors, brushes and paint, and began to obscure or cut out the offensive sections, while Tourolles stood by in agony.

By this time it was nearly midnight. When he heard the hour strike Mazarin put down his tools, remarking that as it was now Sunday morning, he should do no more work. In any case, he was tired and hungry, and supper must be served.

On Monday morning he reappeared with six valets, all carrying hammers; they were told to attack the statues, while he applied himself to the tapestries and pictures. Over the week-end, Monsieur Tourolles, who had friends at Court, had managed to get in touch with Colbert, the King's chief minister; Colbert approached Louis, who agreed to intervene; but by the time his emissaries reached the Palais Mazarin it was too late, and some of the greatest masterpieces in Europe had been irretrievably defaced. Mazarin then turned his attention to his outdoor staff.

The dairymaids were his first concern. It was fearful to think that for years these young women (who, after all, had souls to be saved) had been handling cows' udders and thus forced into contact with lewd images. He directed the men to take over their work, and added that when the cows were not being milked their udders must be veiled. This brought him to another aspect of the same theme. Many of the milkmaids were nursing mothers—an offence in itself—but on this point their master was reasonable, merely giving orders that no child should be suckled on Fridays. Then he perceived that some of the girls were pretty. Here was another danger, the worst, that of concupiscence, which he had been divinely appointed to put down. The suspect dairymaids were lined up and their front teeth were drawn.

Hortense's distress about the collections was forgotten in her fear that Mazarin might now set about herself and her little girls.

They were too young to be placed in a convent, so she sent them to the country, where they remained for the next few years. She was not so alarmed for herself as her family were, partly because Philippe, now Duc de Nevers, was established in a palace next door to her husband's. Mazarin did not know that there was a door communicating between the two; he did observe and resent Philippe's frequentation of Hortense, and became increasingly suspicious about her friendship with the King.

By this time Mazarin was surrounded by sycophants who had everything to gain in alternately flattering him and encouraging his jealousies; such persons had but to hint and angle for him to reward them. These inroads, together with his litigation, had already so diminished his revenues that his children, 'who might have been the richest persons in France,' says Hortense, 'were in danger of becoming the poorest ... I saw every day vast sums go away, movables ... offices ... and all the rich remains of my uncle's fortune ... as much as came to three millions.'

Anxiety made her more reckless than usual. As his poems show, Philippe was passionately attached to her, and she did nothing to discourage him. There seems little doubt that their feeling for one another was highly emotional, as were her friendships with women. She herself refuted the resultant allegations in her memoirs as if touching on a minor issue. She was justified, in that the example had already been set by many others in the highest circles, one of whom was Madame, the King's sister-in-law; her relationship with the Princesse de Monaco was an open secret, and she had been suspected (wrongfully) of incest with Charles II. Mazarin's accusations would have been disregarded if Hortense had not been so foolish as to denounce him for unnatural intercourse with herself, thus recalling the proverb of the precautions advisable for those who live in glass houses ... Similarly, as the King seemed to be supporting her, everyone concluded that they were lovers. 'Her beauty,' remarked Madame de Lafayette, 'together with the advantage of a husband in no sense lovable ... might easily have involved [the King and the Duchess] in a passion, had not Monsieur Mazarin, *with the prudence he has so often since displayed*, removed his wife from the King's proximity.' So it was that Louis refused to intervene when Hortense was summoned by her husband to meet him at Nevers, 'where,' he wrote to her, 'there are, among other *divertissements*, very good comedians.'

She set off to meet that tragic comedian, only to find him on his way back, accompanied by Philippe. All three then went to one of Mazarin's country estates, where he accused the brother and sister of incest. They seem to have agreed to ignore this attack, and the Mazarins left for Paris.

Mazarin's manner now changed from the bullying to the facetious. He replied to Hortense's protests with smiles and jocular remarks. This grinning mockery frightened her out of her wits, and for the first time she began to think about running away — a last, desperate measure, which would cut her off from all her friends, of whatever degree; that a woman of her rank should leave her husband would create a scandal far surpassing that caused by rumours of incest or homosexuality. The climax of terror came during a party at the Louvre, when Hortense saw Mazarin approaching her with that same 'constrained and affected smile'. In a loud voice he began, 'Madame, I have good news to tell you — the King has just now commanded me to go into Alsace.'

This apparently innocuous statement was so delivered that all who heard it recoiled, and the Duc de Roquelaure exclaimed, 'This is fine news indeed, to be told with such joy to a lady of your rank!' — at which Mazarin smiled and moved away. When Hortense appealed to Louis, he replied, 'You shall not stay there for more than three months.'

Three months, in some deserted fortress! There was nothing for it but flight. Hortense decided to take refuge with Marianne while she made her plans. Although she had not a *pistole* of her own, the sale of the jewels left her by the Cardinal would enable her to live comfortably for several years. Late one night she went to fetch them, preparatory to departing the next day. They were gone. She had nothing but those she was wearing. She rushed into Mazarin's bedchamber, woke him up and taxed him with the theft. Smiling — she never forgot that smile — he replied, 'You are of so liberal a nature that I fear you may give some away. I shall presently return them to you — with others.' 'I wish your liberality had been as regular as mine,' exclaimed Hortense. 'I am satisfied with what I already have.' As he said nothing, she added, 'I'll not come to bed until I have them!' Again he made no reply, and she continued to storm and rave. 'To whatever I could say,' she goes on, 'he replied only with unpleasant railleries ... a malicious laugh, or a seeming calmness of voice.' At last she went to the Palais Nevers, and after some discussion with Philippe agreed that he should send for Marianne.

The Duchesse de Bouillon had no patience with her sister. 'You are well enough served,' she said sharply, 'since you have suffered so much already, without saying a word.' She took Hortense back with her, and sent an Italian friend, Madame de Bellinzani, to appeal to Mazarin, who refused to admit her. It was then arranged that Olympe should see the King on Hortense's behalf.

The result was not satisfactory. Louis refused to take sides. When Hortense implored him to help her, he told her that she had put herself in the wrong by leaving her husband. She burst out, 'I see that Monsieur Mazarin is to be favoured against me—his friends are my enemies!' and was dismissed.

In the hope of getting back her jewels she returned home, sending her Groom of the Chambers in advance. He was confronted by his master, who said, 'Who are you? Who has sent you?' and told him to go away. Hortense then appeared to find her husband waiting at the foot of the great staircase. When she begged him to take back her servant, he again assumed his facetious, unreal manner. She tried to push past him. By this time he had discovered the door leading into the Palais Nevers, and knew what she was about. There was a short struggle and then—'grief and vexation supplying me with more than ordinary strength,' says Hortense— she eluded him, dashed down the stairs and across the courtyard. He ran after her, shouting, 'Shut all the doors!' but the servants did nothing and Hortense reached her brother's palace by the front entrance.

From there she wrote to Louis XIV pointing out the danger of remaining with her husband. Meanwhile Mazarin made no effort to get her back. He returned to his semi-religious, semi-hypochondriacal phase, sending for an apothecary to give him a daily clyster. Each time the young man appeared he had to make his confession, lest his sins entered his patient's body.

By this time Louvois, the King's most trusted minister, had convinced his master of Hortense's danger, and it was suggested that she should retire to a convent until her husband calmed down. She refused, remaining with Olympe, who presently announced that she had persuaded Mazarin to be reconciled on condition that Philippe left for Italy.

Hortense returned, and made her usual disturbing effect.

Nevertheless, Mazarin seemed quieter, and she had almost made up her mind to go with him on his next trip to Alsace, when her family expostulated. As if bent on exacerbating him, she ran away to the Hôtel Soissons the night before they were due to leave, taking with her the 'small jewels' she habitually wore. When Mazarin came to fetch her back she refused to see him. 'What does this mean?' he exclaimed. Olympe replied, 'It means that she will not go to Alsace, and demands the return of her great jewels.' 'Those have already been sent into Alsace for safe keeping,' Mazarin replied, and departed.

Colbert then intervened on the King's behalf. Louis's orders were that Madame Mazarin's jewels were to be brought back and placed in the minister's care, while she retired to the convent of Chelles during her husband's absence.

Hortense was deeply depressed—even Alsace would be preferable to a convent life. Then the whole situation changed. She came upon another runaway wife, Olympe's former friend, Sidonie de Lénancourt, now the Marquise de Courcelles. An alliance was formed between the two girls—and soon Hortense was enjoying herself as much as ever.

THREE

I

Sidonie de courcelles was sixteen and had been married for three weeks when she decided that the life did not suit her. As she had no plans and very little money, she had been forced to submit to imprisonment in the Convent of Sainte-Marie-de-la-Bastille, a much stricter institution than that of the Abbaye de Chelles, of which the Superior was Hortense's aunt. Mazarin, finding his wife there in excellent health and great beauty, asked the King to remove her to Sainte-Marie. Arriving under an escort of life-guards, Hortense renewed her friendship with Madame de Courcelles, and they had begun plans for a rebellion, when Mazarin reappeared, and rated her for wearing patches. 'I will not speak to you,' he declared, 'until you take them off. This concerns my conscience.' Hortense replied that she had no intention of offending the Almighty, he expostulated, and they argued for an hour while the patches remained on her face. Then suddenly he asked her to accompany him into Alsace. As Hortense had decided to sue him for her jewels in the Court of Requests, she refused, and he went away.

While the preparations for her suit hung fire, she and Sidonie sent for their lap-dogs and began their campaign. With shrieks of 'Tally-ho!' they organized midnight rat-hunts through the dormitories, and all over the convent; they put ink into the holy water stoups, so that the unsuspecting nuns entered the chapel as if spotted with the plague; and they filled up the ink-pots with water, remaining to watch the effect with suppressed giggles. When the confusion was at its height they asked for water 'to wash our feet', and filled two large receptacles standing above the dormitory, overturning these as the nuns came to bed; the resultant downpour, deprecatingly described by Hortense as 'a mere horse-boy's prank', brought their guardians to a decision, and a group of stern and elderly Sisters was instructed to follow the young ladies wherever they went.

This was just what Hortense and Sidonie were hoping for, and they proceeded to tear about the convent at top speed; the nuns, weighed down by their habits, pursued them with groans and cries; but the girls were long-winded and tireless. Their dogs barking and yelping about them, they twisted and dodged, finishing up with a grand burst in the cloisters. Some of their captors sprained their legs during what Hortense calls 'these little odd follies', which were reported to the authorities. She could not help feeling sorry for 'the poor nuns' and was glad, for all their sakes, when after three months she and Sidonie were sent back to Chelles, 'where I knew we should be more civilly treated, though we could not have so many visits.' But that did not really matter, for Sidonie, 'a very beautiful person, and of a very pleasant humour,' made a delightful companion (it was she who had thought of the booby-traps), and was now working out plans for their escape and departure from France.

Mazarin also had his plan, and a powerful ally, the Archbishop of Paris, who had given him leave to enter the convent and kidnap Hortense. When he arrived with a company of sixty horse, the Abbess appeared at the grille and refused him entrance. She then handed over the keys to her niece, so that she might defend herself. 'What do you want?' Hortense began. 'You are not the Abbess,' protested Mazarin. 'I am Abbess, for you, and for today, since all the keys are in my possession—and there is no entry for you but by my favour,' his wife replied, and Mazarin departed, muttering that he would return that night.

Hortense and Sidonie waited in some alarm, which rose to terror when they saw a large number of horsemen enter the courtyard. They decided to escape by the chimney and climb over the roofs, thence taking refuge at the Hôtel Soissons. Sidonie went first, only to find a grille halfway up, through which she managed to squeeze herself. Hortense followed; but, being pregnant with her fourth and last child, she stuck, waist-high. By this time the troop of horse had surrounded the convent and were beginning to break down the doors. Desperately, Sidonie pulled at her friend's shoulders, while Hortense tried to free her hips. 'Call for help,' gasped Sidonie, but Hortense refused. 'Go on tugging,' she said, and after some twenty minutes of being 'horribly pinched', she freed herself and stepped out on to the roof. Covered with soot, breathless, hardly able to move, the two girls looked down into the courtyard—to be greeted by cheers and laughter from the friends of Olympe and Marianne, who had come to their rescue. Hortense descended to thank them; they were laughing so much that they could barely sit their horses. At last the leaders, all of whom were young men of fashion, assured her of their support and rode away.

Some of this same group heard Hortense's suit in the Court of Requests and decided in her favour. She alone was to occupy the Palais Mazarin and receive 20,000 livres a year, while her husband removed to that of the Arsenal; he must return her jewels and refund the sums he had taken from her dowry.

So Hortense returned in triumph. Mazarin then appealed to the Great Chamber, a body of elderly men who, disapproving of runaway wives (to say nothing of Italians), directed him to occupy the palace and to resume his marital authority. Hortense was in despair; then the King intervened. He ordered the Duke and Duchess to live in separate wings, each retaining their own servants. Hortense was not to be forced to accompany her husband on his journeys; and a committee, headed by Colbert and Louvois, would adjust their financial disagreements. Hortense agreed to these conditions and, ignoring her friends' jokes ('Patched up for the third time, I see,' remarked one when they met at a fair), began to entertain in her usual lavish style. She put up a theatre in her side of the palace, chose a comedy, engaged players and was waiting to receive her guests, when Mazarin burst in and tore down the curtain, shouting, 'It is a saint's day—and this entertainment is profane!'

A few days later he seemed calmer, and she consented to meet him in the afternoons. 'We neither ate nor lay together,' she says, adding that Mazarin gave out that they were doing both. She knew that the present arrangement must fall through, but decided to wait until after her lying-in before taking further action.

A few months later Madame de Courcelles, who had taken refuge in the Palais Mazarin, rejoined her husband. This distressed Hortense; she felt that she had lost an ally. She went to call on Sidonie, only to be told that Madame la Marquise was not at home. She then saw the Marquis de Cavoy's coach drawn up in front of hers. Knowing that he had been her friend's lover, she believed herself betrayed. As she stood there, bursting with jealous rage, de Courcelles appeared. 'In my first transport of passion,' she confesses, 'I could not forbear saying something' — upon which de Courcelles, who had long suspected de Cavoy, but did not care to be shown up as a cuckold, declared that he himself was in love with Hortense, and that de Cavoy had come between them. He challenged de Cavoy, they exchanged passes and agreed to make up their quarrel. De Courcelles then gave out that Hortense had led them on. 'She is a make-bait — she will have other throats cut for her, if she can,' he declared, thus unconsciously revealing that his deepest jealousy sprang from Hortense's relationship with his wife.

Hortense soon got over the chagrin caused by her friend's desertion and continued to go about and entertain; yet her reputation was now irretrievably blackened, not so much on account of her frequentation of Sidonie, but because of her undignified and reckless behaviour at Chelles and Sainte-Marie, her casual reception of de Courcelles's attentions and the unconventionality of her life with Mazarin; this was especially condemned. Appearing with Olympe at the Louvre, she was coldly received. When she defended herself to Louis XIV, he replied, 'I never believed any of the reports,' but in such a manner as to show her that she was out of favour.

She then heard that Mazarin was about to bring a second suit against her in the Great Chamber which would enforce all his rights. She decided to run away, this time for good, to Italy, and appealed to Philippe and her old admirer, de Rohan, to help her. It was arranged that all three should make for Milan where Marie de Colonna would receive them.

Meanwhile Mazarin had once more become violent. When Hortense told him that if he did not behave better, she would leave him, he burst into maniacal laughter. 'Once I am out of your reach,' she cried, 'I'll run far enough, so that you will never overtake me!' 'You would never have the courage,' he replied, reassuming the sinister calm which frightened her so much more than his rages.

She then became aware that Olympe was spying on her with a view to preventing her escape, partly out of spite, and partly because, if Hortense left Paris and abandoned her suit, Olympe would no longer have access to the sums she was accustomed to beg or borrow from her sister's dowry, which would fall into

Mazarin's hands—and thence into those of his lawyers and hangers-on.

Olympe now realized that Hortense was no longer interested in the success of her suit, or in the recovery of her jewels. In fact, she had withdrawn herself, in thought, at least, from a life which had ceased to provide a necessity—the genial welcome of her circle. Hitherto, she had never felt the chilling draught of general censure, for her defiance of certain conventions had been overlooked by all but a few. Now that she knew herself an outcast, she instinctively turned towards another sphere; the alternative, that of submitting to Mazarin, meant destruction, not so much in a physical sense—for she seems not to have believed that he had homicidal tendencies—as in that of the spirit. Her memoirs show that her vitality and her well-being were based on self-confidence and optimism. She was neither vain nor neurotic nor self-absorbed: but she was vulnerable, in that all her life she had been sustained by the admiring affection which produces an atmosphere of gaiety and warmth. Creating happiness and amusement wherever she went, she could not imagine existence without them: nor could she have endured it. Not to be surrounded by happy faces, no matter whose, was out of the question. So it came about that while her plans for escape were in the making she fell back on her private interests and hobbies: music, books and the company of her admirers.

This seemingly carefree attitude enraged Olympe: why did not Hortense intrigue and scheme, and toady the members of the Chamber? 'It is a great shame!' she burst out. 'This is no time to stay all day in your room, undressed, playing the guitar,' and went on, 'It almost makes me believe what is reported, that you intend to fly into Italy. Come with me to St-Germain, to make your court, at least.' 'You must excuse me,' was all Hortense would say. Reserve was as unnatural to her as deceit; if Philippe had not been there to prompt her, she would have told Olympe everything. As it was, she had some difficulty in pretending indifference when one of his envoys visited her and Olympe with a coded message about her route and time of departure.

On the night of June 13th, 1668, Hortense was about to leave when a peremptory summons arrived from Olympe, desiring her presence at St-Germain. 'I will meet the Countess there,' said Hortense, 'after dinner—not later than ten o'clock.' She and

Philippe then set off by separate routes; they were to join up at the frontier. Philippe was stopped by Olympe on the outskirts of Paris. 'Where is Hortense?' she began. 'Have you not seen her?' exclaimed her brother. 'Then she must have taken the other road to St-Germain, for I saw her leave—' and rode on.

I I

A favourite anecdote of the seventeenth century was that in which a grinning landlady interrupted the dinner of a newly arrived guest to exclaim, 'Sir, you must come upstairs—your valet is having a baby!'—thus emphasizing the pointlessness of women's attempts at male disguise. Although Hortense was not in the same case as the apocryphal valet, her efforts at concealment were equally unsuccessful. It was the first time she and her maid, Nanon, had ever worn breeches—to which their respective builds were quite unsuited—and they had the greatest difficulty in keeping on their periwigs. They could not look at one another without laughing; and when, at their first halt, Nanon was overheard addressing her mistress as 'Madame', Hortense decided to resume her usual dress.

By now Paris was far behind them; but they had been delayed at the outset of their flight by having to return to the Palais Mazarin for such jewels as the Duke had not confiscated and which Hortense had forgotten, and by the slow progress of her calèche. At Bar she exchanged this for a horse, and so reached Nancy, where she found a message from the Duc de Lorraine, asking her to stay with him. She dared not accept, for Mazarin's agents were at her heels: but she was thankful for Lorraine's escort of twenty horsemen, who conducted her to the Swiss frontier.

With de Rohan, his page, Couberville, and Philippe, she entered Franche-Comté, pausing to eat and to change horses. Here she and Nanon resumed male clothes, and were chasing one another round the courtyard when Hortense fell and hurt her knee. The injury was more serious than she at first realized, and she had to continue her journey in a litter as far as Neufchâtel, where she remained for several weeks in great pain and threatened with gangrene.

'Beyond despair,' she decided that there was nothing for it but to return to Paris; and then Couberville saved the situation by his skill and knowledge. 'If it had not been for him,' she says, 'I had been forced to have my leg cut off.' A few weeks later, although still lame and ill, she was able to proceed to Milan.

All this time Mazarin had been falling from one paroxysm into another. Discovering Hortense's flight within a few hours of her departure, he rushed to the Louvre and broke into the King's bedchamber at two in the morning. 'Did not the Angel Gabriel warn you of this?' asked Louis. 'Pray give orders for her to be pursued,' Mazarin implored. 'I promised the Duchess that I would no longer interfere in her concerns, and I cannot break my word,' replied the King. 'Nor is it likely that she can be overtaken now.' Next day Mazarin appealed to Colbert, who was kinder. 'Send some person of credit after her, asking her to come back on her own terms,' he suggested, and Mazarin seemed ready to follow this advice.

His envoy caught up with Hortense soon after her arrival in Milan and told her that, contrary to all expectation, the Great Chamber had decided in her favour, but that Mazarin was now accusing her of being de Rohan's mistress, and of 'the highest infamy and lewdness' with Philippe, whose poems to her he had just discovered. Hortense indignantly denied both charges; de Rohan had helped her simply because he was her brother's friend. She had in fact become the mistress of Couberville, to whom she had taken a violent fancy. As soon as she was established in a house taken for her by the Colonnas, she denied herself to all visitors, themselves included, spending hours alone with Couberville, whom she described as the Chevalier, a title to which he had no claim. This enraged her sister and brother-in-law, the more especially because Couberville had begun to give himself the airs of an equal. When Philippe arrived and heard what was going on, he burst in upon the lovers and threatened to throw Couberville out of the window if he did not immediately return to France.

Hortense, who describes her brother's behaviour as 'another persecution, so much the more cruel because it had a specious foundation,' was prepared to dismiss Couberville for the sake of a quiet life; he knelt and begged her to let him stay. Not only was he desperately in love with her, but 'I cannot return to my master,' he said, 'without carrying my head to the scaffold—I shall be utterly ruined if you discharge me,' and she agreed to his remaining.

A series of attacks was then launched against the page by Nanon, Hortense's footman Narcisse, the Colonnas and Philippe, but she continued to protect him, and a few weeks later was carrying his child. Colonna suggested that they should put a stop to the scandal by leaving for Venice, and shortly after they did so Couberville fell ill. He then gave out that he had been poisoned by Philippe, upon which Hortense agreed to dismiss him, and with her sister and brother-in-law left for Rome. She was pursued by Couberville, who rushed to the Colonna palace, and accused her of breaking her word. 'Go!' exclaimed Marie. 'You will get your deserts in the courtyard!' 'Not unless the Duchess desires it,' he replied. 'I will be commanded by none but her.' Hortense got out of the difficulty by taking refuge in a convent of which another of her aunts was the Abbess, 'where,' she says, 'I stayed some time, shut up as in a prison,' and where her child (whom she does not mention) was born and put out to nurse. Meanwhile Couberville was seized and imprisoned. Hortense presently obtained his release, but decided to have nothing more to do with him.

She was thus able to make up her quarrel with the Colonnas and return to their palace; but she was now so desperate for money, having pawned all her jewels, that she decided to return to Paris and ask Louis XIV to force Mazarin to restore her inheritance.

She did not want to leave Rome, where she was surrounded by admirers, who escorted her to the parties given to celebrate the election of the new Pope. To some she gave her portrait, painted on a silver snuff-box. A young man thus honoured sent his to his mother to take care of, adding that it might be shown to their friends, but, 'Do not let it out of your keeping, or allow anyone to finger it.' Two others, disputing the possession of this favour, fought a duel for it; a third, dismissed by Hortense—he had been importunate and tedious—challenged the man who had supplanted him. In all this turmoil she remained as idly good-humoured as usual, denying few, kind to all and more beautiful, according to Marie de Colonna, than ever before. Yet she must go; all her relatives were agreed on that point; Rome was getting too hot to hold her, and she herself felt that she could count on Louis's support against her husband. Philippe, whose marriage with one of Madame de Montespan's daughters had just been arranged, prepared to accompany her.

The brother and sister, now reconciled, took six months over the journey. This leisurely progress threw Mazarin into a frenzy; he was convinced that their relations were incestuous. His impassioned pleas for Hortense's return gave way to threats and orders. He would not receive her until she had spent two years in a convent repenting her sins. He then told his servants that he was a tulip, and ordered them to place him in the sun and pour water over his head.

As Hortense and Philippe approached the frontier Mazarin sent a troop of guards and a company of archers to arrest them; but the Provost on the French side refused to allow this seizure and sent his army to protect the Duchess. They were on the point of joining battle when a courier arrived from the King commanding Mazarin to dismiss his men and sign a truce with his wife. Bursting into tears, the Duke obeyed, and Hortense entered Paris in safety.

She stayed with the Colberts and was received by the King in the apartments of Madame de Montespan. Louis was very kind. 'But,' he said, 'if I have not done better for you hitherto, it is your own conduct that has prevented me.' He went on to suggest that, with his protection and support, she should return to her husband, adding, 'If however you are resolved to go back to Italy, I will see that you receive an allowance of 24,000 livres a year.' Hortense refused to reconsider a reconciliation on any terms, and accepted the pension.

Louis's courtiers were appalled at this improvidence. 'What!' said one, 'you will spend your four-and-twenty thousand at the first inn you come to.' Hortense denied it. 'By this time,' she says, 'I knew how to husband my money.' Nine months later she was back in Rome, while Mazarin protested to the King ('It is unheard of to take a wife away from her husband') and sent messengers to plead with her. She received them with a laugh and a catch-phrase of the Fronde — 'No Mazarin!'

Then, rejoining Marie, she was faced with a new problem: the Princess had decided to run away from her husband, and implored Hortense to accompany her. Colonna was tired of her and already looking out for another wife; this meant that she was in danger of being poisoned. In her anxiety to return to France, Marie may have exaggerated her peril; but private assassination was one of

Colonna's habits; he had been known to dispose of several inconvenient persons in this way.

Hortense did not believe Marie's story, and begged her to reconsider, suspecting, rightly, that she was planning to regain her hold over Louis XIV. As Marie insisted, she gave in, stipulating that if they set off together, they must part at the Swiss frontier, for she herself dared not enter French territory.

FOUR

I

It is unlikely that Colonna would have risked being suspected of the murder of a wife whose protector was the King of France. His conduct after Marie's flight shows that he desired her return, if only to avoid the scandal of a separation, although she had tried him past all bearing. Her friendship with the Chevalier de Lorraine, Monsieur's favourite, whom Louis had exiled; her wild gambling: her affair with Prince Ernst-August of Brunswick-Lüneburg, who had given her and Hortense presents of jewellery: and, most annoying of all, the sensation caused by her sister's bearing Couberville's child—these incidents had destroyed any affection he might have had for her. His intention was to shut her up in one of his country palaces, in the hope that she would die of malaria, and so end their marriage with the minimum of inconvenience to himself. It did not occur to him that she might run away, nor that, through Lorraine and Monsieur, she would obtain a passport and permission to return to France.

Soon after Marie received the necessary assurances and had made her arrangements with Hortense, Colonna announced that he was going to visit one of his stud-farms and would be away three days. So it was that in the early morning of May 29th, 1672, the sisters, with Nanon and Hortense's Groom of the Chamber, Pelletier, left Rome for Civita Vecchia, where a felucca was waiting to take them to Marseilles.

Hortense was well aware of the risks entailed by this change of plan; with her usual optimism she counted on reaching safe territory before Mazarin's agents caught up with her. The Duke of Savoy had promised her his protection, and she intended to remain in his care until her inheritance was restored. To avoid suspicion, she left such jewels as she still possessed in the Colonna palace; Marie took seven hundred *pistoles*, her pearl necklace and some diamonds.

They reached Civita Vecchia at dusk, to find that the felucca was waiting for them some miles down the coast. Having dismissed their coach—they dared not change horses for fear of attracting attention—they sent Pelletier on ahead to tell the captain they had arrived, and took refuge in a wood, where they spent the night. Morning came, and there was no sign of Pelletier. They waited till midday, having had nothing to eat or drink since the previous evening. Marie, declaring that they had been betrayed, proposed returning to Rome. 'Let us wait half an hour longer,' said Hortense, 'and then, if no one comes, I will do whatever you suggest.'

A few minutes later they heard the sound of horse's hooves: and Marie, remembering that Pelletier had left on foot, whispered that they were lost and might as well give themselves up. Hortense replied, 'I shall kill the first person who tries to take us,' and stepped out into the road, a cocked pistol in each hand, while Marie cowered in the undergrowth. The horseman was one of their own postillions who, mistrusting Pelletier, had found and engaged another felucca. It was near by; but he advised them not to take the coast road. He went on ahead; they proceeded by an inland and longer route.

Hortense strode along in the breathless glare, undismayed. Marie, no walker, staggered behind her; every now and then she stopped, crying and gasping, while Hortense urged her forward. As they neared the shore she sank down, unable to move. Then, seeing a peasant in the next field, she called to him to come and carry her. He refused, but gave in when she offered him a hundred *pistoles*. Suddenly, Pelletier appeared; he had had to promise the captain of the first felucca a thousand crowns. 'And,' he added, 'I do not trust him, he looks villainous.' It was agreed that they should sail in the other boat, and they hurried forward. Both feluccas had sailed away.

Marie collapsed, calling for water. Hortense sent Pelletier on a further search and tried to soothe her sister. Eventually he saw and hailed the first felucca and the sisters boarded her, upon which the crew refused to move until they were given more money. 'Have you killed the Pope, then? What have you done?' asked one of the sailors. At last they set sail, and Marie was already beginning to feel seasick when the captain demanded a yet larger sum. A violent quarrel between him and Pelletier ensued, and Marie handed over the money, adding, 'You shall have more when we reach France.'

They had barely started when the wind dropped, and for six hours they remained stationary. As night fell they were approached by another vessel which the captain said was that of a Turkish pirate; they must land rather than risk being captured. They did so, and sheltered in the rocks, waking next day to find that the pirate ship had disappeared. As they re-embarked a storm burst; both Hortense and Marie were horribly seasick; a few hours later they were forced to land in Monaco, leaving there as the sea grew calmer. After a voyage of nine days in hideous discomfort and some danger, they reached Ciotat, where they hired horses and rode on to Marseilles. Here the Intendant was waiting for them with Marie's passport, and they remained hidden in his house for some days, thereafter proceeding by coach to Aix. There the de Grignans, Madame de Sévigné's daughter and son-in-law, sheltered them for a fortnight and provided them with clean linen, for they had lost all their luggage in the storm.

By this time they had been traced. Threatening and peremptory letters arrived for Marie from Colonna: and Hortense was warned that Polastron, her husband's agent, was in the city.

That night they parted, Marie making for Paris and Hortense for Chambéry. Realizing that Polastron would almost certainly overtake her if she went by the direct route, she made a detour through the mountains, stopping in Turin. When she reached Chambéry, he was waiting for her; as he could not use force in the Duke of Savoy's territory, he attempted persuasion, without success, and so departed. Hortense was then established by her old admirer (he had married some years earlier) in one of his castles, 'where', she says, 'I found that quiet I so long in vain had sought for ... with much more tranquillity of mind than a woman as unhappy as myself could hope to enjoy.'

These lines were written some two years later, when Hortense was presenting herself to the European public as a wronged and persecuted victim. In fact, she was radiant; and tranquillity was the very last element she desired or could have achieved. At Chambéry she began another life, filled with interests and pleasures she had never known.

I I

Hortense Mazarin was twenty-six when she settled in Savoy, where she remained for the next three years. Entering on this new existence in her usual light-hearted style, she had no premonition of the change about to take place in her character and habits. Since leaving Italy in her ninth year she had had little time to develop mentally, quite apart from the fact that, although lively and quick-witted, she was rather childish, not highly intellectual and had grown up with the conviction that Marie was, and always would be, the cleverest of the family.

If, at this point in her career, Hortense had continued her cat-and-dog life with Mazarin—if, with or without him, she had returned to the Court circle in France or the fashionable gaieties of Rome, she would have become an entirely frivolous and therefore uninteresting woman, remembered only for her beauty, her adventures and her allure. In Chambéry she discovered, as it were, her deeper nature; and that discovery was facilitated by the conditions of her exile. She turned into, and in a sense remained, a countrywoman. Her restless, energetic temperament was so catered for that her intelligence matured at a speed that would have astonished those who had known her as a child.

The provincial life of the seventeenth century in such a kingdom as Savoy provided a startling mixture of the primitive and the idyllic. The poverty of the country people forced travellers to journey for hours without food or drink and take refuge in verminous and filthy inns, while the aristocracy enjoyed luxurious splendour, surrounded by works of art and exercising the powers of minor royalty. A dialogue between one of Madame de Sévigné's correspondents and a local guide re-creates that semi-feudal world, as it does the sophisticated amusement of the urban reporter. 'Whose is this village?' 'Madame's.' 'And that one, far off?' 'It is Madame's.' 'But down there, that one, and that other?' 'They belong to Madame.' 'And these forests?' 'They are those of Madame.' 'That's a big plain, there.' 'It is Madame's.' 'And that other one, on the hill?' 'That is Madame's property, left her by her ancestors.'

This interchange aptly illustrates the powers of the Duke of Savoy, who, from the moment of Hortense's arrival, gave her all the privileges, and none of the responsibilities, of a petty sovereign. He had long admired her; and although it seems unlikely that he would have treated her in this way without enjoying her favours, there is no contemporary mention of their having a closer relationship than that of host and guest. His wife was, naturally, jealous and resentful of her husband's attitude towards Hortense. Yet if she had consented to be his mistress her position would have been common knowledge, for she had become, as we say now, news; all Europe was talking of the run-away Duchess, much to the annoyance of Olympe and Marianne, who, respectably established at the head of Parisian society, declared that she and Marie were behaving like madwomen and ought to be seized and imprisoned. They were further enraged when they realized that Hortense was living free of charge and enjoying both the amenities of a country life — shooting, hunting, boating — and the entertainment provided by strolling players and musicians. As Charles-Emmanuel's favourite guest, she was more sought after than they were; untroubled by the demands of court etiquette, she was invited everywhere and entertained her friends as freely as, and more informally than, they ever could. She wanted for nothing; that her tastes were simple and her way of life more that of a sportswoman than a patrician hostess, disgusted them; outdoor pleasures were the province of rustic landowners, gamekeepers, peasants, even; ladies of breeding either took carriage exercise or stayed at home. As so often before, Hortense had broken the rules with impunity.

She was about to move into the Château de Chambéry when Marie summoned her to Grenoble. The Duke lent her a carriage and grooms and provided game, fruit and wine for the journey. She found Marie in some distress at being forbidden to proceed to Paris; orders had come from the Queen, now Regent (Louis was invading Holland), that she must remain where she was. Marie decided to ignore the prohibition and persuaded Hortense to take the risk of accompanying her as far as Lyons. Here she was told that the King would not receive her and returned to Turin, while her sister left for Chambéry. Hortense then wrote to remind Louis XIV about her pension; thereafter she received it so irregularly that without Charles-Emmanuel's support she would often have been penniless.

In order to keep watch on her movements the Duke desired two

of his courtiers to follow and report on her: César Vicard, a rather
shady hack writer, who was known as the Abbé Saint-Réal, and
Monsieur d'Orlier, the Intendant of the castle. Saint-Réal became
Hortense's reader and also, briefly, her lover; it was he who
suggested that she should write her memoirs. She would never
have applied herself to the work unless he had insisted and helped
her. In his company her dormant interest in philosophy, theology
and literature was aroused; she began to read seriously, and to
discuss what she read with her visitors. Of these, her particular
friend was a young widow, Madame Deleschereine, a lively and
attractive girl, with whom she made expeditions, sometimes on
horseback, when she resumed male dress, sometimes in one of the
Duke's light carriages, which she drove herself, so fast that she
was frequently overturned. She now entered a religious phase,
attending Mass daily and appearing fervent enough to evoke the
admiration of the rather simple-minded d'Orlier. 'She ought to
be canonized,' he told Charles-Emmanuel, after watching her at
prayers; he was slightly taken aback to see her at a performance
of Racine's *Bajazet* within a few hours of hearing a priest denounce
the theatre.

Hortense's day began early with a warm bath. Then she and
Madame Deleschereine would set off with their fowling-pieces,
bringing down hares, quail and wild duck, and presently calling
on some neighbour to cook what they selected for their midday
meal; a favourite dish was quail in cheese sauce, which Hortense
taught some friendly Carthusians to prepare. On one occasion
after killing a hare, she split it and washed her face, arms and
hands in the blood. 'There is nothing better for clearing the skin,'
she told Madame Deleschereine, who followed her example. Thus
bedaubed, they rode on to the next village, where the children
rushed screaming away, and the monks refused to admit them.
They were very hungry by the time they got to another monastery,
where Hortense sent in one of her grooms to ask for a meal to be
brought to them.

After such expeditions, Hortense would rest in a hammock, and
then feed her dogs and birds, of which she had a large collection. (Waking up one morning to find that rats had devoured her
nightingales, she burst into tears, upon which Charles-Emmanuel
replaced them with a pair of spaniels.) Later she received visitors,
and they would discuss a set subject—men's natural infidelity as

compared with women's, or the theme of *Les Femmes Savantes*;
after which she dressed for a fancy ball, a party or the theatre,
where she had her own box, and where she and her friends ate
bread and cheese in the interval. She then returned to the castle to
gamble, which she did in a mask—'So that no one shall see the
faces I make when I lose.'

On wet days she practised shooting and fencing indoors, tried
her hand at cookery (she invented several sauces), read, wrote and
sketched, breaking off to play Blind Man's Buff or hide-and-seek
with her guests. On summer mornings she swam in the river,
returning to deal, rather cursorily, with her correspondence.
During his absences in Turin and elsewhere the Duke's letters—
which she did not always read—arrived daily. When d'Orlier
reproached her, adding, 'His Highness would like to be near you,'
she laughed and said, 'My sister is the lucky one, she sees more of
him than I do.' Then she would turn away to bind up a lap-dog's
paw, or dash out and spring on her horse; sometimes she rode so
recklessly that she was thrown, and had to go to bed for a day. She
and Madame Deleschereine would cook chestnuts in wine between
their games and fencing lessons. Once d'Orlier took them to a
peasant's wedding, where, to his horror, Hortense tucked up her
skirts to the knee and joined in the dancing under the trees.

The Duke delighted to hear of these exploits; the juvenile side
of Hortense's character, a homosexual attribute which prevented
her from becoming a very remarkable woman indeed, flattered his
sense of superiority. The endemic silliness which marks the Sapphic
type made it impossible for him to take her seriously; she remained
the child houri, who entrances yet never disturbs. She made no
demands; all he need do was to provide such gifts as a set of
fowling-pieces and pistols engraved with her arms in an elaborately
decorated case. She would not let them out of her sight, got up in
the night to finger them and showed them to all her guests. Later
on he sent her a Moorish boy, Mustapha, wearing a silver collar
inscribed with a couplet composed by the giver and carrying a
letter which made Hortense laugh. 'The verses could not be
better,' she said, and made a pet of the little creature, taught him
French, took him wherever she went, drew his portrait and herself
concocted headdresses for him out of muslin and lace. They
bathed together—he swam like a fish, d'Orlier observed—and he
was her slave, in more than one sense, till the end of her life.

222

Those meeting Hortense for the first time were similarly, if not permanently, subjugated. It became the fashion for persons making the grand tour to stop at Chambéry and spend an evening with the famous Duchess, whose memoirs were now being read, translated and pirated all over the Continent; bogus supplements to that brief narrative became a minor industry. To be unable to quote it was to be outmoded; and to have gambled or hunted with the author a status symbol.

Hortense took all this publicity in her stride. Exuberance carried her beyond conceit; her unselfconscious warmth and her interest in others created a glowing welcome. It was impossible to bore or fatigue a hostess whose gaiety infected all her guests; she made each one feel successful. When she burst out laughing, everyone laughed with her, without exactly knowing why. To watch her ride and swim and dance and play children's games was a unique experience; she was irresistible: and yet, curiously withdrawn. Of all her many lovers, none had touched her heart; neither cold nor self-regarding, she remained immune. Her freedom of manner and disregard of fashion—while other women's hair was twisted and tortured into 'fountains' or '*bouquets à la paysanne*', her silky, blue-black curls poured over her shoulders—created envy without spite; she was most often seen either in semi-oriental négligés, or riding-breeches, shirt and cravat, and so sometimes gave the impression that she would accept any approach. D'Orlier found that this was not the case when, suddenly weary of his supervision, she desired him to leave her alone; the rebuff was such that he wrote imploring Charles-Emmanuel to relieve him of his task.

Meanwhile the dispute over Hortense's inheritance continued. Mazarin alternated between imploring her to come back on her own terms and threatening her with years of conventual penitence if she did so. She had almost given up hope of regaining her great jewels, for she now perceived not only that Marianne and Olympe were no longer interested in helping her, but that their influence with Louis had been superseded by that of Madame de Monte-span. As the mother-in-law of Philippe de Nevers, that lady might have worked for his favourite sister, if she had not been afraid of the King's falling in love with her.

So Hortense, cut off from all her family—her children seem to have been left in the care of their aunts—was entirely dependent on Charles-Emmanuel. It did not occur to her to consider what would happen if he died or cast her off; nor did she realize that the full and happy life she had made for herself was built on his favour. She dwelt in the present; and although her intellectual side was developing at some speed, she had no knowledge of, or the faintest interest in, political affairs. She was aware that France and the United Provinces were at war, and that England and several of the German principalities were involved. She may have heard that Charles II's latest mistress, Louise de Kéroualle, now Duchess of Portsmouth, was Louis's envoy. She did not know that among the many cabals in England one was planning to oust Louise in order to sever their master's connection with France, and so strengthen the Protestant cause. This group, headed by Sir Ralph Montagu, formerly Ambassador to the Louvre, and George Villiers, second Duke of Buckingham, was looking for a substitute. But to find an enchantress capable of luring Charles away from the 'baby-faced', hard-headed, intensely correct *maîtresse en titre* was an almost impossible task. He was weary of adventuresses and viragoes; at intervals, the cosy domesticity of his relationship with Louise contrasted agreeably with the bawdy high spirits of two little actresses, Mrs Davies and Mrs Gwynne; so his times of relaxation were fully occupied; and he did not care to have his mistresses chosen for him. The anti-Portsmouth faction had begun to despair. Then suddenly news came which caused Montagu to pack his bags and set off for Savoy.

In June 1675 Charles-Emmanuel died of a heart attack, and as his heir was a minor, the Duchess became Regent. It was therefore obvious that Hortense would be told to leave, but she had made no plans when Montagu appeared and suggested that she should come to England, not with him, but as if she had decided to settle there on her own account. Hortense did not accept out of hand; with characteristic optimism she seems to have believed that she would be allowed to continue as before.

When she received the Duchess's order of dismissal she decided to travel via Switzerland and cross from a Dutch port, so that, if delayed by bad weather, she would not be found on French territory. Then the question of an escort arose. Saint-Réal offered to accompany her, and she was taking a groom, four valets, Mustapha and two maids; but bolder and more experienced protectors would be needed for the war zone. Within a few days a company of some twenty horsemen was at her orders. Early one morning, in brilliant sunshine, they set off, Hortense and the commanding officer leading. She wore riding-breeches and a full-skirted coat; as before, a large enough periwig had been difficult to find; she eventually managed to stuff away her hair, ramming down a plumed hat over the whole. The effect was strange, and far too striking; this did not concern her. In high spirits she was off and away, over mountain passes, across the river, through gorges, meadows and forests, sleeping under the stars or in barns—for the towns must be avoided—till Savoy lay behind her, and she entered Switzerland. The Low Countries and the fighting area must then, somehow, be traversed.

That former unfaithful ally, Madame de Courcelles, with her latest lover, was also running away again, this time from Paris to Geneva, and in that city she and Hortense met once more. Sidonie's attitude was that of a rival. She seems to have resented Hortense's fame; and indeed, when her own memoirs appeared, they had little success. 'This woman', she says, 'triumphs over all her misfortunes by an excess of folly ... She thinks only of enjoying herself. She ... passed through on horseback, befeathered and bewigged ... She talked of nothing but violins and hunting-parties.'

Before Hortense and her party reached Amsterdam her flight was known and Mazarin, who had been told by the Duchess of Savoy that he had her leave to arrest his wife in that kingdom, had sent Polastron and other agents in pursuit with the usual pleas and threats. 'Mad! Mad!' exclaimed Madame de Sévigné, retailing Paris gossip to her daughter, not in reference to Mazarin (he was a little eccentric) but to the untamed creature whom she described as dashing all over the Continent and obeying no rules. 'She may even be in England!' Madame de Grignan was told, 'where, as you know, there is neither faith, law nor priest ... A ballad is being circulated saying that she will bring trouble on the King [of France].'

Hortense's journey was prolonged at various frontiers and by her passion for the chase. Suspecting her identity and fearing espionage, the sentries would not pass her; she spoke to their officers, according to a contemporary, 'in the language of the eyes', and so progressed, pausing for diversion throughout the summer and autumn of that adventurous year, her wild gaiety undiminished. In December, having parted from her cavaliers, she crossed from

Brill in a storm, was driven out of her course and landed at Sole Bay, where Montagu was waiting for her. With Saint-Réal, Mustapha, Nanon and her other servants, they set off for London. A fortnight before Christmas, her breeches and boots caked with mud, her wig awry, her plumes bedraggled, Hortense was riding up Bedford Street into Covent Garden Piazza, where a house had been taken for her. She then told Montagu that she wished to remain incognito; no one must know her address.

She was soon traced and her doorstep thronged with sightseers and journalists, who presently made way for His Excellency the Marquis de Ruvigny, His Most Christian Majesty's Ambassador to the Court of St James, and the Comte de Gramont. They stayed with her some time and then, departing, de Gramont made a single comment. 'She is the most beautiful woman I have ever seen,' he said. What had she come for? How long would she stay? Ruvigny only knew that Madame Mazarin was in a strong position, for the Duchess of York, Charles II's sister-in-law and wife of the heir-presumptive, was her first cousin once removed. Mary of Modena, a Martinozzi on her mother's side, had already asked her to a reception. Then Ruvigny had to hurry away, to Whitehall; he had been sent for by the Duchess of Portsmouth, who, falling from one hysterical fit into another, was in an agony of fear and hatred.

FIVE

I

HORTENSE was in her eleventh year when a fortune-teller told her, 'Your husband will be very rich, and he will adore you, but you will not love him,' adding, 'You will have many lovers and a happy life.'

She did not meet the most famous and remarkable of her lovers till she was twenty-nine. His influence was beneficial and permanent, and his hold over her may be partly accounted for by his semi-paternal attitude and unselfish care. She never became his mistress: nor did he seriously suggest that she should. Their *amitié amoureuse* provided a support on which she became entirely dependent.

Charles Marguetel de St Denis, Seigneur de St Évremond, a retired soldier who had achieved renown as a philosopher and essayist, was in his early forties when the Peace of the Pyrenees was signed in 1659. As some of its terms seemed to him dangerous and absurd, he attacked it with the satiric wit for which he was celebrated, and so was forced to take refuge from Cardinal Mazarin's wrath in the United Provinces. There he met the Duke of Buckingham, who invited him to England. St Évremond then settled in London; but as Villiers was financially unreliable, he soon found himself in difficulties, for he earned little or nothing. Buckingham put his case before Charles II, who gave him an allowance, and, when criticized for this extravagance, blandly replied that he had made his new protégé Governor of the ducks in St James's Park.

St Évremond was nearly sixty and had been living in England for some fourteen years when Hortense arrived. He had known her as a child and was partly responsible for her leasing a house from the Duke of York at a peppercorn fee in the parish of St James's. His devotion to her and her affectionate trust in him were deep and lasting. No great nobleman, neither the Yorks, nor the King himself, could have done for her what this brilliant, eccentric old

227

man did; he taught her how to develop and use her assets and how to surmount her difficulties; their intimacy brought her pleasures and interests of which she had never dreamed.

They made an incongruous pair. Shabby, tall and gaunt, his white hair falling below the cap he preferred to a periwig, St Évremond was disfigured by a huge wen, which protruded from between his eyebrows. Those meeting him for the first time were repelled by this deformity; within a few minutes of listening to his talk they forgot it. Kind, courteous, amusing and sympathetic, he was, although differently, as irresistible as his new pupil, his dear, beautiful Duchess. Their daily companionship, their untroubled intimacy, at first a subject of mocking wonder, became a legend in a circle where corruption and self-seeking were taken for granted.

St Évremond, who took no part in politics, would have nothing to do with the cabal formed round Hortense and aimed at the Duchess of Portsmouth. He had been Louise's friend when she first came into England, and had advised her not to delay too long in becoming Charles's mistress. Now he saw her only at court; they had nothing in common, for she seldom read anything but novels, and did not care for music, his great passion. Discussion bored her; and she suspected clever men, believing, not without reason as far as the King's intimate circle was concerned, that they were bent on getting rid of her.

For Madam Carwell, as the English people called her, was the most unpopular of Charles's mistresses—even more disliked than Nell Gwynne, whose consciously exploited Cockney insolence was much resented by the class from which she sprang. A fictional dialogue, circulated at the time of Hortense's arrival, shows that anyone likely to oust Louise or Mrs Gwynne was welcome in the eyes of the public. The scene is Garraway's establishment in the Strand. Two Frenchmen are talking to a group of coffee-drinkers.

The visitors call Hortense 'the Queen of the Amazons' and describe her arrival, all splashed and muddy, upon which one of their hosts exclaims, 'She could not have taken a better way of recommending herself!' Another gloomily remarks that she is likely to cost more than His Majesty's faithful subjects can afford, adding that her beauty will give her a greater power over him than any of his other mistresses have ever enjoyed. 'They are fools who fear that,' his friend replies, ' ... I think it much more honourable for Great Britain to have its monarch subdued by a great Roman dame than by an obscure damsel from Little Britain [Brittany] or by a frisking comedian ... No woman was ever likely to be so cheap a mistress to the King as she, having fair pretensions to great sums of money ... And who will blame His Majesty to take his pennyworth, if he can, out of so fine a creature? And a Duchess already to his hand,' he thoughtfully adds.

Hortense's political value is then touched on, as likely not only to ruin Carwell but also Lord Danby, that lady's supporter. Will the Duke of York reconcile Madame Mazarin to her husband, is the next point—or does he desire her for himself? 'All things are possible in this world,' is the profound reply, upon which a Frenchman strikes in with, 'Je me contenterai de vous dire que la Duchesse Mazarin est en vérité si charmante, que si votre Roi la baise seulement une fois, je tiens la Portsmouth pour foutue'— and on this delicate augury the scene closes.

In fact, the political rivalry of Hortense and Louise existed only in the imagination of the spectators. No one, not even those who had known Charles II all his life, realized that in this respect his mistresses never had, and never would have, the slightest influence. Louis XIV and his plump little Breton envoy were similarly deceived; for Charles masked his ingenious machinations by appearing to comply with their wishes—so well, indeed, that he could nearly always count on Louis for financial support. Thus the conjectures caused by Hortense's arrival, the prophecies of Portsmouth's downfall, the fears of the French ambassador, the hopes of the English politicians and the hysterical appeals of his Fubbs, as Charles called Louise, must have amused him very much indeed.

This attitude was shared, unknowingly, by Hortense. She was perfectly willing to become Charles's mistress; but, as she was once more penniless, her serious purpose was that of renewing the struggle for her inheritance. She therefore co-operated with Ruvigny and his successor, Courtin, who warned their master that unless he forced Mazarin to restore her jewels and give her an allowance, she would defeat Louise and turn Charles against the French interest. Neither Ruvigny nor Courtin grasped that their supposed ally had less knowledge of, and care for, European politics than a street urchin. Amiably agreeing to all their suggestions, Hortense concealed her total indifference to the diplomatic issue, and so unconsciously combined with Charles to fool these two clever gentlemen and their employer.

Urged on by Courtin, Pomponne, Louis's minister, interviewed Mazarin and suggested that he should return his wife's jewels and give her an allowance. With her absence, some of the Duke's obsessions had diminished; but his concern for his position caused him to reply, not unreasonably, that he could not be expected to support her in the present circumstances. When this statement was reported to Hortense, she said that she would not return unless she and her husband occupied separate portions of the Palais Mazarin, while she remained his wife in name only. In a letter of eight folio sheets Mazarin refused these terms and outlined further conditions: before he consented even to receive Hortense she must undergo a conventual repentance lasting two years. When she rejected this proposal Louis XIV was appealed to, and refused to interfere. So once more deadlock was reached, to the delight of the anti-Portsmouth faction. Some months later, Louis was persuaded to speak to Mazarin, with no result. 'It seems to me', Ruvigny told Pomponne, 'that the King of England takes the interest of this lady more to heart than he did ... and that he may well become passionately attached to her. From her behaviour, one would think that she is not aware of it.'

By this time Hortense, who was meeting Charles two or three times a week in the Duchess of York's apartments, had resigned herself to the loss of her jewels and her allowance. Although it had become obvious that the alternative must be a pension from him, she made no advances, and he seemed equally indifferent. This delay alarmed Hortense's backers, but they were unable to influence her. Advised by St Évremond, she then organized her household so as to be able to entertain lavishly but informally, with the result that Charles visited her almost daily. 'She is very beautiful, and I would rather talk with her than with any other,' he told Courtin, adding, 'But I will not allow myself to be won over,' in his most reassuring manner. The ambassador's incredulity was justified when he heard that Hortense was receiving £4,000 a year, that parties were given for her at Whitehall and that His Majesty visited her at night, returning in the small hours. His hopes rose when Louise came back from taking the waters, and Waller published a poem entitled *The Triple Combat*, in which he described Little Britain, the Amazon and Chloris (Nell Gwynne) competing for first place.

Then the situation became clear. There were no places. Charles divided his time, according to his mood, between the three god-desses. Louise made a series of scenes, and Mrs Gwynne evolved a rather laborious joke about going into mourning for Her Grace of Portsmouth's hopes. Hortense was perfectly satisfied. She now had her own court, one much more amusing than that of White-hall. St Évremond was her Prime Minister, Saint-Réal her private secretary; her Cabinet consisted of Buckingham, Philibert de Gramont (author of the best-selling memoir of Anthony Hamilton) and Ralph Montagu. Among her most assiduous courtiers was a group of young women—Lady Harvey, Montagu's sister, Char-lotte Beverwaert and Lady Sussex, Charles's daughter by the Duchess of Cleveland—who were joined by Sidonie de Courcelles, now a widow but still on the run, this time from her creditors, and full of stories about her misfortunes. Hortense, very much bored by her demands, gave her money and encouraged her to resume her travels. Lady Harvey was equally importunate (Charlotte Beverwaert gave no trouble), and poor little Sussex, a neurotic sixteen-year-old, married to a brutal husband, became emotionally devoted. Hortense was kind to them all, and lazily responsive to the King; but she made no secret of her preference for St Évremond, who not only entertained and educated her, but provided the domestic, fatherly devotion she had never known.

So she began to lead an ideal existence. Unless she joined the Court at Newmarket, Windsor or Tunbridge Wells, Hortense spent the afternoons with St Évremond, who arrived for dinner at two o'clock with some little contribution: peaches, butter, a bottle of wine. Then they would talk alone, of what they had been read-ing, or of household matters, or go to the play. In the evening their friends arrived and sat down to Crimpo and Ombre, or joined in discussions on philosophy, history and literature; this last covered the widest range, as both Hortense and St Évremond were well read in Italian and French, and she was studying Spanish and English. Then there was music, the latest airs of Lully and Chambrunières alternating with those of the older composers, and St Évremond would accompany Déry, Hortense's soprano page, on the lute. In their talks alone the two friends interchanged recipes for new ways of cooking cheaper dishes, such as rabbit and mutton. As housekeeping bored Hortense, she delegated this duty to Charlotte Beverwaert ('Lot') who came every morning to help her dress and try out new ways of doing her hair. Hortense then fed her bullfinch, Boule, Jacob, a starling, Loteret, the parakeet, and her dogs and monkeys; these were the principal charge of Mustapha and a solemn English valet, Stourton, whom St Évremond called the Young Senator. He and Hortense had their private language; her house became the Little Palace, she was Dulcinea, he Don Quixote, and Mustapha, Pompey. When she came to spend the day with him she brought clean linen — he kept some of the rarer breeds of ducks in his rooms, and shared their habits — game and sweetmeats. They disagreed on three points: opera — which St Évremond described as impure and unrealistic — Hortense's passion for cleanliness, and her regret for her jewels. 'Those who keep them from you are better friends than you imagine,' he would say, and advise her to appear at some Court function as 'a country nymph', thus outshining all the other women. (Hortense generally did this, with or without jewels.) When she complained of the stink in his lodgings, he provided scented cushions; he insisted on her living frugally and dressing simply, and tried, unsuccessfully, to prevent her going for long walks after dark; with the adoring Lady Sussex, cloaked or in men's clothes, Hortense often went on foot as far as Chelsea Fields.

St Évremond was not possessive. He encouraged Hortense to sup alone with Lady Harvey, because the King could then 'surprise' her, thus avoiding Louise's spies and the resultant scenes. When, in the Italian custom, she cheated at cards, he would tell her guests, in a stage whisper, to look the other way; and she would join in the laugh. One of her most frequent visitors was Henry Jermyn, Lord St Albans, once a famous beau, now old and frail, and so blind that he could not see his cards; Hortense always sat next him and helped him play. Watching them both, St Évremond would lean over and kiss the tip of her ear; then Hortense, turning from one old man to the other, would ask, 'Have you been courting Marie de Medici — or Gabrielle d'Estrées?'

There was an upheaval when Déry, whose voice was breaking, decided to be castrated in order to keep it, and St Évremond persuaded him not to take this desperate step. When Hortense flew into a rage, he alone knew how to soothe her; her naïve surprise at his lack of jealousy amused and touched him. 'Should I ask you to love a man of my age? I do not expect miracles,' he said, adding, 'A man can never be ridiculous in loving you.' When her admirers complained he would say, 'She is born to be loved rather than to love.' During her absences from London he wrote to her every day, reporting on her menagerie (the new parrot, Pretty, was desolate), promised a loin of veal from a friend of his in Rouen, on her return, and begged her not to drink spirits (he enclosed a little poem about this), receiving in return letters beginning 'Dear Knight of the doleful countenance,' and ending with a new recipe or a sharp remark about his latest pupil, the Marquise de la Perrine, and 'that villain', Frank Villiers, who had entertained them both while she was away.

St Évremond refused to take part in the quarrels caused by Lady Sussex's passion for Hortense, which reached a climax in the winter of 1676. The young Countess went everywhere with the friend whose tolerant kindness seems to have given her the impression that her love was returned and that they need never be separated. With the Prince of Monaco and the Portuguese ambassador they were watching the Lord Mayor's show when Lady Sussex was hit by a squib, which nearly blinded her; she refused to admit that she was seriously hurt, put on a patch and remained where she was. This incident roused Lord Sussex's possessiveness. He ordered his wife to leave the Court and return with him to their country estate. Naturally, she refused; but she would have been carried off by force, if the weather had not made the journey impossible. She and Hortense were now taking fencing lessons; as there was not enough space to practise indoors, they did so in St James's Park. Very soon a crowd would collect to see them come out in their dressing-gowns, which they discarded to reveal themselves in shirts and breeches, with drawn swords; their mock duels became one of the sights of the city.

Then Sussex descended and removed his wife. She at once collapsed, and became so ill that the King's doctors were summoned. One, more sensible than the rest, advised Sussex to let her take up hunting and coursing, which she did, feverishly kissing Hortense's portrait before she left her rooms and returning to weep alone. The enraged husband enforced his rights, and although she had not long recovered from her first lying-in (when Hortense had nursed her, a rapturous time), she became pregnant again. In that state she could no longer pursue her idol—who had forgotten all about her.

Less harm but greater scandal was caused by the Prince of Monaco falling in love with Hortense; that would not have mattered, if he had not disregarded the fact that she was the King's property. His advances, which she did not discourage, became common talk, and although Charles remained amiably inscrutable, Hortense's friends felt sure that if she were openly unfaithful His Majesty would cut off supplies. St Évremond implored her to use discretion, at least: how could she expect to live in comfort if she cuckolded the King himself? Hortense appeared to accept the warning. But Monaco was young, handsome and persistent ...

For some time she alternated between the two men, while St Évremond expostulated—and then the blow fell; her income vanished. Presumably Monaco and the anti-Portsmouth group contributed to her upkeep; but he could not long remain in England, and they were always short of funds.

Meanwhile, Charles visited her as usual—they seem never to have interchanged an angry word—delighting in the entertainment she and St Évremond provided. The literary and philosophical arguments amused him, and he would join in the gambling. Best of all were the moments when Hortense, teased beyond endurance, would burst into tears, or spring up to illustrate her point with a recitation from Racine or La Fontaine; and the climax of pleasure came with her laying aside her guitar to dance the tarantella or the *furlana*. And Charles appreciated, more than most of her guests, her capacity for listening. She never interrupted; yet she knew exactly how to divert a flagging or irritable discussion. Such a creature made her own rules; she was unique; and presently her allowance, prudently halved, was restored. Her memoirs, now in translation, were endlessly talked of; her salon was the most famous in Europe; she seemed, Charles declared, to grow more beautiful every day. Finally, the Puritan and dissenting section of the English public took up her cause, representing her as a martyr to the popish tyranny of her husband and Louis XIV.

Courtin was in an agony, Portsmouth on the verge of a serious breakdown, and constantly in tears. 'You must get her back *at all costs*,' the ambassador wrote to Louis XIV. 'She is dangerous to France, because of her beauty, and her resentment towards Your Majesty.' Then Hortense suddenly announced that she was tired of England, and intended to return to Paris.

II

For the rest of her life Hortense remained in a state of delusion about her inheritance; either through Mazarin's death or her own efforts, she felt sure of getting it back, and so St Évremond's attempts to curb her extravagance were gradually abandoned. Although he had little difficulty in persuading her that to return to France would be worse than useless, she continued to borrow on her expectations, gambled more heavily as she reached middle age, and gave money to anyone who asked for it.

Frustration began to affect her temper. The first to suffer was St Réal, who, bitterly jealous of St Évremond, had taken to sitting in corners and sulking. Hortense's impatience, added to worry about her finances, ended in a quarrel, followed by his departure to Paris. His reports to Louis XIV strengthened that monarch's conviction that as Hortense was indifferent to French interests there was no point in supporting her against her husband.

Courtin, now desperate, decided that he must divert Hortense's influence by allying her with Louise and making them work together. So he gave a party for them at which everyone was encouraged to drink more than usual, and instead of dancing or sitting down to cards, played rowdy games, organized by the host. What Courtin euphemistically described as *les goûts spéciaux* of Hortense, Lady Sussex and Lady Harvey, were catered for by a horse-racing competition, in which the women bestrode one another, while the men betted on them. Then came hide-and-seek, also in couples, and somehow Courtin, relying on Hortense's powers, contrived that she and Louise should be locked up in a cupboard. They emerged holding hands and shrieking with laughter. Mrs Gwynne was then heard telling a group of courtiers that her Charles III, as she called the King (he had been preceded by her fellow-player, Charles Hart, and Charles Lord Buckhurst), slept more often with her than with either of his foreign mistresses. When Vasconcellos, the Portuguese ambassador, who had been hoping to succeed the Prince of Monaco, complained of Hortense's profligacy to St Évremond, he was told, 'Tout sexe a pour elle fourni des amants,' and retired in disgust.

Louise was then persuaded to call upon Hortense, who received her with the utmost amiability; but Courtin sadly noted that while the King spent some time each day with the French Duchess, he returned in the evenings to the Italian, generally at Lady Sussex's house, who had got permission to leave her husband by pimping for her father. Courtin's account of Portsmouth's sobs and howls, in which all her women joined, amused Louis, who thereafter referred to her as *La Signora adolorada*.

Meanwhile Hortense, after a series of lectures from St Évremond, made some effort to economize. She went down to the docks to buy silks and *objets d'art*, thus cutting out the middlemen; but she was gambling more wildly than usual. When she won 6,000 crowns from a Portuguese nobleman she spent the whole sum on gold liveries for her footmen. Then the ballad-mongers began to turn against her. 'Cloister up fulsome [spendthrift] Mazarine, And once more make Charles king again,' became a popular chorus. The shadows were beginning to fall.

Having lost all contact with her family, she was in no position to protest when her eldest daughter ran away from a convent to marry the Duc de Richelieu, by whom she had a child. Then Philippe de Nevers came to London, made impertinent advances to Louise and was told to leave. The brother and sister did not meet again; nor did Hortense ever see Marie, who, still forbidden to enter France, wandered about the Continent till she died in Spain at the age of sixty-seven.

Hortense did not miss her relatives; nor was she troubled by the attacks of Titus Oates who, achieving his first sinister notoriety in 1678, denounced her as a Popish whore and a French agent. For the Duke of Monmouth, the hero of the Country Party, was her friend, and the Dissenters still maintained that she was the victim of Louis's tyranny; also, the fact that her librarian and her croupier were Huguenot refugees was in her favour. Then Barillon, succeeding Courtin, reported Louise's return to favour.

Yet Hortense continued to live as before, a little more recklessly, borrowing money from all her friends, riding out at dawn over the Newmarket downs, attending cock-fights, betting, adding three more dogs and several cats to her menagerie (St Évremond bought her a white sparrow that whistled, for eight shillings) and ordering delicacies from France for her parties. Her cook, Galet, was famous; her laces came from Flanders, her fans from Spain, her jewels from Italy, and her *grandes toilettes*, naturally, from Paris. A black flowered satin trimmed with gold lace and its accompanying gold and silver cloak were paid for by the King.

She and St Évremond would take refuge from the terror and turmoil of the Popish Plot at the Duke of Richmond's, or at Boughton, Ralph Montagu's great palace, where they spent whole days in the gardens. Here the three friends had their special jokes: about the pike, which they pretended were dangerous and as big as crocodiles; about the truffles, of which Hortense ate so many; and about St Évremond, who, Montagu said, was one of the *Depontani*, 'old men, good for nothing, thrown from bridges into rivers'. When they returned it was observed by Barillon that Hortense, having put on weight, was lovelier than ever, at her zenith. Louise, trying in vain to gain flesh, was thought to be out of favour again: but she had nothing to fear. Hortense's relationship with Charles was more friendly than amorous. The Earls of Derwentwater, Arran and Devonshire pursued her, without success. She was unattached, carefree but for her financial worries, which her husband tried to enhance by sending an agent to tell Charles that her I.O.U.s were valueless. 'That is a matter which troubles me not at all, as I never take any,' the King replied. 'But it would be as well if M. Mazarin continued her allowance.' He was in financial straits himself, and ageing rapidly.

In the summer of 1683 a Swedish nobleman, Baron de Banier, arrived in London, was presented to Hortense and made the usual advances. Within a few days she became his mistress. That was to be expected. Then suddenly it dawned on St Évremond that in her thirty-seventh year she was in love—for the first time.

Nothing in de Banier's appearance or personality set him above or apart from Hortense's other lovers. His ascendancy was caused by the sudden need of change, of a revolution in behaviour which marks the course of most lives. Standing as it were at the cross-roads of her development, he subjugated her completely, and happily. Then her nephew, Philippe de Soissons, arrived and fell in love with her. Absorbed in de Banier, Hortense was hardly aware of Philippe's passion, or of his jealousy. Within a few weeks of their meeting he challenged de Banier—and killed him.

Somehow, the scandal was hushed up, the Swedish government appeased and Philippe de Soissons smuggled out of the country. Within a month the incident was forgotten. But Hortense had been struck down by a blow from which she never recovered. Her grief was so desperate, its demonstrations so violent that St Évremond began to fear for her reason. She hung her rooms with black, refused to see anyone and spent her days and nights in an orgy of sorrow. St Évremond, forbidden to approach her, pleaded in vain. When she did admit him, it was with the news that she intended to join Marie in her convent at Segovia. She had finished with the world.

St Évremond knew better than to burst into expostulations. He let some days pass before he wrote to her in loving sympathy, going on to describe the consequences of such a step. She had not the religious temperament; convent life would merely increase her misery. 'In the present disposition of your mind,' he added, 'it would be impossible for you to bear with the disgusts of such a solitude.' And as she had never been a dedicated worshipper of the God to whom she proposed to give herself up, 'Who knows, Madame, whether you will believe but one quarter of an hour in what you must ever believe?' She had lived triumphantly in the present—therefore 'Don't imitate Dido or Thisbe, but Helen, who caused both gods and men to fight ten years together.'

Presently her mood of self-immolation passed. She sent for Madame de Ruz, whom she had not seen for fifteen years, and they wept together, the older woman urging her to take the vows. St Évremond remarked that Madame de Ruz 'insisted on melancholy', and was a bad influence. 'In the name of God, Madame,' he wrote, 'rid yourself of a contagious converse with wickedness and folly'—and Madame de Ruz was sent away.

With her departure Hortense regained much of her gaiety and returned to her usual manner of life; but now her high spirits were flawed with bouts of violent irritation and attacks of rage, chiefly directed at the only person on whom she could rely. 'You old scoundrel,' she burst out to St Évremond, 'you have spoken against me!' and dismissed him. He remonstrated gently. 'You are cruel ... I never spoke ill of you ... Bring back those happy days.' The quarrels were made up, recurred, were made up once more. Then St Évremond observed, as did others, that Hortense, generally abstemious, was drinking, not to excess, but in such a manner as to enhance her moods of anger. 'Everything I do displeases you,' he said sadly, and again they were reconciled, resuming old jokes and interests. He engaged a famous flautist to play for her, organized a picnic party on the Thames during the

great frost of 1684 and teased her about her latest conquests—
Godolphin, a respectable widower, was one, Bonrepaus, replacing
Barillon, another—as in their happy days.

They were again on the best of terms, and Hortense seems to
have reached a more regular way of life, when Charles II died of a
stroke on February 6th, 1685. Evelyn's famous description of the
King on the night before his last illness, quietly chatting with his
three middle-aged sirens—Hortense, Louise and Barbara Duchess
of Cleveland—while a page sang to them and the courtiers played
cards ('A scene of the utmost vanity') gives an impression of
general friendliness and peace.

Hortense was greatly shocked by this fresh loss. St Évremond
thought her grief exaggerated in view of her behaviour to Charles.
'He was just another lover,' he said; but she would not be com-
forted. James II then continued her allowance; as the new
Queen's cousin, she could count on his favour; Mary of Modena
was very fond of her, and they met nearly every day.

With Charles's death came the thought of her own. That sudden
interest in the next world which so often arises when grief and
discontent combine with the awareness of middle age—and in
Hortense's case, with intemperance—to reject the present and
settle for the future, absorbed her. At a later period she would have
taken up spiritualism with its appendages of apports, séances and
communication with 'discarnate' persons. As it was, she could
only arrange with a new admirer, Madame de Beauclair, to meet
in the next world—would she have remembered her, if they had?
—thus taking out an insurance policy against the obliteration she
could neither face nor imagine, although her religious beliefs had
long disappeared. This phase did not last; during a short illness
she fell back on wondering what people would say of her after she
was dead: and St Évremond at once produced a witty and affectionate rhyming obituary in which she delighted. Once more, she
seemed to be entering calmer waters; but this stage came to an end
with the Revolution of 1688, the accession of William and Mary,
and the withdrawal of her allowance. There was nothing for it,
she decided, but to return to France. To many of her friends this
seemed a sensible resolve; St Évremond told her that it would
result in her being forced to become a professed religious.

Preparation for the next world no longer concerned Hortense:
at least, not in that form. After consulting Marianne de Bouillon,

239

who was staying with her, she moved into a smaller house, one of a new block in Kensington Square; finding this more than she could afford, she rented a modest establishment from Lord Cheyne, in Paradise Row, near Chelsea Fields.

In this suburban retreat she received a letter from Mazarin, begging her to return, on the grounds that, as the subject of a heretic monarch, her soul was in danger and that she would perish from 'spiritual gangrene'. Hortense replied that she would come back if he paid her debts. He then appealed to the Council of State to extradite her and deprive her of the settlement made by Cardinal Mazarin. Her family engaged a lawyer for the defence, but eventually the Council decided in her husband's favour. She was ordered to return within three months; if she failed to obey, her entire fortune would revert to him.

By this time Hortense's pension had been restored; and although her debts were such that she was in danger of imprisonment, her friends stood surety for her and she continued to live as before. Gambling parties alternated with debates on theology and philosophy; these were attended by Vossius and Bayle. The Frenchman, who had no use for fine ladies with intellectual pretensions, as he had shown by his treatment of the Electress Sophia, was entranced by her gaiety and her teasing of his Dutch rival. ('You, Monsieur Vossius, who read all the good books but the Bible, you can answer that question.') The philosophers were followed by La Fontaine, now very old and feeble; his admiration for Hortense burst forth in the last poem he wrote about her.

> Hortense eut du ciel en partage,
> La grâce, la beauté, l'esprit; ce n'est pas tout:
> Les qualités du cœur; ce n'est pas tout encore.
> Pour mille autres appas le monde entier l'adore ...

In fact, Hortense's circle of adorers had greatly diminished. St Évremond, more than ever devoted, remained, unresentful of her bouts of bad temper and of her debts to him, which now amounted to some six or seven hundred pounds. Her drinking absinthe and whiskey (this last was sent her from Ireland by Lord Galway) distressed him; but his mild expostulations and the reports of Hortense's contemporaries show that she was very far from becoming an alcoholic. Her health was excellent, her beauty but little impaired and her capacity for enjoyment that of a young woman. At a supper and ball given by Lord Rochester she danced all night; for another party she contributed forty dozen fireworks.

St Évremond was now told that he might return to France, and refused. He could not contemplate leaving Hortense, who seemed to have entered another religious phase. Then, coming into her private chapel, he saw her on her knees before her confessor, her arms about his neck. He was about to withdraw when she got up, bursting with laughter. She had been piercing Father Milon's ears so that he might wear the ear-rings she had given him.

The printed version of the lawsuit reached her in 1696. She was so enraged at the virulence of the attacks made on her that she at once dashed off her own account of Mazarin's behaviour. St Évremond said, 'It is too long and too passionate,' and begged her to let him shorten and modify it. Hortense indignantly refused. 'You know very well', she said, 'that a wife ought not to leave her husband, and therefore nothing but a lively representation of the Duke's exorbitancies can justify me to the world. And', she added fiercely, 'his lawyer shall not be spared—he has broken all the laws of truth, judgment and decency.'

Eventually she allowed St Évremond to issue a précis of her defence—unnecessarily, for by this time Mazarin's contemporaries had turned against him. 'He is a madman,' wrote Madame de Sévigné. 'He dresses like a beggar; piety runs riot in his brain ... His wife ... is exempted from ordinary rules; and one recognizes that she is justified, when one sees Monsieur Mazarin.'

Hortense's fury at the Council's decision became more frenzied as her circumstances declined and the majority of her acquaintances dropped away. The pretty little house with its panelled rooms, tiled roof and view over the river (it was replaced in 1906 by a block of flats) only reminded her of what she ought to have had—jewels, palaces, vast estates, an income not even she could have exhausted. 'God give me patience!' exclaimed St Évremond, when her anger burst forth; but to a friend he wrote, 'The rigours of Hortense do not disturb a man of my age,' presumably in the very natural belief that she would outlive him.

He was perfectly happy in these altered circumstances, so long as they remained together, visited by the faithful few who contributed to her housekeeping in kind, or in small sums left under the plates after a meal. Hortense may have been further exacerbated by this reminder of her deprivation. Her temper grew more uncertain; the greater number of her servants left; her invitations (she still arranged banquets) were ignored; she was in debt to the tune of some £7,000, and, when remembered at all, had become an object of pity. 'Never have I been in better health, never more beautiful!' she defiantly declared: and it was true. 'Everybody from England speaks of the Duchess of Mazarin's beauty,' wrote Ninon de l'Enclos in 1699, 'just as they talk of that of Mademoiselle de Bellefonds [Hortense's granddaughter] which is now in the bud.'

By the spring of that year Hortense's circle had sunk to half a dozen friends; of her servants, only Mustapha and a valet remained. Still St Évremond came every day, with his little presents, now so sadly needed, of wine, fresh butter and made-up dishes; then they would talk, or play and sing, or read aloud. Somehow Hortense managed to scrape together half the sum she owed him, which he accepted in order to help her in what he described as 'such extremities as are not to be believed'. She was his whole life. Her hair might be grey, her moods increasingly difficult; but she was still, in his eyes, the most beautiful woman in the world, and the dearest. He loved her even more than when he had known her first, twenty-four years ago.

In the first week of June Hortense collapsed and lost consciousness. She was put to bed and remained in a coma for a fortnight, deserted by all but St Évremond, Mustapha and an under-valet. As soon as he realized that there was no hope, St Évremond informed her family; her son, Paul-Jules, and Marianne de Bouillon set off for London. She then recovered consciousness, and St Évremond asked her if he should send for a priest. She refused, and when the doctors came again would not have them admitted. So she and St Évremond were left alone.

On June 23rd she again lost consciousness. St Évremond, unable to believe that she might not rally once more, and perhaps even recover, dosed her with brandy; she swallowed enough to keep her alive, but neither recognized him nor took in what was happening. St Évremond then ensured her eventual entry into paradise – even he would have admitted that her term in purgatory must be a long one – by summoning Father Milon, from whom she received the Last Sacraments, without, it seems, much awareness. She was drifting away, in no pain. Hour after hour St Évremond sat by her, his hopes fading with her heavy breaths. Then, as he watched, he saw her regain a strange, a transcendent beauty. At eight o'clock on the morning of July 2nd, she died.

St Évremond did not know that Marianne and Paul-Jules, arriving at Dover some two days earlier, only to read in the news-sheet that Hortense's survival was a matter of hours, had taken the next boat back to France. Knowing that she had nothing to leave but her debts, her animals and slave-boy, they took no steps about such valueless effects as remained.

These were at once impounded by Lord Jersey, William III's Secretary of State. On August 13th, escorted by St Évremond, Mustapha and her executors, Lord Feversham and Sir Ralph Montagu, the body of Hortense was conveyed to France and received by her husband at the church of Notre-Dame-de-Liesse in Normandy.

She had been forgotten by all but these few some time before she died. But the great persons who still desired St Évremond's company set about cheering him up; he was, after all, a valuable guest, and now that he was freed from attendance on a woman who had long ceased to matter, he would no doubt be as entertaining as before.

In order to bring him back into circulation, Montagu asked him to Boughton. At first, all went well. They walked about the gardens and fed the carp. Then they went into dinner, and the preliminary course — truffles — was served. The poor old man burst out sobbing. *She* had so loved truffles — and now he must eat them alone ...

Very soon his friends saw that there was nothing to be done with St Évremond. When they condoled with him, he wept; if they did not mention Hortense, he did, recalling their happy times, their jokes and parties, her goodness and beauty — 'the choicest, richest, most lasting beauty that woman ever had' — until he grew wearisome. So he would go back to his lodging to write of her, describing in minutest detail all that he had lost. He survived her by twenty years, and was buried, at the age of ninety, in Westminster Abbey.

Hortense had one other mourner, more distraught and no less sincere: the husband from whom she had been parted for thirty-one years. Mazarin refused to leave her after the funeral. As if determined that she should continue the wanderings which had been part of her saga—and perhaps to ensure the companionship she had denied him in life—he took her coffin with him all over his estates: Vincennes, Brittany, Bourbon, Alsace. Within a month or two, these journeyings created a legend—Duchesse Mazarin was a saint. Peasants brought their rosaries to lay on her coffin; they carried their sick children to touch it; many cures were reported. Mazarin might have taken her about indefinitely—for he too survived her by twenty years—when, pausing at a convent in Normandy, he was persuaded by the Abbess to leave in peace the woman he had persecuted and ruined, and who had helped to drive him to madness and despair. In 1700 Hortense was deposited in the vault of the Collège des Quatre Nations, and laid beside Cardinal Mazarin, its founder.

It was not to be her final resting-place. Ninety years later the Paris mob broke into the chapel, dragged the coffins from the vault and threw the skeletons on a bonfire. What they could not burn was scattered and lost.

PRINCIPAL SOURCES OF INFORMATION

with dates of the most recent editions

Aulnoy, Madame d',   *Mémoires de la Cour d'Angleterre* (tr., London, 1927)

Bertrand, L.,   *Louis XIV* (tr., New York, 1928)

Bussy-Rabutin, R.,   *Histoire Amoureuse des Gaules* (Paris, 1938)

Choisy, Abbé,   *Mémoires* (Utrecht, 1727)

Courcelles, Marquise de,   *Mémoires et Correspondances* (Paris, 1869)

Delpech, J.,   *Louise de Kéroualle* (Paris, 1949–50)

Domestic State Papers, 1675–99

Érard, C.,   *Plaidoyers* (tr., London, 1699)

Evelyn, J.,   *Diary* (London, 1955)

Fea, A.,   *Some Beauties of the Seventeenth Century* (London, 1906)

Gravigny, J.,   *Abbés Galants et Libertins* ... (Paris, 1912)

Hartmann, C. H.,   *The Vagabond Duchess* (London, 1926)

Historical Manuscripts Commission,   *Bath MSS, Belvoir MSS*, vol. II

Jesse, J.,   *Memoirs of the Court of England during the reign of the Stuarts* (London, 1840)

Latour, T.-Louis,   *Princesses, Dames et Aventurières* ... (Paris, 1923)

Luttrell, N.,   *Brief historical relation of state affairs from Sept. 1678 – April 1714* (London, 1857)

Mancini, Marie,   *Apologie ou les véritables Mémoires de Marie Mancini* (Paris, 1881)

Mazarin, H.,   *Mémoires* (Cologne, 1675)

Motteville, Mme de,   *Mémoires* (Amsterdam, 1723)

Perey, L.,   *Le Roman du Grand Roi. Louis XIV et Marie Mancini* (Paris, 1894)

Renée, A.,   *Les Nièces de Mazarin* (Paris, 1856)

St Évremond, C. M.,   *Works of M. de St Évremond* (tr., London, 1700)

Saint-Simon, Duc de,   *Mémoires* (Paris, 1951)

Sévigné, Mme de,   *Lettres* (Paris, 1953–7)

Sutherland, M.,   *Louis XIV and Marie Mancini* (London, 1956)

Williams, H. N.,   *Five Fair Sisters* (London, 1906)

THOMAS BRUCE, EARL OF AILESBURY

(SEPTEMBER 1656 — DECEMBER 1741)

What though I cannot see my King,
Neither in person nor in coin;
Yet contemplation is a thing
That renders what I have not, mine:
My King from me what adamant can part,
Whom I do wear engraven on my heart?

PERCY'S Reliques

ONE

I

In the year 1884 Ernest, third Marquess of Ailesbury, withdrew from the muniment room at Savernake a folio manuscript of nine hundred pages bound in red morocco, tooled in gold and labelled *Memoirs of Thomas Earl of Ailesbury, Written by Himself*. He had a copy made, which he submitted to the Roxburgh Club, and in 1891, a hundred and fifty years after the death of the author, the printed version of his book appeared under those auspices. He himself had called it *A Domestic Diary*—wrongly, for he never kept one—adding, 'For the sincere part I answer. At a great feast, very ill dressed, one finds some dishes that relish amongst a quantity of very ill ones, and the comparison I make is true and just. I have an upright meaning in all I have set forth, and if I displease any, I am heartily sorry for it.'

The dish thus modestly presented is rich and varied. It contains intimate portraits of Charles and James II, William III, Mary II and Louis XIV; records of conversations with such statesmen as the Earls of Danby, Halifax and Nottingham; studies of the Dukes of Monmouth and Marlborough; and sketches of a number of Dutch, French and Flemish grandees. Throughout this concourse of seventeenth- and eighteenth-century celebrities the solid figure of the chronicler moves deliberately, with the purposeful confidence characteristic of those incapable of compromise, treachery or disingenuousness.

Ailesbury has been described as a typical Englishman; and he himself would have preferred this designation to that of Jacobite, expatriate and plotter, all of which he became. In fact, his political activities so fluctuated as to arouse the censure of certain historians; yet it may be possible, now, to see his apparent inconsistencies and divagations as the outcome of a single principle —loyalty, not to an individual, but to an ideal, that of the monarchical system. A hundred and ninety years before his birth his views were perfectly expressed by the Duke of Norfolk, when

249

Henry VII asked him how he had dared to fight for Richard III in the battle of Bosworth Field. 'He was my crowned King,' replied that nobleman, 'and if the Parliamentary authority of England set the crown upon a stock, I would fight for that stock. And as I fought for him, I will fight for you, when you are established by the said authority.'

So it was that Ailesbury, the devoted servant of the last two Stuart kings, submitted to and was employed by William and Mary, while working to restore James. In his opinion, William had become the stock, by Parliamentary authority. James was his crowned King.

Thomas was the eighth of seventeen children, seven of whom died in infancy; he became the heir at his brother Edward's death in 1663, when he was seven; this may have influenced his parents' decision to educate him and his two younger brothers privately, at Houghton House in Bedfordshire, a vast Jacobean mansion (later described by Defoe as 'a noble and magnificent palace') surrounded by park lands and overlooking the river Ouse. Their London home was in Clerkenwell; but they preferred country life for themselves and their children, although Thomas's father, who was Lord Lieutenant for the counties of Huntingdon, Cambridge and Bedford, appeared regularly at Court, bringing the boy with him. After waiting on Charles II, who was very fond of him, he would go on to St James's Palace to pay his respects to the Duke and Duchess of York. By his first wife, daughter of the disgraced and exiled Lord Chancellor Clarendon, James of York had two surviving children, Mary and Anne, both of whom were to become Queens of England. Thomas was sent to play with them during these visits and Mary, the elder, always remembered him with affection; his gentleness and courtesy were well set off by his good looks; and he seems to have had what would now be called an old-fashioned dignity of manner, the result of his Cavalier background and training. All his long life, he gave the impression of belonging to an earlier day.

His forebears were of ancient Scottish stock. When his grandfather, Lord Elgin, died in 1663, Thomas's father received his English earldom from Charles II, and could therefore have styled himself Elgin and Ailesbury; he dropped the Scots title, and Thomas became Lord Bruce until he succeeded as second Earl of Ailesbury in 1685.

During these years, although he wanted for nothing, his up-bringing was rather that of a country squire than of a great nobleman. He preferred outdoor sports to indoor amusements, and was not much interested in books. 'God Almighty', he says, 'endowed me with common reason and understanding for to jog on with the world, and as for learning, my good father was too indulgent.'

When the first Lord Ailesbury perceived that his seventeen-year-old heir was lacking in accomplishments and polish, he sent him, with his tutor, to Paris, where he remained for a year. During that period (1673–4) Thomas's natural intelligence took charge. 'It grieved me much', he recalls, 'that I had so mis-spent my time.' By now, he had seen something of both the French and the English Courts, came to the conclusion that a career therein was 'the finest way of living possible', and resolved to train himself to that end.

With this ambition at the back of his mind, he returned to Houghton and renewed his boyhood friendships, specifically that with the only child of his nearest neighbour, Lady Philadelphia Wentworth: this was Henrietta, who had become Baroness Went-worth in her own right after her father's death; she was also the owner of Toddington Manor, an estate equal in size to that of Houghton. Thomas now discovered that he had fallen in love with Henrietta. She was of his own standing, their lands marched, and her mother was eager for the match. 'I greatly esteemed and loved her,' he wrote, fifty years later; but, 'God be praised, I was reserved for a more happy fate in marriage.' Yet he never forgot or, in a sense, ceased to love this strange, quiet, intensely forceful girl. She was like no one else. Her beauty, neither voluptuous nor flamboyant, was that of another epoch, and her temperament, according to Thomas, 'visionary'. Their friendship lasted through-out her short, tragic life.

When Bruce asked his father's leave to court the fourteen-year-old Henrietta, Lord Ailesbury made inquiries about her prospects, and finding them much inferior to his son's, desired him to think no more of her. 'Out of duty to so good a father,' he says, 'I laid aside all thoughts, but my esteem I could not blot out so soon.' He would no more have broken the Second Commandment than he would the Sixth; and in the two years which followed this dis-appointment he accepted the fact that his wife would be chosen for him. Meanwhile, in view of his hope, encouraged by Lord Ailesbury, of obtaining a Court appointment, he began to study the political situation and the history of government during the last quarter of a century. Here again he was guided by his father, whose principles and ideals were those of the generation preceding his own, and of such statesmen as Clarendon, Ormonde and Nicholas, ministers long despised or forgotten by the advisers of Charles II. So it was that the political and moral outlook of young Lord Bruce was that of fifty years ago; he became, and remained, a Royalist in the completest and most old-fashioned sense of the word.

Looking over the crises of the last fourteen years, Bruce came to the conclusion, from which he never afterwards diverged, that His Majesty's mistakes had been caused by his being wrongly advised; left to himself, he would not have made them. The subtlety and unscrupulousness, the convolutions, the broken promises, the half-truths and bare-faced lies, which, together with the sudden and startling exercise of his prerogative, eventually enabled Charles to achieve a form of absolutism, were not seen as such by this faithful servant. He perceived, simply, the result; that of the King's hard-won triumph, which produced 'the golden age' of his last years, and which Bruce never ceased to look back on with love and longing.

Such a single-minded and limited view might be described as that of a bigot or a dolt. Bruce was neither. His judgments, often contemptuously dismissed in his own day, reflect in part those of a number of twentieth-century historical experts, who have the benefit of hindsight and access to a mass of information unknown to him. Naturally he simplified what they elaborate; but his opinions of such persons as Shaftesbury, Monmouth, Danby, York, Jeffreys and Nottingham may be closely identified with theirs.

Before he received his Court appointment and became the confidant of Charles II, Bruce's opinions on certain aspects of government were, he says, already formed; he recorded them many years later in such statements as 'The nation is ever safe when the counties, cities, etc. are represented by men of substance and natives of the county from which they come, and never safe when 'tis otherwise,' going on to denounce the hysteria and tyranny created by the 'devilish artifices' of the extreme Whig or Country Party. Of course he was prejudiced and partisan; but his bias is no longer thought of as degraded or absurd.

While Bruce was wondering whether he was fitted for the career on which he had set his heart ('My chief study was to examine ... what I could ever be good for'), his parents were looking for a suitable wife. Their choice eventually fell on Lady Elizabeth Seymour, daughter of the late Lord Beauchamp, and thus the direct descendant of Lady Katherine Grey, the great-niece of Henry VIII. They approached her mother, now Marchioness of Worcester, whose insistence on lavish settlements delayed the betrothal for two years. During that time the young people met seldom and formally; at last the marriage took place at Badminton in August 1676. In his *Memoirs* Bruce makes no mention of these proceedings, or of his wife; shortly after they settled in at Houghton it was observed that they were very happy together. When Elizabeth recovered from the illness caused by the birth of a dead son they came up to London, and Thomas, having obtained the Court appointment he had so long desired, took a house in York Buildings in the Strand.

He was now Gentleman of the Bedchamber to Charles II. 'Your coming into my service will be most acceptable,' said the King, 'and', Bruce complacently adds, 'I soon found it was so in reality.' He seems not to have been singled out in any way for the first few months. But Charles had been watching him. At last, shortly after Bruce's twenty-second birthday, he drew him aside and said, 'You are young, and I will breed you up and instruct you for my service — and principally, learn to keep a secret, and on the trust I have in you as to that good maxim I will inure you.'

From that moment onwards Bruce's whole life changed. He loved his wife: he was devoted to his parents and fond of his brothers and sisters. But his adoration of Charles II overrode all other loyalties and bound him closer than all family ties. He lived for his 'good and gracious' sovereign, who, he fondly records, 'was pleased to distinguish me far beyond my age, and I was never at rest till I was placed near that incomparable prince.' For the next eight years he existed only to serve and worship, to study the moods and listen to the talk of His Sacred and Blessed Majesty, 'the best of kings and masters ... ' who, he firmly believed, 'had no ambition but the good of his subjects.'

And yet Bruce was very far indeed from being a stupid man; he could not know that the exercise of that particular magic was Charles's speciality, nor that it partly consisted in the jovial, fatherly attitude towards his people (as he himself once remarked, he *was* the father of a good many of them) which masked his undeviating resolve to stay where he was and to live as he chose. He was well aware that he could be irresistible; now, ageing and weary, he turned the full lustre of his fascination, his wit and gaiety, on the most fervent devotee of the many he had enslaved.

II

The King's subjugation of Bruce needs no explaining. But that he should have made a favourite of this rather simple, modest, and comparatively inexperienced young man is not so easy to understand. Hitherto, his intimate circle had been composed of sophisticated, unconventional, talented worldlings and wits, whose derision was as incisive as his own, whose repartee met his mockeries with cool insolence and bold understanding. He and they had spoken the same language for seventeen years; indeed, for some of them it had been evolved even earlier, in the squalor and degradation of exile; it sprang from shared disillusion, destructive cynicism and bitter mirth. And now this long-established group observed, with mounting resentment and surprise, that their former boon-companion was turning from them to a country-bred, downright, respectable youth whose only assets were his gentle breeding and the height and fairness with which his unassuming address contrasted so agreeably; a lad who could be trusted to hold his tongue, do his duty and be there when he was wanted. What could His Majesty find in such a being that he should set him above themselves?

Charles II, whose mistresses exceeded in number those of the Duke of York and Louis XIV, the father of fourteen acknowledged bastards, and the most popular and the most accessible of all the English kings, was in fact a lonely, secretive, melancholy man, loving few, distrusting all, respecting none. James Duke of Monmouth, his eldest and idolized son, was becoming politically disloyal; his other children were affectionate but uninteresting; his brother and heir was a wrong-headed liability, his wife pathetic but physically repulsive ('a virtuous princess, but so disagreeable in many respects as not fit to mention', according to Bruce), and his oldest friends were ready to betray him to his enemies. As one nauseated by rich food and spiced wine longs for home-baked bread and spring water, so Charles seized upon Bruce's undemanding love and selfless loyalty. This courtier, alone among the tosspots and sycophants of Whitehall, wanted nothing for himself, neither honours nor power, nor any place but that he already had, at his master's side. And — best of all — *he believed what he was told*. The mistrust, the smooth incredulity, the polite withdrawals of those he had fooled too often and too successfully were becoming wearisome to Charles. He knew that they knew most, though by no means all, of his little ways, and that they saw through the charm to the shifting depths of his deviousness, his intricate scheming. Bruce stood apart from these, a little bewildered by his good fortune, yet neither presumptuous nor overwhelmed. In the frenzied, unending feast of snobbery, jobbery, place-hunting and corruption which composed Court life, he and the King remained sober. They understood and valued one another on a separate level; whether higher or not, it was healthier, calmer and perfectly defined. Charles told Bruce what he had done and how, even, sometimes, what he intended to do; and Bruce asked no inconvenient questions, expected nothing that the King could not give.

When Bruce walked beside the King in the Park or climbed after him on board his yacht or stood behind the throne in the Presence Chamber, they matched yet contrasted with one another. Charles was six foot two, Bruce about the same height, or perhaps a shade taller. The King's sombre colouring, heavy eyes and lined features appeared startlingly Italianate and exotic beside the younger man's ruddy freshness and smooth cheeks. (Charles was shaved only three times a week, and on the intervening days must have looked unkempt and dirty.) Both carried themselves well, striding 'fastly', as the onlookers put it; but there the resemblance ended. The King was a great talker; jokes, anecdotes, comments succeeded one another, even on the tennis-court or in his laboratory. Bruce was silent and attentive, storing up every word, every look and gesture. And while Charles still seemed tireless, riding his own horse at Newmarket, walking from Whitehall to Hampton Court and swimming in the Thames, Bruce was an ailing man, often in agonies from the stone. In search of a cure, he went abroad during the first years of his service, to Spa, Bourbon and Montpellier, returning to find himself little better. No one but his wife realized how ill he sometimes felt; the King lent him a yacht and encouraged him to stay away till the waters took effect; at the same time he was told to make secret inquiries about Louis XIV's scheme of a canal between the ports of Cette and Bordeaux. Bruce came back with a complete plan of the work, obtained from a dismissed clerk. His Majesty need not fear for English trade; Louis's contractor was a fraud, who did nothing to prevent the canal silting up as soon as it was formed.

These absences partly account for Bruce's simplified version of the troubles into which the kingdom was plunged from 1677 to 1681, and the appalling problems—financial, political, religious— which broke down Charles's health and helped to bring on the stroke from which he died. The King's version of his methods for dealing with these dangers was reserved for Bruce alone; but so much was left unsaid that the young man's description of those terrible years, while reliable, is incomplete. Yet he knew more and judged better than many persons twice his age, who had been concerned with government since, and even before, the beginning of the reign.

The principal protagonists in the attempted revolution which came to a head with the Popish Plot were Shaftesbury, Monmouth, York, Buckingham, Halifax, Danby and Louis XIV. With the exception of Louis, who had received him formally during his year in Paris, Bruce came to know all these persons very well. To him, the situation seemed simple enough. The evil, 'hot-headed' men, led by Shaftesbury and Buckingham, with Monmouth as their dupe, were on one side, York and Charles their victims, Halifax and Danby, although self-interested and corrupt, their opponents, while Louis XIV was a potentially dangerous spectator. When Bruce came to the conclusion that Charles stood alone in the turmoil while controlling it, he was right, although he knew little of the undercurrents caused by the struggle between France and the United Provinces.

When these two powers temporarily ceased hostilities with the Peace of Nimeguen in 1678, Charles was two million pounds in debt, and the only person from whom he could borrow was Louis XIV. If he did so openly, the violence of the anti-papist factions in Parliament and throughout the kingdom might force him into abdication and exile, if not to the scaffold. The Commons would not grant him the money needed to run the country; they trusted neither him nor James, his successor; for James was a declared Catholic (as was his second wife, Mary of Modena), and Charles suspected of being one, partly because, ever since he had agreed to the secret Treaty of Dover in 1670, it was rumoured that he had sold out Protestantism and English liberty to Louis XIV. (In fact, if he had once entertained such a scheme, he had long abandoned it; he got the money for promising to do so, which was all that concerned him.)

Charles thus had to appear anti-French in order to reassure both Houses, while relying on Louis to help him support York and defeat the Country Party led by Shaftesbury and Buckingham, with Monmouth, the people's Protestant hero, as its figurehead. Shaftesbury and Buckingham were working for the dissolution of Parliament, so that they might organize a general election which would eliminate York from the succession and inaugurate an oligarchy. They therefore instigated and encouraged horrifying reports of a Catholic invasion, which (they implied) would be submitted to by Charles, financed by Louis and the Pope, and enforced by James.

Danby and Halifax stood apart from Charles's supporters and the Country Party. While hating each other, neither wished to interfere with the succession. Danby, now Lord Treasurer and a first-class business man, planned to free the King from his French obligations by reorganizing the Treasury, and Halifax was backing York because he saw through Shaftesbury's propaganda to his plan of a crypto-republican tyranny.

Meanwhile, the Commons refused to vote supplies until they knew for certain what alliances Charles had made; he appeased them by marrying his elder niece, the Princess Mary, a Protestant and second in the succession, to her first cousin, William of Orange-Nassau (later William III), Louis's greatest enemy and the representative of Continental Protestantism; he then sent James into exile, first to Brussels and then to Scotland, while keeping in touch with him through Bruce.

Louis XIV partially hamstrung the combatants by bribery. He paid Shaftesbury's faction to prevent Parliament meeting (and thus voting for war with France), and financed Charles for the same reason. These bribes were accepted, and used for the recipients' own ends.

Charles temporized in his usual masterly fashion, not by immediately proroguing or dissolving Parliament, as Louis and Shaftesbury wished, but by adjourning it for a few weeks at a time; he was rewarded with a million livres from his cousin. English troops, led by Monmouth, had been fighting the Dutch under the French command. They were recalled in 1677, and took the field with the Spanish against the French in 1678, when Louis captured Ghent and Ypres, then part of the Spanish Netherlands; for this Charles received a handsome subsidy from the King of Spain. Three months later he signed a secret treaty with Louis promising to maintain his neutrality during the continuance of the war; his reward was to be six million livres, which did not materialize; but he at last had the standing army voted him by Parliament, who were now in terror lest he should use it on behalf of Louis and the popish tyranny. Meanwhile Danby temporarily halted the machinations of the Country Party by counter-bribes, borrowed from the City of London.

Rumours of all these intrigues contributed to the hysterical anti-popery of the common people; they suspected everyone but Shaftesbury, Buckingham and Monmouth, adored Charles, whom they thought of as persecuted and wrongly advised, and detested James. James's attitude was one of stubborn patience and outraged pride. He refused to abandon his faith, urged his brother to resolve the struggle by executing the Whig rebels—which might have caused a second Civil War—but obeyed his orders. He was fond of, and trusted, Bruce, sometimes even asking his advice.

Bruce's opinions, shared by a small minority, placed him above intrigue, quite apart from his personal horror of such activities. He thought that James should succeed, and believed in his promise of not interfering with the national religion; he scouted the idea of a Catholic invasion, and deplored the King's apparent tolerance of such politicians as Shaftesbury ('turbulent and fiery'), Buckingham ('flashy and vain'), and Monmouth—'that unhappy Duke, my good and noble friend.' He was sure that the King, that 'master of statecraft', would overcome them all in the end, and here again he saw further than most. But he was not prepared, any more than anyone else, for the shock tactics of Kirkby, Tonge and Titus

Oates, which were sprung on Charles and his Cabinet in August 1678.

Tonge and Oates, using Kirkby as their intermediary, presented Charles with an indictment in which they stated that the Pope and the Jesuits, financed by Spain, were about to invade England, overthrow the Government, murder the King, massacre all Protestants and put James on the throne. Charles's contemptuous disbelief in the story was shared by Bruce, and the young man was horrified when 'that vile fellow Oates' was allowed a public hearing in the Commons. Oates's rise to power and Shaftesbury's exploitation of his fantasies inaugurated a reign of terror, in which thirty-nine innocent Catholics were executed. Charles did nothing to save them; if he had, it would have cost him his throne. When the still unsolved murder of Sir Edmondsbury Godfrey, the magistrate who had heard Oates's depositions, was ascribed to the Jesuits, thus giving the Country Party another weapon, the King could no longer interfere, except to protect the Queen; Oates had accused her of planning, with her physician, Sir George Wakeman, and the Earl of Castlemaine, to poison Charles.

In the summer of 1680 Bruce and his wife returned from France to be given an example of the general atmosphere by the Mayor of Hastings, who greeted them 'with a grave countenance'. 'What news?' asked Bruce. 'Sad news,' was the reply. 'Lord, is the King dead?' Bruce exclaimed. The Mayor shook his head and answered that Wakeman and Castlemaine had been acquitted. 'No doubt they were not guilty,' said Bruce. The Mayor was deeply shocked. 'O my lord,' he said, 'if they had not been guilty, they never would have had their trial.' Violently irritated, Bruce replied, 'I am sorry the King has not a wiser magistrate to represent him.' What credulity — what doting folly! He returned to Whitehall in great indignation.

By this time, Danby had been impeached on the grounds that he was privy to the secret agreement between Louis and Charles, and had accepted a bribe of £231,602 from the French King, and James was excluded from the succession, while Charles categorically denied all the stories put about by Shaftesbury of Monmouth's legitimacy. The King then formed a new Privy Council which included both these men. This bewildered Bruce. His Majesty could do no wrong; but — this was his nearest approach to criticism — he did not always give himself time to think. Charles, whose processes of thought sometimes achieved the speed of light, 'spoke to me', says Bruce, 'for the first time, some natural, obliging things ... suitable to my young years.' 'Your father,' he said, 'looked out of humour when in my presence.' Bruce, unaware that he was being tested, respectfully denied the suggestion. 'Oh,' said Charles, 'I am sure he would die at my feet, I know him so well. Doth he imagine I left him out [of the Council] because I did not love him? He was left out because I do love him.' After a pause he added, 'Godsfish! They have put a set of men about me, but they shall know nothing, and this keep to yourself.' This was the first of many similar confidences lovingly recorded fifty years later.

Charles's plan of controlling his adversaries by appearing to consult them would have suited his sardonic humour and strengthened his optimism if Monmouth had not been among them; but he sadly recognized that his over-indulged son was being fooled by Shaftesbury and the mob, and may have foreseen the breach which eventually parted them. His contempt for those of his courtiers who professed subservience while working against him was expressed shortly after Bruce returned to Whitehall and went to wait on him in Arlington Garden. He found Charles on the terrace ('his usual walk') with his gentlemen, and accompanied them to the bowling-green. As he strode along, the King continued his satirical attack on two-faced statesmen, talking at his hearers in such a way that they were deeply embarrassed. Then he turned to Bruce and said, 'My lord, come hither. You must carry a message from me to your father,' and as soon as they were out of hearing went on, 'Did you ever see such guilty and hanging faces as they made when I was drawing their pictures?'

The 'trimmers' then attempted to eliminate Bruce when he waited on the King in the Matted Gallery. 'He received me', says Bruce, 'in a most gracious manner; those about him looking on me as a monster come out of the woods. I followed him, by order, towards his bed-chamber, the door of which they shut against me. The King ... was never seen in such a passion, asking with a most fierce countenance (very rare for him) why I was not let in.' When Bruce appeared with letters from the Yorks, Charles said loudly 'I am glad my brother has chosen so good and trusty a person,' adding, 'I am sorry you found no more benefit by the waters.'

A cause of jealousy unperceived by Bruce was Charles's habit of addressing him formally when they were in public. The King generally referred to his intimates as Tom, Ned, Nelly, etc. or by nicknames (the Duchess of Portsmouth was Fubbs, or Fatty), and when he used the youthful newcomer's title, he was drawing attention to a tribute denied to others. Bruce, trained in the fashion of an earlier day, did not realize that he was being subtly favoured. Nor had he any idea that this was the preliminary to a series of confidences by which Charles fulfilled his promise of instructing him for his own service. Within two years the King's peculiar and highly specialized blend of ruthlessness, cunning and patience was used to destroy his enemies coolly, without mercy and single-handed; and Bruce alone was allowed to observe the drama from behind the scenes.

TWO

In October 1680 Bruce took his seat in the Commons as M.P. for Marlborough, where the second Exclusion Bill was passed by a large majority. It was thrown out by the Lords, and York's succession seemed temporarily assured. The King, who had been seriously ill in the preceding year, then dissolved Parliament until the following spring. Meanwhile, 'it is very certain', says Bruce, 'that never was a Court seen of such a composition, and a melancholy sight for a true and good subject to see ... There were but very few that the King could confide in, and none but those ... that were the chief instruments of bringing in the Bill of Exclusion.' Yet Charles appeared curiously serene. 'Give [the Council] but enough rope,' he told Bruce, 'and they will hang themselves'—a euphemistic announcement of the revenge he was planning. It then dawned on Bruce that the exclusion of York was still on Shaftesbury's agenda, and that it might be followed by Charles's deposition and murder through the 'miscreant and insatiable measures' of that nobleman's party. 'But,' he goes on, 'God be praised, His Majesty was endowed with a great temper of mind and kingcraft, and knew men to a hair (it had to have been wished that his brother had enjoyed that most useful talent).' When he told Charles that the Whigs, under Lord Russell, would oppose the Tory interest in Bedfordshire, the King replied, 'I shall not long be troubled with him and his party, for I tell them nothing, and it will not be long before we shall part.'

Before the new Parliament was summoned to meet at Oxford, Louis offered Charles two million crowns to dissolve it, thus ensuring York's succession; the King's further independence was to be guaranteed by an annual allowance of half a million crowns. No one but the French ambassador was privy to this deal, and so Bruce came to attend his master at Christ Church in low spirits. The Country Party's organization had been so widespread that their victory seemed inevitable. As he went out for a ride he met

Monmouth, arriving at the head of a thousand troops, and was greeted affectionately by the Protestant hero, to the disgust of his followers. On March 28th Bruce entered the Geometry School, where Charles was sitting crowned and robed. He caught his young friend's eye and smiled. 'I never saw him', says Bruce, 'with such a cheerful countenance.'

Charles might well look cheerful. Secure in the knowledge of financial support, he had already rejected Shaftesbury's proposal that Monmouth should be made his successor, on the grounds that it would be contrary to law and justice. 'If you are restrained only by law and justice,' said the great Achitophel, 'rely on us, and leave us to act,' adding that the necessary laws would be made and passed by his party. 'My lord,' replied the recipient of French Catholic bounty, 'let there be no self-delusion. I will not yield. For what may remain of my life, I am determined that nothing shall tarnish my reputation. I have the Church on my side' — pointing to the Bishops' bench — 'and nothing shall part us.'

With the entry of the Commons and the Speaker, Bruce retired into a corner, and there heard the Serjeant-at-Arms call for silence. The King turned to the Lord Chancellor. 'Do your duty,' he said. The Chancellor rose and announced, 'It is His Majesty's royal pleasure and will that this Parliament should be dissolved.'

After joyously observing the 'dreadful faces and loud sighs' of the defeated members, Bruce went to help the King disrobe. 'With a most pleasing and cheerful countenance,' Charles clapped him on the shoulder and said, 'I am now a better man than you were a quarter of an hour since; you had better have one King than five hundred.' He and Bruce then left for Windsor, and in the course of the next few months Charles confided his plans to the disciple who acclaimed him as a political genius. 'I will have no more Parliaments,' he said, 'unless it be for some necessary Acts that are temporary only, for, God be praised, my affairs are in so good a posture that I have no occasion to ask for supplies.' (He did not add that by threatening to summon that body of 'devils', he had screwed another million livres out of his long-suffering cousin.) He talked of paying his debts, and made mock of those courtiers who, to flatter him, spoke of his government as supreme and inviolable.

'Nonsense!' he said. 'A King of England that is not slave to five hundred kings is great enough,' adding, 'I will have all my subjects live under their own vine and fig-tree, but I will not have them give me the law. Give me my just prerogative, and I will never ask more.' This ingenious parade of toleration was rapturously greeted, not only by such dyed-in-the-wool Tories as Bruce, but by a number of persons who were imploring His Majesty to summon a Parliament. To a deputation from Berkshire he genially observed, 'I marvel that my neighbours should meddle with my business—but when we meet over a cup of ale at Windsor, I have no doubt we shall agree upon the matter'—and they retired, bewildered but submissive.

So Bruce, himself well supplied with vines and fig-trees, could reasonably describe the last years of his master's reign as a golden age, and record the elimination of such 'loose and buffooning persons' as Buckingham with approval, as he did Shaftesbury's downfall and Oates's removal from power. The Earl, tried for high treason, received a verdict of *Ignoramus* and escaped to Holland, where he died in 1683. Charles then ensured his personal dictatorship by depriving the boroughs of their charters; when they refused to give them up, a writ of *quo warranto* was issued and new charters enforced installing civic authorities approved by himself; so a Tory constitution masked an absolutism almost equal to that of Louis XIV. Meanwhile, Monmouth had pursued his own campaign for the leadership of the Country Party by semi-royal progresses in the West; and it was at this point that he and Bruce renewed their friendship on painful and embarrassing terms.

Bruce detested the Duke's politics and was pained by his ambitions; he loved him, nevertheless. Now he became aware that Monmouth, married at fourteen to a Scots heiress whom he had long deserted for a series of mistresses, was the lover of Henrietta Wentworth. Bruce was deeply distressed; although happily married and the father of two sons, he retained strong feelings for 'my poor Lady Henrietta'. He tried to reason with her and Monmouth, only to be told that they regarded themselves as man and wife, 'before God'—deplorable! Then he realized that the Duke was living with Henrietta, more or less openly and with her mother's connivance, at Toddington. 'I respect [the Lady Henrietta's] memory so,' he goes on, 'that I am sorry I cannot justify these unheard of steps, but on the contrary.' Yet with his disapproval, his old romantic passion seemed to revive, and he not only supported Monmouth in this relationship, but tried to protect

Henrietta from censure, in the *amour courtois* style of a hero in a novel.

Monmouth's penultimate disgrace came about with the imaginary Rye House Plot—that of planning to murder the King and York on their return from Newmarket—in 1683. The informers who revealed this scheme were almost certainly paid to say that Monmouth and his supporters were privy to it, which was not the case, although the Duke's party had planned a rising from the City to enforce the calling of Parliament. The incriminating evidence against Monmouth and his Council, which Charles knew to be partially false, enabled him to arrest and condemn the remaining leaders of the Country Party. For the sake of appearances Monmouth must be seized; so Charles sent for Bruce, who found him setting his watch by the sundial in the Privy Garden. 'Go forthwith', said the King, 'into Bedfordshire, to surprise and take into custody by my warrant, James, who is at Toddington.' Guessing his master's real wishes, Bruce replied, 'I am and shall be ever ready to obey Your Majesty's orders—but the house is surrounded by vast ponds, and there are many vaults by which the Duke might escape.' As the King's face lightened he went on, 'And if I raise a militia troop, he will hear of it,' upon which Charles, 'full of joy', said, 'Well, come to me again for further orders,' and dismissed him.

A few weeks later Lord Ailesbury and Bruce were hunting from Houghton and found the quarry in the park at Toddington. 'I was accidentally thrown out,' says Bruce, 'and in a lane beyond the park I saw a tall man in a country habit opening a gate for me. I … perceived it was the Duke of Monmouth, who … mingled with the crowd at the death of the stag.' In order to prevent Lord Ailesbury recognizing the Duke and thus, as Sheriff of the county, arresting him, he held his father 'in continual discourse' and was accused of being tipsy. Next day, Lady Philadelphia asked him and Lord Ailesbury to dinner, to show that she was alone; a neighbour then told Bruce that she had come upon Monmouth sitting by the fire in Henrietta's room while she was dressing. It was all very regrettable: but Bruce could not find it in his heart to blame Henrietta. 'Had she been brought up by a discreet and good mother, she would have made a perfect good wife.'

Six months later Monmouth was received and forgiven by his father and York, who thanked Bruce for his discretion in protecting

'that unfortunate great lord ... charming both as to his person
and engaging behaviour ... but of a most poor understanding as
to ... politics.' This was proved when Monmouth, having submitted several statements owning to his and his friends' share in the
plan of the City rising, realized, too late, that they had been used
to execute a number of persons whose lives Charles had promised
to spare; he asked the King to return this evidence, in order to
save those that remained. 'The King', says Bruce, 'was never
known to be in such a passion' when the Duke insisted. Charles
wanted to destroy all Monmouth's group, on the grounds that
they were involved in the Rye House Plot; Monmouth, by
refusing to give any more of them away, spoilt this plan. The King
returned the papers, telling his son to go to hell, and the Duke
joined Henrietta in Holland.

When appealed to on behalf of the condemned Whig leaders,
Charles replied, 'The law must take its course,' just as he had in
the case of Titus Oates's Catholic victims. So the heads fell, his
subsidy came in, and 'we breathed nothing but peace and happiness,' according to Bruce, who entered his last term of waiting in
the autumn of 1684. It seemed to him that the King, although
distressed at parting from Monmouth (whom he secretly financed
and planned to recall), was in excellent health and spirits. 'He was
free from Parliaments ... those yelping curs ... that so greatly
disturbed him, and the succession was settled.'

The yachting trips were the most enjoyable part of this time.
'He is young and lazy,' the King would say to his Page of the
Bedchamber as Bruce came aboard. 'Get him one of the best beds
under mine.' As they dropped down the river Bruce and his
companions would eat with Charles, laughing at his jokes and
stories; while they played cards he would sit and watch, himself
'all mirth and of the most pleasing conversation'. In such surroundings Bruce was able to forget one of the few duties which
troubled him — that of arresting those Dissenters who refused to
conform, with the result that many died in prison. Somehow, he
felt this to be wrong. 'Those that persecute find persecution sooner
or later, [it] is not agreeable to God, and is next to murder, and a
murderer never goes unpunished, either in this world or in the
world to come.' His Majesty was blameless, naturally; he merely
gave the orders and then let the law take its course.

There were other disadvantages during the periods of palace

duty. The two gentlemen-in-waiting slept in the King's bed-chamber; between their shared truckle-bed and his curtained four-poster lay the dogs, who made messes, littered, barked, snuffled and whined, sometimes jumping on top of Bruce and his companion; the smell was dreadful, the noise ceaseless. And Charles's clocks, some thirty-odd, were as ill disciplined as his pets, unsynchronized, striking the quarters throughout the night, while the Scotch coal, crashing in the grate, added to the din. Charles slept through it all, seldom even turning over. Bruce's health made rest impossible, and he was glad when morning came and the King called for him, 'before anybody came in, [when] we might entertain him ... at pleasure, and ask of him anything.' After dressing, he returned to stand behind Charles's chair while he was being shaved; then came the *lever*, then chapel, followed by a visit to the Queen and later a walk in the Park or the galleries; and always, this best of masters, God bless him, was 'so affable ... that he would pull off his hat to the meanest; gave great liberties,' although he could 'take on majesty' with terrifying suddenness. Once Bruce ventured to wonder at Charles's tolerance of those 'ancient persons ... of limited sense' whom he employed because they had served his father. 'Their blunders and bulls make me laugh as well as the good sayings of others,' the King replied. And his royal kindness — 'he was so gracious and great in his expres-sions ... he could send away a person ... pleased at receiving nothing ... talking to each according to their genius.'

In the last week of January 1685 the King, who had a sore heel, drove out instead of walking; that night, seeing Lord Ailesbury enter the Presence Chamber, he said with a smile, 'My lord, you make me blush whenever I see you, for whom I have done nothing in recompense for your constant adherence to me and mine — but your son is now near my person, and I will make it up to him, and he shall never quit me as long as I live.' This promise, so easily given, was as easily kept. He had six more days of life.

After supper, at which the King ate heartily, beginning with a couple of goose's eggs, he went as usual to the Duchess of Ports-mouth's apartments, where he sat talking to her and two former mistresses, while his courtiers played cards and a little French boy sang to them. When he got up to go Bruce, carrying a candle, preceded him to his bedchamber; at the threshold he handed the taper, a very large one, to Chiffinch, the senior page of the back

stairs. Although there was no draught, it went out, and they interchanged glances, Chiffinch shaking his head in what seemed to the
younger man superstitious alarm.

As soon as Charles had undressed he went to the privy and there
remained, talking and laughing with Bruce and Henry Killigrew.
Bruce then asked him for a commission in the Guards for a cousin.
'Trouble me not with trifles,' was the smiling answer. 'The Colonel
will be most glad to oblige you therein.' The King went on to
describe the palace he was building at Winchester. Turning to
Bruce, he said, 'My lord, I do not remember that I ever saw you
there.' 'I did not wish to intrude upon Your Majesty.' 'Godsfish!'
said Charles with a laugh. 'Modesty must sooner or later be
rewarded—and when 'tis otherwise, 'tis the fault of the sovereign,
and not of the subject. I will order John [an old comrade, the Earl
of Bath] to put you into waiting the first time I go thither, although
it be not your turn, so that I may show you the place I so delight
in. And', he added casually, 'I shall be so happy this week as to
have my house covered with lead.' On the following Saturday his
coffin was lined with that metal.

After some more talk the King climbed into bed, and Bruce
prepared for the usual uneasy night. He heard his master turn over
several times, but thought nothing of it. He did not accompany
Killigrew to the King's bedside in the morning, and went to dress,
returning to find the surgeons waiting to bandage his heel. 'How
did His Majesty sleep?' asked Howard, the gentleman on day
duty. 'He turned sometimes,' Bruce replied. 'Lord!' said Howard,
'that is an ill mark, and contrary to his custom,' adding that the
King had got up looking very pale and was now alone in his closet.
Bruce sent for Chiffinch and suggested that he should take in His
Majesty's dressing-gown—'for a more bitter morning I never felt.'

When the King came out to be greeted by Lord Craven with the
password for the day, he tried to speak, and failed. He then sat
down to be shaved and as he did so fell back into Bruce's arms.
One of the surgeons was still in the room, and Charles was bled,
while Bruce ran for the Duke of York. By the time they returned
the King had been put to bed and seemed more like himself. As
Bruce bent over him, he gripped his hand and whispered, 'I see
you love me dying as well as living. I found myself not well,' he
went on, 'and took some of my drops, and then walked about,
hoping to be better—coming down, my head turned round, I was

in danger of falling.' Here the physicians begged His Majesty not to talk, and Bruce withdrew.

So began the last, slow, strange scene of that extraordinary life. From the thronged, stifling bedchamber came the bulletins: His Majesty was very ill—much better—out of danger, ring the bells— an apoplexy—he could not last the night—had rallied—might even yet recover—spreading through ante-rooms and corridors and courtyards to the crowds outside the palace. With the rest, Bruce came and went, half dazed. Sometimes he held his master in his arms; on the fifth day he himself collapsed and had to leave, returning on Friday February 6th at ten in the morning, to find the King conscious and longing for death. The bishops encircling his bed had implored him to take the last sacraments, only to be told, 'Time enough—I thank you—time enough.'

Time enough: just time to break one last promise, that of his coronation oath. At eight o'clock that morning Charles had been received into the Catholic Church by Father Huddlestone (who had saved his life during his flight from Worcester, thirty-four years ago), York and the Earls of Bath and Feversham remaining in sole attendance.

With the departure of Huddlestone, some fifty courtiers, the bishops, four ducal bastards and Bruce were readmitted. They watched and waited while the King gave York his final directions and messages. Monmouth was not mentioned. Then he looked towards the window, and asked to be lifted up. Bruce supported him on one side, York on the other. The King raised his hand and pointed to the nearest press. 'That clock', he said, 'must be wound tomorrow.' Then he sank into a stupor. Two hours went by; he breathed more heavily; was bled again. 'Just at high water and full moon at noon,' says Bruce, 'he expired.'

As he relinquished his master's body Bruce broke down; between his sobs he asked to be allowed to watch over him till the embalmers came. He remained in the darkened room for many hours, trying, between the bursts of weeping, to accept his loss. It was hard: very hard. Only a few days since, His Majesty had never seemed so well or so gay. 'His heart was set to live at ease, that his subjects might live under their own vine and fig-tree; but the good God thought us not worthy of these blessings ... '

All joy, all hope, were gone. Thinking of his wife and boys, Bruce had a moment's thankfulness. Then he remembered that he now had another master. The contrast between the wonderful being whose voice he would never hear again, and his successor, to whom 'I bore, according to my duty, all respect,' broke him down afresh. 'Thus ended my happy days at a Court, and to this hour I bewail my loss, and that of the three kingdoms. God's will be done, in earth, as in Heaven!'

It was over, everything he had lived for. One poor comfort remained in the bitter years that followed—the manner of His Majesty's death—and to that Bruce returned, in humble gratitude. 'My good and gracious King and master, Charles the Second, the best that ever reigned over us, died in peace and glory—and the Lord God have mercy on his soul.'

So at the age of twenty-nine, Thomas Bruce resigned himself to sorrow. For eight years he had been the most honoured, the most devoted of confidants in a thrilling drama. He was now to become one of the principals in an ironic farce.

I I

James II was fifty-two when he succeeded and, although physically vigorous, had the outlook and mental ability of an old and ignorant man. He can now be seen as totally unsuited to his position, and therefore pitiable. The brilliantly villainous image created by the genius of Macaulay—that combination of Iago and Richard III—has faded into a dimmer and less interesting figure. James had always been stupid; now his stupidity, enhanced by arrogance and self-will, was geared to an obsessive energy, which drove him to liquidate all the assets accumulated by his brother, so that within less than three years he was politically bankrupt.

Bruce's account of James's behaviour bears out his self-destructive qualities while explaining the persistent and widespread Jacobite feeling which survived him by nearly a century. Unwittingly, Bruce makes it clear that James was charmless and dreary; yet he himself thought him 'a most good and worthy Prince ... that had all moral virtues ... He was the most honest and sincere man I ever knew.' And Bishop Burnet, James's adversary, detested by Bruce, says, 'If it had not been for his popery, he would have been if not a great, yet a good prince.'

In fact, James's actions during his brief reign show him as a bigot, a muddler, a liar, a lecher and a coward. He was always a kind father, and during his last years he became a good husband — and also a bore. Yet he called forth loyalty and devotion from persons much more experienced and cynical than Bruce, who was aware of his faults, but not of the range and depth of his deceit. He considered James unwise, limited and 'snappish', and deplored the amorousness he describes as being 'more out of a natural temper than for the genteel part of making love'. This lack of fastidiousness was atoned for, he adds, by the King's 'hearty penitence' during his final exile.

When James publicly announced his intention of supporting the Church of England, 'as by law established', and encouraging religious toleration, it did not occur to the majority that his ultimate purpose was the reconciliation of his subjects to the old faith; and indeed, it is possible that in the long-awaited triumph of his accession, he may have meant what he said. The attempted enforcement of his Declarations of Indulgence has been quoted as proof of an enlightenment which placed him in advance of his age, while alarming many of his contemporaries and destroying their belief in his integrity. Bruce was one of those who continued to believe in the King's good intentions.

His appointment having lapsed with Charles II's death, Bruce was somewhat taken aback when James sent for him and asked him to form a group of influential persons who would support his demand for increased revenues for life when the new, and strongly Tory, Parliament assembled in May 1685. Bruce did this successfully, but received no reward and no renewal of his appointment. His desire to serve was not affected, and he began to work out further plans for increasing the subsidies desired by James.

Before Parliament met, the King sent for him again. Bruce's account of this interview shows James as practical and patriotic; also, his abrupt, intensely serious manner concealed the vacillations which underlay his apparent resolve. 'I will not have one farthing laid on land,' he began. 'That is the last resource, if God Almighty should afflict us with a war. Lay it on luxury, as chocolate, tea, coffee — and' — with warmth — 'on wine — who obliges people to make themselves drunk? But if they will drink, let them pay for it.'

Bruce then suggested that a tax should be laid on all private buildings put up since the Restoration, and the King gave his approval. When Bruce put forward this plan in the House, those who had spent vast sums on palatial residences were enraged, and one, Sir Thomas Clarges, complained to the King's brother-in-law, Lord Clarendon. James censured Bruce, and his proposal was rejected. Exclaiming 'This is too much!' as he left the Presence Chamber, Bruce retired to Houghton, where he remained until June, when news came of the Duke of Monmouth's having landed at Lyme Regis and thereafter being proclaimed king at Taunton.

The greater number of landowners then offered to raise and lead troops against the rebels, and the Houses were desired to pass a Bill of Attainder against the Duke. Bruce's behaviour was anomalous, and typical of his future actions. 'I stepped out of the House so that another might carry up the Bill,' he says. 'I abhorred the Duke's presumption as much as anyone, but I was glad that another carried it up, I loving the Duke as much as my King's natural son, but not as my own king and sovereign.' He was then given a troop and a commission, but not called upon to serve, much to his relief. While he waited for news from the West his elder son, Robert, became very ill, and he retired again to Houghton. When he heard that Monmouth's army had been defeated and himself taken prisoner, Bruce returned to wait on the King: but he could not bring himself to kiss his hand in congratulation. 'I, coming to the city by water, unfortunately landed at the same moment and saw [the Duke] led up the stairs ... lean, pale, and with a disconsolate physiognomy ... The Yeomen of the Guard were posted, and I got behind one of them that he should not perceive me, and I wished often and heartily since that I had not seen him, for I could never get him out of my mind for years, I so loved him personally.' Two days later young Robert died, and Bruce's 'unfortunate friend ... the finest nobleman eyes ever saw as to his exterior,' was beheaded on Tower Hill. Henrietta Wentworth then returned to England; in horror and pity, Bruce perceived that at twenty-eight her appearance was that of an old woman. A few months later she died of lead poisoning as the result of painting her face, and was buried at Toddington. Bruce mourned in secret 'my poor Lady Henrietta', whom her lover had called 'his wife before God to the last', to the disgust of the bishops who accompanied him to the scaffold.

Then followed the Bloody Assize, approvingly described by James as Judge Jeffreys's 'campaign in the West', and supported by him to the utmost measure of cruelty. Bruce blamed Jeffreys — 'a man of great and fiery passion' — and believed the King when he said, 'I abhorred what passed in that Commission.' It did not occur to him, any more than it did to the majority of his contemporaries, that James might have deliberately lied about such a matter. The hideous tortures inflicted on the rebels by Colonel Percy Kirke were done, he concluded, 'To render the King odious in the eyes of his subjects.' Bruce was in attendance when Kirke, returning to report on his activities, was proselytized by his master. 'Kirke,' said the King, 'you do not much mind religion, and why cannot you be of mine, as well as of another?' 'Sir,' replied that officer, 'I am very sorry for to be pre-engaged.' 'To whom?' 'When I had the honour to command at Tangier as Governor, I promised the King of Morocco that if ever I changed my religion, I would become a Mahometan.' Bruce was shocked. He did not consider the King's approach as a sign of what was to come, for once more family troubles occupied all his thoughts, recalling him to Houghton to attend his father's death-bed.

As he leant over him to ask if there was nothing more he could do, Lord Ailesbury took his hand. 'I thank you,' he said. 'Dear son, you will see melancholy days; God be thanked, I shall not.' Twelve hours later 'the best subject, patriot, husband, father and master that ever lived' was no more, and Bruce, now second Earl of Ailesbury and third of Elgin, succeeded him as Sheriff of Bedford, Huntingdon and Cambridge; summoned to Whitehall, he once more became Gentleman of the Bedchamber. Then, gradually, he became aware of the 'wrong measures' taken by the King, which were to lead to the utter ruin of himself and of all his schemes.

The rout of Sedgemoor had put James in a very strong position. In the months which succeeded the Bloody Assize, Tory ascendancy was strengthened, and with it his conviction that his first steps towards re-establishing Catholicism would not be criticized, far less resisted. And as England's financial dependence on the bounty of Louis XIV was enhanced by that monarch's belief—fully justified—that James, unlike his slippery brother, could be trusted to keep his word, so Barillon was instructed to increase his allowance and to promise further subsidies with the progress of his

Catholic campaign: a promise greeted by James with tearful gratitude.

While continuing to promote religious toleration for Dissenters and Roman Catholics, James deliberately contravened the Test Act—which obliged all those in official positions to deny the doctrine of transubstantiation—by placing a number of Papists in authority, specifically in the standing army, now, as a result of the Monmouth Rebellion, a larger and better equipped force than in the previous reign. He then turned from the influence of Clarendon and his other brother-in-law, Lord Rochester, to that of two persons detested by all loyal subjects: Lord Sunderland and Father Petre. Sunderland was brilliant, unscrupulous, and self-seeking to the point of monomania; he knew how to twist his master and proceeded to do so, thereby vastly enriching himself. Later on the new Earl of Ailesbury considered that Sunderland 'had nothing in view but the King's ruin ... pen cannot describe of him worse than he deserved'; while Petre, bursting with conceit and even more besotted than James, was, 'as to state affairs, a perfect novice'.

After the next meeting of Parliament an official deputation, headed by Ailesbury bearing the sword of state, waited on James to ask him to inform and discuss with them any further defiance of the Test Act. As some eighty Catholics had been given commissions in the forces, this request was not only reasonable but subservient. The King told them sharply that he was not, and would never be, answerable to Parliament in any way. The Lords left the Presence Chamber in deep depression; some shed tears; Ailesbury was so miserable that he could only just hold up the heavy sword. He then went to visit a Catholic friend, the aged Earl of Bellasyse, who had been imprisoned in the reign of terror caused by the Popish Plot; that nobleman exclaimed, 'My dear Lord, who could be the framer of this speech? I date my ruin and that of all my persuasion from this day!'

A more influential Catholic than Bellasyse was also appalled by the crude tactlessness of James's actions. Pope Innocent XI instructed his envoy to beg His Majesty to behave with greater caution and to adopt the *suaviter in modo* tactics which alone might bring his subjects back into the fold—and was ignored. Meanwhile the Queen, a foolish, unhappy and vain young woman, who, after thirteen years in England, was as out of touch with national feeling as if she had just arrived from Italy, tried to convert Ailesbury in the same blatant fashion. If he became a Catholic, she said, 'I and the King will stop at nothing that will be for your interest.' Detesting bigotry, of whatever denomination, Ailesbury respectfully replied that he preferred to remain in the faith in which he had been baptized. This angered James and put Ailesbury out of favour with the Queen. Sadly, he began to recognize the truth of his father's forebodings. Melancholy days were dawning upon England; he had no notion of how dark and perilous his own were to become.

In October 1685 Louis XIV revoked his grandfather's Edict of Toleration for Huguenots, and his persecution of that body sent a flood of refugees into England; their reports of the *dragonnades* increased the national horror of popery, with the result that further protests were made about James's employment of Catholic officers. With a view, presumably, to reassuring his subjects, he subscribed £500 to the relief fund for the Huguenots, at the same time writing to congratulate Louis on the success of his crusade. A month later, when the Houses objected to his abrogation of the Test Act, he prorogued Parliament, continuing to replace Protestants by Catholics in various posts. His substitution of the Catholic Tyrconnel ('lying Dick Talbot') for Clarendon as Lord Deputy of Ireland horrified Ailesbury, who, although he and Talbot were friends, thought him 'of all men the most improper to be thus dignified'. He said nothing of his disapproval until James asked him what the general feeling was as to these and other such measures. 'I beg Your Majesty's pardon,' Thomas replied, 'but when I take the liberty to tell you the truth, you seem to be in some passion. None are so blind as those that will not see. I am a good subject, but no flatterer.' James took this plain speaking impassively, and desired him to proceed. After some discussion, Ailesbury's advice was ignored and Tyrconnel's appointment confirmed.

In the following year James set up his famous Ecclesiastical Commission, which enforced his jurisdiction over the universities and the clergy. This right was in a sense legal, but had hitherto been used with tact by the sovereign and was, according to the tenets of James's faith, an outrageous example of heresy, as he should not have claimed royal supremacy. He exercised it arbitrarily and unjustly, thus challenging the Church he had sworn —

heretically—to defend.* He then called a Cabinet Council of which Ailesbury was one, and ordered all the Lords Lieutenant to ask their Deputies and Justices of the Peace (a) whether they would vote for the repeal of the Test Act; (b) if they would support those who did; and (c) if they would promise 'to live neighbourly and friendly with those of a contrary opinion ... in religion.'

This interference with personal principles distressed Ailesbury; he sent for the Deputies and Justices in his district and told them to act according to their consciences. None agreed to the first and second questions and all but one agreed to the third. His report on these answers was censured by Sunderland, upon which he refused to discuss the matter with anyone but the King, and left the meeting. In James's name Sunderland then desired him to dismiss his subordinates and submit a fresh list of officials. Ailesbury obeyed the first order; his new list contained the names of all those dismissed. He expected to be deprived of his position, but was retained, 'full weary' of these ordeals, returning to Court in March 1687 to hear of the death of the President of Magdalen College, Oxford.

By this time Parliament was dissolved, the papal Nuncio had been publicly received, houses of Franciscan and Benedictine monks were established in London and a Catholic press was issuing propagandist literature. In December of this year a more vital question arose: that of the Queen's latest pregnancy. If her child was a boy and survived, the succession of the Princess Mary of Orange would be superseded by that of a Catholic sovereign and, in the event of James's death before his majority, by the regency of a Catholic Queen even more fanatical and doltish than himself.

Ailesbury's heart sank when James began to discuss the appointment of the next President of Magdalen. 'The late Dr Clarke', said the King, 'was an honest man—but I have named one to succeed him that will repair that loss.' As this Catholic nominee, Mr Farmer, had been dismissed from Cambridge for drunkenness and debauchery, the Fellows rejected him. A few months later a Catholic convert, Mr Charnock, known to Ailesbury as being 'of a dark temper', was made Vice-President. By now the Fellows, having refused to accept James's jurisdiction, had been turned out

* Also, this Commission contradicted the Statute of 1661 which forbade royal visitatorial powers.

and replaced by Catholics; the new President was Giffard, formerly Bishop of Madaura. Magdalen had become a papist seminary.

Yet James was within his rights. When they heard the full story of the results of these efforts, the Cardinals at the Vatican were at first incredulous and then amused: how could such a person be taken seriously? It became a joke amongst them that he ought to have been excommunicated for losing the Catholic cause in England. Several eminent historians have suggested that he had become senile. With the greatest respect, it is submitted that this was not the case. Ailesbury's account of the King's conversation and behaviour before his final exile shows him as he had been for the last decade: old for his age, crassly complacent and blockheaded, but perfectly able to take in and then reject any advice which did not suit him. His comments were sometimes apt; he had, on occasion, a certain grim humour; his bearing and appearance were generally impressive; and he could be extremely alarming.

He was now less under the influence of his latest mistress, Catherine Sedley, whom he had made Countess of Dorchester, than under that of the Queen; for Mary of Modena's violent temper—she boxed Lady Peterborough's ears during a religious discussion, and threw a hairbrush at the Princess Anne when she made a tactless remark at a *lever*—had begun to dominate him. Ailesbury, unaware of this change of attitude, and fearing the worst from the 'melancholy and fatal transaction' of Magdalen College, asked for a private audience, and implored His Majesty not to proceed, adding that his advisers were to blame. 'Believe me, Sir, on my honour and conscience, you are grossly imposed upon.' When James replied that his mind was made up, Ailesbury pursued, 'Sir, if you *will* have a Romish college foundation, though it be against the laws, rather than take the bread out of the mouths of the others in possession, I will lay a thousand pounds at your feet, for to contribute.'

This extraordinary offer, which Charles II would have greeted with peals of laughter, seems to have been made in the manner of one trying to distract a passionate child with a new toy. It was solemnly (and not very gratefully) refused by James, who in the summer of 1688 issued his second Declaration of Indulgence, commanding the bishops to read it in all the churches; in fact, they were ordered to contravene the laws of the realm by pronouncing the Test Act null and void. When seven refused, James committed them to the Tower for seditious libel. Their trial and acquittal was preceded by the birth of the Prince of Wales, to be followed, a little later, by the circulation of the warming-pan story. This enraged Ailesbury. 'None but knaves,' he says, 'invented that calumny, and fools ... came into that vile and ridiculous belief.' As its acceptance by the common people increased, James summoned some thirty witnesses, of whom Ailesbury was one, to give evidence of the birth. This, Thomas thought, 'was below the King, and it signified little, for all persons of honour and conscience ... firmly believed the reality.'

Although Ailesbury knew that William was assembling his forces in order to establish the Princess Mary's claim against that of the infant later known as the Old Pretender, he thought, as most people did, that this venture had little chance of success. Nevertheless, he now decided to resign his post, partly for reasons of health, and partly because he felt unable to serve a master who had placed himself in an impossible position. 'If you give up,' Lord Dartmouth told him, 'I fear many more will do the same. For the love of God, lay aside your rash design.' Ailesbury stuck to his resolve, and was admitted to the King's private closet. James thanked him for his 'constant attachment'. Then he said—and it was almost as if his brother were speaking—'I will let you into a secret that I have not communicated to my Cabinet and Council, under oath of secrecy.' This obtained, he went on, 'According to all the advices I have received from the Hague and from Paris, these great armaments from Holland for sea and land are certainly designed against me. I am well assured that you will stand by me.'

Thanking God that he had not resigned his position, Ailesbury fell on his knees. 'I assure Your Majesty of the last drop of my blood and of that of my brothers,' he exclaimed. 'I will obey your orders—I will make no step until I know your pleasure'—and repeated his promise of secrecy on a matter already known to the Cabinet and to more than half his fellow-members in the Upper House.

A few weeks later, having obtained his commission in the cavalry, Ailesbury prepared to accompany the King and his staff to Salisbury Plain. By this time William of Orange, having accepted the invitation of 'the Immortal Seven'—Shrewsbury, Devonshire, Danby, Bishop Compton, Edward Russell, Lumley and Henry Sidney—had embarked and was on his way. He landed at Brixham on November 5th, 1688.

It was fortunate, Ailesbury thought, that James's appeal was made before he had given in his resignation; for if he had retired to Houghton, he would have been accused of sitting on the fence, or even of treachery. In the weeks preceding William's arrival he was approached by a number of persons in high places suggesting that he should abandon his master, to whom he replied, 'I cannot change kings as one doth a suit of clothes.' He was worried about leaving his wife, now seven months pregnant, for what he thought would be a dangerous campaign—and then surprised to find her taking his departure quite calmly; for as a rule she could not bear him out of her sight when she was ailing. Later on, she told him that her half-sister, the Duchess of Ormonde, seeing her distress, had got leave from the Duke to reassure her. Ormonde was committed to William: and he believed that 'there would not be a blow struck' in James's defence. Sunderland was now in Holland; Clarendon, Rochester, Charles II's eldest bastard, the Duke of Grafton, and Churchill (recently ennobled by James and at the outset of his dazzling career) had decided to desert as soon as the opportunity arose.

Ailesbury was then ordered by James to restore the dismissed Deputy-Lieutenants and Justices in his district. (This was one of a number of the King's useless, last-minute concessions.) He returned to London to find James refusing to admit the possibility of being betrayed, not only by his ministers and the army, but also by the navy. The news of William's landing was followed by a report that no one had joined him and that he was about to return to Holland. On November 17th Ailesbury followed the King to Salisbury to find him much weakened by nose-bleeding, and inactive. A few days later he returned with him to London to hear that the Princess Anne, with Sarah Churchill, had left for Nottingham. By this time, her husband, Prince George of Denmark, with Grafton and Churchill, had joined William. James then made arrangements for the flight of his wife and son to France, intending to follow them before William entered London.

Yet even now an appeal to the people and to those of his officers who remained faithful would almost certainly have been effective. His army was more than double the size of William's, and his subjects, dreading a prolonged civil war and willing to believe in his promises to call a Parliament and dissolve his Ecclesiastical Commission, might have rallied to him if he had marched to do battle with his son-in-law. Nothing that Ailesbury or others of his calibre could urge had any weight. James was determined to fly, while giving out that he would remain.

When Ailesbury heard that a large body of cavalry under reliable officers was ready to march with the King, and that the ranks of the infantry were loyal, he decided to make a last appeal. He knelt and, with tears, humbly besought His Majesty 'not to think of going'. 'That is a coffee-house report,' James replied, 'and why can you imagine it?' 'For the love of God, Sir,' Thomas exclaimed, 'why will you hide it from me, that knows your horses are now actually at Lambeth?' and proceeded to give all the details of his plans. James, although considerably taken aback, still persisted in his denials. Then he said, 'If I should go, who can wonder after the treatment I have found?' going on to bewail his daughter's flight and the treachery of Sunderland, 'on whom I heaped all favours. If such betrays me,' he added, 'what can I expect? I know not who to speak to or who to trust.' Ailesbury told him of the forces on whom he could count, 'to the last drop of their blood.' 'To what purpose?' demanded James. 'The Princess your daughter, Sir, is at Nottingham, the concourse there seems great, but of what do they consist on?' said Thomas, and implored him to march to that city, or else to York, where he would find only the Earl of Danby, 'with his broomsticks and whish-tail militia and some raw bubbles he has drawn in.' As James took no notice, Ailesbury begged him to stay until his messengers returned from interviewing William, who was now at Hungerford. 'I will speak to you in the morning,' was all the King would say, and Ailesbury, knowing that this was a lie, retired.

While James, disguised, made his way to the coast, Ailesbury and his companions formed an unofficial Regency Council, and under their aegis the city became quieter. At Faversham James was stopped and manhandled by a party of fishermen, who took him for a Jesuit. He was finally sheltered at Lord Winchelsea's house, where Ailesbury, after a journey through panic-stricken and furious crowds, found him 'sitting in a great chair, his hat on and his beard being much grown, and resembled the picture of his royal father.' James said angrily, 'You were all kings when I left London.' Thomas did not attempt to conceal his resentment. 'Sir!'

he exclaimed, 'I expected another sort of welcome from you, after the great dangers I ran last night.' 'I know you meant well,' said the King. 'It is certainly so,' Ailesbury pursued, 'and give me leave to tell Your Majesty that your going away without leaving a Commission of Regency, but for our care and vigilance the City of London might have been in ashes.' The King made some sort of an excuse, and they went in to dinner, where Ailesbury served him on the knee. After the King had changed his shirt, which was full of lice, and shaved, he cheered up, made a few mild jokes and eventually agreed to return to London, where he was rapturously acclaimed. The Prince of Orange, who had now reached Syon, suggested that he should retire to Ham House, while the Dutch guards took over Whitehall, Somerset House and St James's. The King replied that he would prefer to go to Rochester, and William, realizing that he would thence leave for France, agreed; only so could he be sure of a bloodless and peaceful entry into London. When James said to Ailesbury, 'I am sure you will not quit me,' the young man replied, 'Sir, I will die first,' and broke down. They then entered the royal barge and proceeded to Gravesend. Just before his departure James received a letter from William's Council, signed by a number of his former ministers, warning him that he would not be safe if he stayed in England. Even at this point, an advance on London might have restored him; but the fishermen's attack had broken his nerve, and his wife had implored him to follow her.

At eleven o'clock on the evening of December 21st James sent for Ailesbury and began, 'You have on all occasions and in the worst of times stuck so firmly by me, that on my part I ought to study your security as well as my own, and therefore you shall not this night lie in my bed-chamber, but I will direct my Lord Dumbarton to supply your place, for I will not think of your attending me. He hath nothing to lose, and he is to follow me.' He then desired Ailesbury to report his departure to the Prince of Orange, told him about the warning letter, and went on, 'If I do not retire, I shall certainly be sent to the Tower, and no King ever went out of that place but to his grave. It is a cruel thing for a subject to be driven out of his native country, much more for a King.' After some further explanation, he concluded, 'Can you advise me to stay?' 'Sir,' said Ailesbury, 'this is a matter of the most nice nature, that I will not take on me to give you any advice, nor be so presumptuous.' James held out his hand, and the young man kissed it, weeping.

The King then summoned his gentlemen; they undressed him, and he got into bed. As they retired he told Ailesbury to remain, and embraced him. Nothing more was said, and Thomas went to his own room. Lying awake, he heard no sound; at last he fell asleep. He was woken at dawn to hear that His Majesty had gone. He then returned to London to interview William.

He told himself and always maintained that James was not to blame; he was 'a good and gracious king; and had he been less devout, it had been better for us, and, I may add, had he not been too credulous.' Petre and Sunderland—the fool and the knave— were responsible. Those two villains had 'walked him out of three kingdoms'.

THREE

I

FROM December 11th, 1688, to February 12th, 1689, there was no King in England. During that time Ailesbury continued to work for James's cause, but with divided feelings; for his reception by the Prince of Orange showed him that James's supplanter was superior in every way to the uncle and father-in-law who had fled before him.

Ailesbury had heard of William as a scheming, false, hard-hearted climber, who was preparing to seize the English crown in much the same way as Henry IV took it from Richard II. Also, it was common knowledge that the Prince had a Dutch heart, no use for his Stuart relatives, despised the English courtiers, and seldom troubled to conceal his contempt for them. But when Thomas, within a few hours of parting from a master who had shown, if belatedly, concern for his safety and gratitude for his services, found himself talking to that master's enemy, he was agreeably surprised. William received him with quiet courtesy and invited him to dinner. As Ailesbury was highest in rank that day, the two men sat together and got on very well. The Prince, usually so taciturn, 'entertained me the most part of the time with discourse ... insomuch that a spectator ... came ... with the news that no doubt I should be a great man at that Court.' As Ailesbury left St James's he was approached by the Clerk of the Kitchen, who asked him to speak to the Prince in his favour. 'Sir,' said the young man, smiling, 'if you design to succeed in your pretensions, do not employ *me*,' and passed on. Some time afterwards he realized that William, as brilliant a ruler in his own way as his uncle Charles, knew that the majority of his ministers were for sale. What he had heard of Ailesbury convinced him that he could not be corrupted; at this moment he had no fear of his Jacobitism, for he could rely on James to let fall any weapon, whether supplied by English loyalists or French politicians.

So it was that Ailesbury spoke openly in favour of King James.

During a debate in the Lords it was maintained that he had abdicated, and that therefore the throne was vacant—and elective. Although enraged by this 'revolution doctrine', Ailesbury, knowing himself no speaker, was silent, until the Earl of Chesterfield said, 'The King hath neither abdicated nor deserted. I have been convinced to the contrary by a noble Lord of this House.' 'Name him!' came the cry, upon which Chesterfield blushed and hesitated. Thomas, resolved to behave 'like a gentleman and a man of honour', stood up and called out, 'Name me, my Lord!' Desired to proceed, he then repeated the gist of his last talks with James; His Majesty had been driven out by threats against his life; his abdication was therefore not in question. 'I had this', he wound up, 'from the mouth of a prince endowed with all kingly virtues, and you must therefore give me leave, my lords, to enter my dissent, in case the vote be carried against us.' (It was.) During a later debate Ailesbury declared, with stubborn boldness, that the Prince of Orange had not, as he gave out, come over to protect the Protestant faith, 'but for to set the crown on his own head.' William of all men must have appreciated the outspokenness despised by such as Danby, who asked Ailesbury how he had dared advise James to march on York, adding, 'Was the devil in you, and what did you mean by it?' 'To knock you on the head, in the first place, if you had resisted,' Thomas replied. 'Your most humble servant and good friend and kinsman is much obliged to you,' said Danby. 'I sucked in with my milk a principle I can never swerve from,' Ailesbury went on, 'to stand by my King with my life and fortune. Pray, my lord, what course would you have taken, had we marched to York?' 'What course?' exclaimed the minister, exasperated by such a silly question. 'To submit ourselves, and to crave his pardon.'

On February 15th William and Mary were proclaimed joint sovereigns, upon which Ailesbury gave in his resignation as Lord Lieutenant. He then took the oath of loyalty to the new King and Queen, but refused to attend their coronation. This seemingly inconsistent attitude was the result of what he thought of as very simple reasoning. The Prince and Princess of Orange had become monarchs by Act of Parliament and therefore protectors of the realm and of the Protestant religion; as such, they must be obeyed. This oath in no way cancelled that taken by Ailesbury to King James in the House of Lords, where 'I answered only to

God Almighty for my actions', for James was King of England by the grace of God, and not by election. It therefore followed that the coronation of William and Mary was not sacramental. In fact, as there could not be two grace-of-God kings, the anointment of James's daughter and son-in-law was not only meaningless but blasphemous, and Ailesbury would have nothing to do with it. He then informed William that he should continue to uphold James's rights in the Lords, and would accept no position during the exile of that King, or of the Prince of Wales.

The non-juring Earls, who had to pay double taxes, seem to have hinted that Ailesbury had taken the oath in order to avoid this heavy fine, to which he replied, 'I should have lost nothing by so paying, for I would have reduced my yearly expenses.' He had thought of retiring to France, for reasons of health and economy; now he decided to remain in England in order to further James's restoration. His career at Court having ended, he was much impoverished, so he retired to the country with his wife and their son and daughter.

Shortly after the coronation Ailesbury renewed his rather uneasy acquaintance with the Countess of Dorchester who, while appearing at Court, had proclaimed herself a Jacobite and behaved with great insolence to Queen Mary. She asked him to spend Sunday at her house in Weybridge, presumably in order to involve him in one of the many plots against William. On the way there he called at Hampton Court Palace, where he was coldly received by the King; he was then told by some official (who may have wished to effect his outward adherence to the sovereign) that he must carry the sword of state before Their Majesties into chapel, 'which I did with all respect and decency.' As the service was followed by Communion, he did not get to Weybridge till two o'clock, when he found Catherine Dorchester in a rage, having waited dinner for him since twelve. She greeted his explanation with, 'Did you not wish the sword in his body?' This attack infuriated Ailesbury, who 'sharply reprehended' the lady. 'In Parliament,' he added, 'I have done all that lies in my power to keep him from the crown, but now I must submit. Besides, as a Christian, and having the fear of God before my eyes, I hold [murder] a most damnable sin even to hope it, much more the putting of it into execution.' Catherine, equally enraged, then began a private feud with him; but of this he was not immediately aware.

A few weeks later William declared war on France, and James, having raised an army in Ireland, was defeated at the Battle of the Boyne in the summer of 1690. This, and the rout of the Jacobites in Scotland, put an end to all his hopes. Ailesbury would not accept the situation, and continued to work for him openly and unmolested till the Anglo-Dutch fleet lost the Battle of Beachy Head to the French. As invasion now seemed imminent, warrants were sent out for the arrest of a number of Jacobites, of whom he was one.

Warned by a friend in the Council, he made his plans. He believed that if he were arrested and sent to the Tower, his attainder and execution would follow (in the two previous reigns this would certainly have been the case), while at best he could only hope for a long imprisonment; this would result in his death from the disease which tormented him till middle life. So he decided to avoid capture until he got in touch with Danby, now President of the Council. He disguised himself with 'a brown periwig, eyebrows black and a Church habit,' and took lodgings in Berkeley Street, where he wrote to Danby, saying that he would give himself up on bail, and that he was hiding to avoid being sent to the Tower.

While he waited for an answer, a message came from the exiled Court at St-Germain that no invasion had been planned. Through his wife Ailesbury sent this news to the Queen (William being in Ireland), and received a reassuring answer. He then went to report to Lord Nottingham, Mary's Secretary of State. They argued, amicably enough, about politics for some time. Then Nottingham said, 'My Lord, I must send you to the Tower.' 'I came out on the public faith,' Ailesbury protested, 'and the Queen hath declared that I should be treated with all distinction—what can be worse than going to the Tower?' Eventually he was allowed bail, and through Elizabeth and Lady Derby sent a message of thanks to Queen Mary. 'Tell my lady of Ailesbury,' Her Majesty replied, 'that I love to do good to all persons as far as I can, but more especially to her husband and his family, whom I knew so well in my youngest years,' adding that she would receive him at four o'clock that afternoon.

Ailesbury found the Queen at cards with Lady Derby and two other courtiers, all old acquaintances. Mary acknowledged his bow and played on for a little while; then, smiling, she turned and

said, 'My Lord, do you play at Basset?' 'I used to play, Madam—
but prisoners are poor,' Thomas replied. The Queen said, 'Your
old friends'—indicating the gentleman that kept the bank—'have
money at your service,' and he sat down. She then engaged him
in talk about his family in such a way as to fascinate him.
Although unhappy, anxious and over-worked, Mary was still very
beautiful; and her gay, gentle manners were entrancing. Ailesbury
observed the amazement of the spectators with great glee; two
days earlier he had been wanted for high treason, and now—!
'I shall have sufficient matter', he recalled, 'to continue the praises
of that incomparable Queen, for her great judgment, as well as for
her compassion.'

A few months later, after a chance meeting with William,
Ailesbury realized that he was cleared of all suspicion, but, 'this
sunshine also lasted not long ... He became cold and dry, I then
retired.' He now began to assess the efforts of the Jacobites, and
decided that their 'hot heads, empty purses ... and disunion in
thoughts' were fatal to their cause. Any underground movement
was bound to fail; open invasion must be tried. In the summer of
1691 this attempt failed, and once more he fell under suspicion;
but Queen Mary refused to sign the warrant for his arrest.

By the spring of 1693 Ailesbury had come to the conclusion that
William's wars and his system of taxation were bringing ruin upon
England. King James must be restored, and this could only be
effected by the navy. He therefore got into touch with Admiral
Killigrew, Sir Ralph Delaval and Sir Cloudesley Shovel, and a
plan was evolved, which he was to put before James. After a prolonged and adventurous journey, in which he several times risked
his life, he came secretly to St-Germain in order to confer with the
King and Queen he had not seen for five years.

As Ailesbury left his curtained sedan chair for Mary of Modena's
closet, the fact that he was breaking his oath to the reigning
sovereigns did not trouble him; his explanation was as simple as
his reasoning was confused. 'I own plainly', he says, 'that then ...
I did all I could ... to get ... my master reinstated ... by a revolution [i.e. as William had been installed in 1688], and not by fire
and sword.' Elsewhere he speaks of his horror of warfare as being
unChristian and pointless. He regarded his promise to William
and Mary as a 'garrison' oath—one taken to the person temporarily in command. He obeyed all the laws but that forbidding

his adherence to King James, which was God's law, and must precede man's. Politically, he was, of course, in a fine muddle. The Jacobites thought him double-faced and feeble; the ruling clique (nearly all of whom corresponded with James and assured him of their loyalty) regarded him as a traitor in the technical sense, and a nuisance rather than a danger. Every man's hand should have been against him; yet it was obvious to all who had to do with him that he was not only truthful and courageous, but extremely acute, and well worth consulting.

Ailesbury was now, although he did not know it, in James's black books; for he had advised him to dismiss his chief advisers, the Earls of Melfort and Middleton, as being responsible for his proclamations to the English people ordering them to refuse to pay taxes, while giving no assurance of the retention of the Test Act. James would not admit the folly of this procedure, and had much resented Ailesbury's writing to say that he would be restored in six weeks if Melfort were sent away. He therefore received him correctly ('in a most distinguished manner') but coldly, leaving the Queen to say, 'My lord, no person can be in more joy than I am in for to see you, but I tremble when I consider the danger you will run at your return.' As Thomas glanced at her in some distress—for she had left off painting her face, and was much aged—she added with a sigh, 'Afflictions alter people fast.' This, and her 'genteel' manner of expressing her gratitude, further endeared her to him.

They then discussed Middleton, Melfort and the proclamations. James would not move an inch—'a bitter pill to swallow,' Ailesbury felt, 'but down with it I must.' When James spoke of the English ministers' readiness to restore him, Thomas said, 'I must beg Your Majesty's pardon, but it is my humble opinion that your return is the furthest of their designs.' James was horrified. 'Why so?' he exclaimed. 'They never durst look Your Majesty in the face, being conscious of what they have done against you,' said Ailesbury, adding, 'Perhaps, Sir, they may have an eye on the Prince your son, who was but just born when they had played their pranks.'

That son, now in his sixth year, was sent for—'a lovely child,' Ailesbury noted, 'from the nose upward all of the Queen, and the lower part and the mouth resembling his uncle, my royal master.' When the Prince left the closet he was surrounded by his father's courtiers. Who was with Their Majesties—what did he look like? 'I did not know him,' said the little boy, 'but he must be some great person, because the King ordered me to kiss and embrace him. He is the tallest man I have ever seen,' he added. 'By God! it is Ailesbury, then,' said one gentleman, and the rest agreed.

Next day that nobleman was visited in his lodgings by Middleton, who asked him to read James's latest declaration, and required his advice. 'Advice, my lord?' said Thomas. 'It hath been printed in London a fortnight since, and I doubt not but that the printer is hanged by this time, or will be soon,' and handed it back. In his next talk with James, Ailesbury repeated this view, which 'a little stunned' his master. Ailesbury went on, 'Is Your Majesty ready to go over with a competent force to support it?' James, feeling himself baited, said angrily, 'Over? Over? You know the contrary.' 'Sir,' Ailesbury said, 'I never read in history of a declaration set forth and published until that Prince or King was ready to support it, either by a legitimate right, or a usurping one,' he added. This silenced James. 'Well, Sir,' Thomas continued, 'I see that what is done cannot be retrieved. Give me the original declaration, and I will carry it on board the Fleet, that so the Admirals may accept and declare for you. But I will not go without my Lord Middleton and he can assure the Admirals that he saw Your Majesty sign it.'

James took this suggestion, which terrified Middleton, fairly well, and arranged for Ailesbury to confer with Louis XIV about the invasion; it was to be financed and ordered by that monarch. Thomas guessed that Louis had wearied of his cousin's cause, and that he no longer desired his restoration; also that, having lost two-thirds of his ships at the battle of La Hogue in 1691, he had decided to attack William by land only. He admired Louis for his generous chivalry towards James and his wife and family (their daughter, Louisa Mary, was now a year old), and was much impressed by his clearsightedness and grasp of essentials.

Louis began by complimenting Ailesbury on his excellent French ('his smiles ... were most affable') and then said that he had no intention of risking what remained of his fleet in the English Channel. He suggested Torbay, as better for retreat in the event of failure. Ailesbury replied that this was not practicable, and went on, 'If Your Majesty designs to settle the King on his throne by fire and sword—which in good English would be termed a conquest—I cannot treat with Your Majesty. Although you are respected and termed a great King by men of honour, amongst the generality in England Your Majesty's name is not in good odour.' 'I see you are a plain speaker,' remarked Louis with a smile. 'There is great reason in what you have said.' Ailesbury then explained that James must be landed under the protection— no more—of his foreign ally, and so wait for the acclamation of his people, who were discontented with the regime (this was true) and desired his return. This last assumption was one of his comparatively rare errors of judgment. Later that day Louis said to James, 'This lord is the first man of quality with a great estate that hath repaired to you; the first man that came over about an affair of the most high importance—and the first that never asked anything for himself.'

This excellent summing-up was ignored by James. Ailesbury might be loyal: but he was a heretic, and therefore not worth more than cursory consideration. Worse still, he had views of his own, and stuck to them. That was unforgivable.

I I

Ailesbury's journey home nearly killed him, for he caught a fever and became, at intervals, delirious. Yet he struggled on, arriving at his new house in Leicester Fields in such a state that his wife fainted when she saw him. After three weeks' hovering between life and death he went to Houghton to convalesce, having resolved temporarily to give up all attempts at James's restoration. There was nothing to do but wait upon events, his plan for a landing having failed.

This was not the view of the other Jacobites who, when not intriguing against one another, continued to evolve a series of imbecile schemes. Their hopes were raised by the death of Queen Mary in the last week of 1694; for it seemed that she alone had controlled the general discontent by her administration during William's absences; now, surely, the love of her people must turn them towards her father. Ailesbury knew better. Mourning her, and guessing what she had had to put up with ('she suffered inwardly, and to a high degree'), he still maintained the efficacy of the plan rejected by Louis XIV. Yet 'the Jacobites could never be quiet ... and because I would not enter into their vain schemes they began to be jealous [suspicious] of me.'

Princess Anne, now heiress-presumptive, was much attached to the Ailesburys; but Thomas realized that she had no power to protect him, partly because she and her husband were ruled by the Churchills (now Earl and Countess of Marlborough) and partly because William detested her. He therefore tried to detach himself from the plotters, while they pursued him. Rejoiced to be at home and well, he 'thought of nothing but diverting myself,' and so fell into great danger.

Ailesbury was a sociable man; he loved to see his friends, whether privately or at the play or in taverns; and it was his habit to speak freely, wherever he was. After dining with Sir John Fenwick, a violent Jacobite, Thomas and a friend were talking by the fire, when Fenwick and the other guests began to discuss the rewards and places they would get after the restoration. 'What shall you choose?' Ailesbury was asked. 'I should like a large income and no work,' he replied, 'as, for example, Auditor of the Exchequer.' There was a general laugh; Sir John hoarded up the joke for future use.

In 1696, Fenwick's plot to assassinate William was discovered. A few weeks later Catherine Dorchester, with whom Ailesbury was in dispute about leasing her house in Weybridge, burst out, 'I will make King William spit on you! Go to your——King James!' adding that she would report him as having wished the sword of state 'in the guts' of William four years earlier. She did so, and presently received the pension for which she had been angling. Ailesbury then retired with Elizabeth to Tunbridge, 'where dinners went round, and no talk of kings and governments.'

The Duke of Berwick, James's son by Arabella Churchill, then came secretly to England and conveyed a message to Ailesbury from his father desiring his co-operation in another plot. Ailesbury refused, and advised Berwick to return to France, which he did. Meanwhile, Fenwick's plot having been reported to the Privy Council, Thomas was advised to hide or leave the country.

He decided to do nothing of the kind, and informed William through an intermediary that if he had known about the assassination plot, he would have warned him. He then told the Duke of Shrewsbury, now Secretary of State, that he was ready to give evidence as to his innocence, and continued his social round. On March 21st, 1696, he was arrested for high treason and brought before the Council. 'On what grounds am I charged?' he asked. 'Two witnesses will be called against you,' was the reply. 'If there were fifty,' said Ailesbury, 'they would all be proved to be perjured rascals. But, my lords, I know very well that I have a good estate coveted by others [he was referring to Bentinck Lord Portland, whom he had long suspected of this design] and so do what you please.' A few minutes later he was placed under escort and taken to the Tower.

Although Ailesbury had always felt that imprisonment in the fortress would result in a slow and painful death from the stone, he was not unduly cast down; for, quite apart from his having had nothing to do with either Fenwick's or Berwick's plot, his actions during the last eight years had not been, from his point of view, treasonous. He had never concealed his Jacobitism, and his plan for James's landing was an exact replica of William's, who, escorted by Dutch guards and foreign mercenaries, had peacefully entered the capital and taken over the government at Parliament's request. Secretly, Ailesbury may well have doubted James's ability to carry out these tactics; but as William had several times told his ministers that he was ready, at any moment, to return to Holland and let England be governed by Mary, Anne, or their father, Ailesbury could not be blamed for taking him at his word. In fact, he was the only person of any consequence who had worked for a bloodless counter-revolution; it was rather his attitude than his actions which had brought him to this pass. Too many people wanted him out of the way.

He was courteously received at the Tower by Lord Lucas (who had been appointed Governor at his suggestion) and consigned to a warder who was 'a very knave', and determined to make money out of him. After some weeks Ailesbury was allowed larger rooms, the attendance of his family doctor and accommodation for his wife. Besides writing materials and other comforts, Elizabeth brought with her a cook and a chambermaid, to whom the warder behaved so insolently that Ailesbury told him, 'Go downstairs, or I will kick you down.' This man was replaced by an 'honest and humane creature' who was constantly drunk.

The Footguards on duty presently informed the Ailesburys' maid that they were at her master's disposal and that, 'if I would make my escape, I had but to give the word.' Ailesbury would not break the law; in a note he replied, 'Honest Friends—if this proposal be sincere, I am much beholding to you all; if not, God forgive you. The power which brought me here may free me, but if the gates were open, I would not stir from hence.' He was not allowed to ask the officers to dinner, so he sent them venison and wine through his steward. He cheered himself and Elizabeth by teasing Lord Lucas with pretended plans for escape, tried his hand at verse-making, and designed a formal garden, while privately preparing for death on the scaffold; for Fenwick's defence—in which Thomas's remark about becoming Auditor of the Exchequer was one of the principal items—had implicated him to a high degree. He was living in great discomfort; his height made it impossible for him to stand upright. 'My health and consequently my life was at stake; so I resolved ... to walk in my rooms at full speed for five hours the day ... and the door being too low, I was forced to stoop'—which he did to the end of all his adventures.

It then occurred to him that, with the adherence of the Guards, and the friendship of their officers, he might seize the Tower and thence declare for James. He rejected this plan, although 'I had rather have died on the breach than on Tower Hill,' preferring to prove his innocence to his peers. Lady Mary Fenwick then suggested that she and he should inform against Marlborough, Shrewsbury and two other lords, thus purchasing his and Sir John's lives. Ailesbury replied, 'No person of honour and in his right senses can expect from me an answer to so ridiculous and preposterous a proposition.'

He was now in grave danger; and his anxiety was increased by Elizabeth's fourth pregnancy, which enforced her returning home. When she clung to him, sobbing, 'My dearest, I shall never see you more!' he assured her that his innocence was known and that they would soon be together again. She would not believe him.

In the tenth month of Thomas's imprisonment William drove to the House of Lords to pass the Bill of Attainder and execution against Fenwick, to the accompaniment, as was then the custom, of a salute of guns. Elizabeth, who was just sitting down to dinner, asked why the cannon were being fired. She understood her servants' reply to mean that Ailesbury had been condemned, and fainted. A few hours later she gave birth to a daughter, and died at midnight. The child survived her by eighteen months.

Next morning Ailesbury's servant came as usual with food and linen from the house in Leicester Fields. Looking down from a window as the man handed them over to a warder, his master saw that he seemed much depressed, and called out for news of Elizabeth. 'She has been ill, but is better,' was the answer. A few hours later he was again at the window, when he overheard another servant say to his valet, 'I am sorry for the loss of your lady.'

Ailesbury lost consciousness. He revived to find himself lying on his bed; his valet and the maidservant were standing on either side. They heard him murmur, 'I shall go to her, but she shall not return to me.' Then he collapsed again.

He continued very ill for some days. His children were allowed to visit him, and they wept together. When he asked if he might drive out under guard, the request was refused; a clergyman – not the one he had asked for, but the Bishop of Lichfield whom he did not like – came to see him, and did nothing but gossip. Wearily, Thomas lifted his head from the pillow to say, 'My lord, must I perish here?' 'No, my lord,' the bishop replied, 'God forbid that you should,' and promised to approach Ormonde and Devonshire on his behalf, but did not do so.

Ailesbury did not much care what happened to him, so long as he could prove his innocence. At last, on February 12th, he was summoned to Westminster Hall. The Lieutenant-Governor, Colonel Farewell, who came to escort him, said, 'I fear, my lord, that I shall bring you back again.' 'I assure you, Colonel,' his prisoner replied, 'that I shall not return. 'Tis a maxim with me that I never show my teeth but when I am able to bite' – and with a smile he told his maidservant that, nevertheless, she had better prepare the Colonel's favourite dish for dinner at two o'clock. Having been bled the day before, he was still very weak, and when he took his place, had to ask leave to sit down.

The trial did not last very long, and the charge of high treason was not proved. In view of Ailesbury's declared adherence to King James, he was released on bail for £10,000. The spectators cheered the verdict, and he left the court in triumph. As he came out the Tower-Major was waiting to return his sword; Ailesbury made a present of it to the warder who had been so kind to him and Elizabeth. In the Bishop of Lincoln's lodgings his brothers and sisters, the fifteen-year-old Lord Bruce and his daughter Elizabeth, all in deep mourning, were waiting for him; in the cloisters two friends had a meal ready. Ailesbury, now feeling very faint, could eat little. He then drove to his house. The rooms were still hung with black, and that broke him down. He managed to speak cheerfully to his steward, who presented him with a list of callers. Next day, from nine in the morning till ten at night the house was thronged with congratulating friends. The tall, stooping figure of their host—he would never again walk like a young man—moved amongst them with an appearance of happiness. But he was so exhausted, so dazed with grief that on the third day he denied himself to all but the Duke and Duchess of Ormonde. The quiet hours with them restored him a little, and within the next week he received some hundred and fifty guests. He was then warned that this general acclamation ('There was scarce a tavern or ale-house ... but there were rejoicings') had enraged King William, and that he would be well advised to retire to Houghton without notice, so as to avoid another welcome. But the news had preceded him; he rode into Bedford to the sound of bells, thence proceeding through cheering crowds—'and at a bridge above a mile from my house there were upwards of three thousand on horse and on foot, cutting down branches ... and strewed rushes and flags.' He did his best to appear grateful; as he passed the church where Elizabeth lay, he burst into tears.

Next day he asked a dozen neighbours to dinner, and a week later was able to hunt. At intervals he tried to pet the little Lady Mary, but could never get her to smile—did she know her loss? Then came another warning from London—'for that the King was in a great passion when some Court earwig set out with malice my reception.' So he left the peace of Houghton for the city in deep depression and strong resentment; it seemed that he was never to be let alone.

He then found out that certain members of the extreme Whig party were added to his enemies, and planning to get him and the Duke of Shrewsbury impeached for treasonous correspondence with St-Germain. Their scheme fell through and Ailesbury returned to Houghton; he was discharged from bail a few weeks later. This did not diminish the hostility of King William's Dutch entourage, specifically that of Portland, of Keppel (now Earl of Albemarle) and of Zulestein Lord Rochford. 'I had become their beast, and they had me in horror.'

It is possible that Portland, although acquisitive, was not quite so unscrupulous as Ailesbury believed; the two younger men were certainly out for what they could get. They thought of him as just another perfidious and greedy nobleman, of the same type as Danby, now Earl of Caermarthen, or Marlborough; and his actions, from their point of view, had been highly suspicious. A man who took the oaths and then planned King James's return with a French army was far more dangerous to the regime than the inefficient and blundering Fenwick. With a fairmindedness most uncharacteristic of his day, Ailesbury followed their reasoning, and realized that William, trusting the Dutch alone, had to take their advice. 'Had I been in his place,' he says, 'I should have done as he did.'

Meanwhile, he was temporarily unmolested, entering, 'God be praised, into a calm harbour,' and making up his disagreements with his Whig neighbours, whom he entertained throughout the summer and autumn of 1697, although he felt his loss increasingly, and had much illness and pain. When he came up to sit in the Lords he found himself cold-shouldered and was advised to stay away, which he did, but 'that hindered me not from diverting myself with my friends,' at the theatre especially. Ailesbury was a great playgoer, and in old days had made friends of several stage celebrities.

After a pleasant Christmas at Houghton he decided to approach King William and declare his resolve 'to live most respectfully under his government'. The King, who had been informed that Ailesbury was still in touch with James, chose, not unnaturally, to believe this report, and refused to see him. Ailesbury told the intermediary, an English friend of Keppel's, who had promised him an audience, 'I will have nothing more to do with you or the new favourite,' and again retired, but renewed his hopes of a quiet life with the signing of the peace of Ryswick between England and France in December 1697. Now, surely, he thought, William would take this opportunity to reconcile all the parties within his kingdom; for without Louis's support, Jacobitism must cease to exist. To his amazement and horror, a Bill was passed in January 1698 rendering anyone guilty of high treason who had visited France without permission during the last nine years. This retrospective law was to operate from February 1st.

On January 24th Ailesbury met his family and friends in

London. They implored him to leave. He could not bring himself to consent at once, although he was sure that if he did, his exile would not be prolonged, for William's health was failing, and with the accession of Anne he would be restored to favour. Nevertheless, he shrank from saying goodbye to his children, and abandoning all his schemes for renovating his estate and enjoying a quiet country life. Thinking of himself as 'a true Briton', he could not imagine living abroad; and he was now in his forty-third year. Finally, he consulted Marlborough, who said, 'Go—or you will certainly lose your head, for though I suppose you have not been in France during these years [a characteristic evasion, for he knew all about the visit of 1693] yet they will get witnesses to swear they saw you there.' 'This', says Thomas, 'clinched the nail, and ... the 29th was the most melancholy day I had seen ... My separating from my children and nearest relations was a dismal sight.' In a fearful storm he sailed from Dover on February 1st, and was nearly washed overboard. The foremast broke, rain and mist descended and the master lost his bearings, so that Ailesbury had to take command, calling out, 'Starboard!' or 'Larboard!'—'as one or the other was proper.' They reached Calais on the afternoon of the 2nd, where 'I failed not to acknowledge the great mercy of God that had delivered me from the roaring of the lions and the waves of the sea ... I might add, from the madness of the Court.'

There had been very little time for him to decide where to live. After staying in Bruges ('that melancholy town') and Antwerp, he settled in Brussels, reaching that city on March 21st, 1698, with three gentlemen of the horse and five servants. He was homesick, lonely and ill. Yet one of the happiest times in his life was now approaching.

FOUR

I

WHEN Ailesbury established himself in the capital of the Spanish Netherlands, the Viceroy, who held his Court there, was also the Elector of Bavaria, and the principal citizen was the Governor-General, Count Bedmar. While in Antwerp Ailesbury had been warned that the Elector, now representatively allied to William III, would not be able to receive him officially; nor could Count Bedmar. But as soon as he arrived both gentlemen sent word that they would be delighted to entertain him privately; thus he was launched into Brussels society, and became a frequent guest of its two principal hostesses, the Comtesse d'Egmont, and Olympe de Soissons, *née* Mancini, who had been exiled by Louis XIV some thirty years earlier. His friendship with both ladies made him feel as 'one born and bred' in this cosmopolitan circle.

Yet during these first months he so pined for 'his most noble and dear wife' that his health deteriorated, and he concluded that he had not long to live. In these circumstances his first duty was to forgive his enemies and achieve resignation. Thus his need of spiritual support and direction was paramount. As Protestant worship was forbidden, and to practise his religion secretly and against the law was against all Ailesbury's instincts, he became a Catholic. He makes no reference to his conversion in his memoirs; in his will he mentions it as having taken place at the beginning of 1698.

That a middle-aged Church-and-King man of the most orthodox type should suddenly and, as it seems, without hesitation, become a member of the Church hated and feared by the majority of his compatriots may be partly accounted for by Ailesbury's reverence for the hierarchical system, his dislike of underground activities and his innate tolerance. He had always respected piety, of whatever creed; and so, in this colony of the most Catholic country in the world, he found consolation, and perhaps also a discipline of the kind not exercised by Anglican divines. He had known and liked several Catholic priests before his exile; one, Father Mansueta, had been a friend. 'God Almighty', he says, recalling this time, 'had endowed me with that Christian temper [of forgiveness] and I praise daily His Holy name for that and all His other blessings.' This statement is not pharisaical. Ailesbury's nature was fiery; he achieved self-control with difficulty. 'I take a violent passion', he noted, 'to be a great sin before God' — and now, more than ever, he required help in overcoming his furious resentment of the injustice which had been meted out to him, and the spite and malice with which he was still pursued. When rumours of his apostasy reached his brother Robert, that gentleman wrote describing the story as ridiculous and urging him to put an end to it, if only to protect the family reputation. Thomas neither affirmed nor denied his change of faith. Detesting religious controversy, he avoided it by maintaining a silence which lasted all his life.

Having made friends with the Prince de Hornes, whose house became 'as free to me as my own', Ailesbury settled in the Place du Sablon, where he entertained the principal residents and a number of English travellers and exiles, while steadfastly refusing to be drawn into correspondence with St-Germain. His children came to stay, also his steward, Mr Beecher, who presently informed him that if he gave Zulestein's French mistress five hundred guineas, he would be allowed to return home. After hotly refusing, he consented: but the deal fell through; and then, by remaining where he was, he achieved a greater happiness than any he had dared to hope for — his meeting with Charlotte-Jacqueline d'Argenteau, only child of the Comtesse d'Esneux. That 'noble and virtuous lady, born to make any man happy', was then twenty and should long since have been married; but, although beautiful, elegant and 'the admiration of all that knew her', she was slenderly dowered, delicate, and dominated by her mother, a moody and tyrannical widow. From the moment he saw Charlotte, Ailesbury was 'never quiet in mind', and desperate for marriage; but there were many difficulties, one being his duty towards his own family. He could provide a small jointure only, for which he presently obtained young Lord Bruce's consent. He then consulted the Comtesse d'Egmont about approaching Charlotte's mother. 'I should myself have proposed the design to you,' she said, 'as I esteem and love the young lady. But I pity you for to have to do with a person of so jealous and most suspicious temper [as Madame d'Esneux], never knowing her mind two days together. Else', she hastily added, 'a person of great worth.'

Ailesbury then asked how he ought to proceed. He was told 'not to be too hasty, which agreed wholly with my intentions.' 'I know well', his mentor continued, 'that you have too noble a spirit for to be a flatterer—but on the other hand, do not contradict her; hear her with patience, and take another day for to tell her your mind. Get good admittance, that all may be done by degrees.' The suitor 'resolved to pass a noviciate before I took the last resolution'—how many persons had he known who 'jumped headlong into marriage without considering'—and so set himself to observe the young lady. To this end, he invited mother and daughter to his house, was entertained by them, and mingled with their circle in the public assemblies; he found Charlotte 'always charming, gracious, and of a most even and sweet temper'. He then prepared to besiege the Comtesse.

The only person of whom Ailesbury had ever asked a favour was Charles II; and he knew that in spite of his financial commitments and past adherence to a lost cause, he was a desirable match. Determined to behave according to custom, he began by approaching Madame d'Esneux through a third party, a nun, related to her, who 'had wit and judgment, and understood the world.' His opening proposals were rejected, but the nun persisted, reporting slow progress to the lover through the grille. When he himself raised the subject with the Comtesse she flew into a temper; then he would say, 'Pray, Madame, moderate yourself, and tomorrow you may be of another mind.' Oddly enough, this seemed to irritate her further.

Madame d'Esneux's violence had estranged her from most of her acquaintances, so Ailesbury visited her and Charlotte in the afternoons, and very soon realized that his love was returned. He suggested bringing a friend with him, and all four sat down to cards. This phase lasted some nine months, the unfortunate Charlotte being kept as a prisoner, until at last her mother consented to the match. Next day she changed her mind; in despair, Ailesbury divagated between Madame d'Egmont and 'the poor worthy nun', with no result. He then called in a lawyer trusted by Madame d'Esneux, who convinced her that he was not a penniless adventurer, upon which she and Charlotte shared his box at the opera and went to the ball with him afterwards, where he was careful 'not to play at the young fop' by whispering to Charlotte or singling her out at the card-table.

After another six months the Comtesse gave in, the contract was signed, orders were sent to Paris for Charlotte's trousseau and Ailesbury bought the ring. That evening, he called on Madame d'Esneux to be greeted with a flood of tears. 'I cannot part with my only child, and for her to go into a strange country!' she sobbed out, adding some abuse. Ailesbury, violently irritated, let her go on; then he said with a smile, 'Sleep well, Madame, and ruminate upon your pillow, and I am assured that you will tell me to-morrow that you are sorry' — and took his leave. Next day, when they met at an assembly, Madame d'Esneux flung her arms round him and apologized, greatly embarrassing Charlotte, 'who was ready to sink down'.

At last the date of the wedding was settled. The Comtesse then insisted on its being celebrated in absolute secrecy. 'What all this was for,' says the bridegroom resignedly, 'I know not,' adding that the trousseau did not arrive till a fortnight later. Finally they were established in the Place du Sablon, to his 'unspeakable joy', which reached its climax with his children's next visit, when they became devoted to their kind, pretty stepmother. Charles went home to finish his education; the eleven-year-old Elizabeth stayed on, and they were all very happy together. The Ailesburys then set off on a honeymoon tour, returning to find that the Electress Sophia and her daughter the Electress of Brandenburg had arrived and were receiving, incognito, at an English convent. Ailesbury went to pay his respects, and there, walking in the garden, the magnificent old lady, then in her seventy-first year, and the stately, stooping Englishman made friends. He recounted his misfortunes and she listened sympathetically. At a party that same evening, she put her arm round Charlotte, and smiling at him, said to the Comtesse d'Egmont, 'Madame, here is one that hath undergone great troubles and afflictions out of honour and conscience.'

Ailesbury then gave a reception for the Electresses. Wisely disregarding their supposed incognito, he told his pages to serve them on the knee with chocolate and lemonade, upon which Sophia remarked to one of her ladies, 'It is evident that my lord has been bred at a Court.' Tables were set out for basset and ombre, while the Ailesburys ushered the royalties to a dais, and pyramids of China oranges, sweetmeats and hot pastries were presented. After supper he conducted them to their coach, preceded by two of his gentlemen carrying flambeaux.

When the Electresses left for Antwerp, Sophia asked Ailesbury to accompany them, and he followed their barge in a post-chaise. During another talk, 'Give me,' she said, 'a whole account of what preceded the Revolution.' When he finished she went on, 'Tell me in what I can be useful to you, and I will do it with all my heart.' She was very like his first good and gracious master, 'affable and courteous' in just the same way; but nothing came of her pleas to William for his return.

In 1701 King James died at St-Germain. 'Give my Lord Ailesbury my hearty recommendations,' he said to his confessor, 'and mention ... that if I had taken his advice ... I had never rendered my soul to God my Creator in a foreign country.' In the following year William died; and now, at last, Ailesbury could count on his return. With the accession of Anne the Marlboroughs became supreme, and they had promised to send for him. The Queen too was his friend, for he had been one of those who had voted her an increased allowance in the last reign. She would remember, and let him come home.

As before, when he had taken the oaths to William and Mary but refused to attend their coronation, Ailesbury's position seemed to him clearly defined. He was, and always would be, a Jacobite; but he had given his word to remain neutral in all circumstances. Now, however, Louis XIV's acknowledgment of the Prince of Wales as James III and his acceptance of the Spanish Throne for his grandson resulted in the war of the Spanish Succession; this put Ailesbury, with many other exiles, under suspicion. He had become, against his will, the antagonist of Queen Anne and her Government. When the war, with France and Spain on one side, and England, Holland and Austria on the other, began in May 1702, Ailesbury's difficulties were added to by his residence in enemy territory; with Charlotte and Elizabeth he moved to Aix-la-Chapelle, then a free city.

Here he was approached by a Mr Cayley, an old friend, formerly his elder son's governor, and now empowered to ask him whether he would take the oath of abjuration against James II's heir; if he consented, he would not only be allowed to return home, but to resume his place in the Lords. Ailesbury felt himself insulted by such a proposal. Determined not to lose his temper, he replied calmly, 'Mr Cayley, what do you see in my face that bespeaks me to be a villain, and a double-dealing man? You know what I have suffered for following my conscience in regard to the father—and will you have me abjure the son? No, sir, I will rather die first!'—upon which Mr Cayley apologized.

Yet Ailesbury believed that his promise of obedience to Queen Anne must bring about his return, especially as she herself, now childless, had expressed a wish that her fourteen-year-old half-brother, although a Catholic, should succeed her. Through Sarah Marlborough she told Ailesbury that she would certainly recall him when she could do so 'without prejudice'. He did not know that she had been advised not to, although he became suspicious when Marlborough, now Commander-in-Chief of the allied forces, asked him not to visit his headquarters in Holland.

Ailesbury continued to hope during the victories which brought Marlborough his dukedom; after that of Blenheim he took a house at Liège, and there he and the great General met again. Marlborough advised him to stay where he was, charmed Lady Ailesbury and made himself most agreeable. But Thomas saw that the brilliant genius who had betrayed two Kings and now ruled a Queen was not going to help him. 'He was timorous in council, and cunning and politic, and I ... had obliging words, but no performances, and that and his avarice were his prevailing vices,' he says, going on to praise the Duke's sweet temper and superb courage.

In 1705 a daughter, Marie, was born to the Ailesburys, and they returned to Brussels, now in allied hands, the following year. In 1707 Elizabeth went back to England and became the wife of Lord Cardigan. Still there was no word of Ailesbury's recall. He realized that Marlborough had no time for him, Ramillies and Oudenarde being now added to his laurels, followed by the crowning triumph of Malplaquet in 1709. Then, in the autumn of that year, he received the Queen's official licence 'to return and abide in this realm'. After all his adventures (he had been taken prisoner by 'an old, doting Brigadier-General' in 1703) his eleven years' exile was at an end.

I I

Ailesbury's sufferings had made him extremely cautious. Having been told that it would not be advisable to return till the war was over, he wrote to the Queen, asking her if she personally wished him to come back. He and Charlotte then left to take the waters at Aix, where he was so troubled by his old malady that he had to stay in bed most of the time. On their return to Brussels he was told that Her Majesty preferred to leave the question of his recall to his 'usual discretion'. While he was considering, Charlotte caught a fever. Eight days later she was dead.

Once more, he was alone; and his loss seemed greater then he could bear. He left for the country; there his loneliness was unendurable, and he returned so broken that he could barely eat or drink. His friends, the women especially, were very kind; but he knew that his grief made him 'ill company'—and, half dazed by such narcotics as were then available, he spent hours thinking of his first wife, sunk in misery. The six-year-old Marie was some consolation; Charles and Elizabeth wrote in loving sorrow; but they were married and far away. He was utterly bereft.

No word of sympathy had come from the Marlboroughs; this upset Ailesbury very much, and when the Duke arrived in Brussels he did not call. Marlborough did, and spoke so gently of Charlotte that he was won over. Then Marlborough described his own troubles. He had been dismissed from all his commands, and Sarah had been ousted by Abigail Hill. 'I thought', said Ailesbury, 'that you understood an English court better than to be surprised at changes', and advised him to 'live quietly and retired, and you may laugh at your enemies.' He added, 'Lay yourself, my lord, at the Queen's feet, and let her dispose of you as she shall think fit, and you know by experience that she is a most gracious Princess.' The Duke replied that he had already done so, and they parted.

Ailesbury believed that the disgrace of the Marlboroughs precluded his return; in any case, he was in no state to travel. With the Peace of Utrecht in 1713, he decided to go to Paris to consult a doctor famous for his cures of the stone. He was not very hopeful. To his amazement, 'that great artist' (whom he does not name) set him on the road to recovery. When Mary of Modena wrote reproaching him for not calling on her, he excused himself; news of their meeting might prevent the reinstatement for which he still hoped. Then he returned to Brussels to convalesce, and began to share in the mild gaieties of the city. His younger brother James, who had been made one of the Comptrollers of the army, was negotiating his recall through the party now dominating the Queen, and, by the early summer of 1714, Ailesbury's hopes were justified. In August Queen Anne died, and with the accession of George I his permit lapsed.

He wrote asking for its renewal, and received a courteous but noncommittal answer. Friends and relatives continued to work for him, and at last he was told that he would be able to return almost at once. In 1715 James Francis Edward Stuart, the uncrowned King he had refused to abjure, landed in Scotland. Jacobitism was once more a danger — and in his sixtieth year all Ailesbury's hopes were destroyed.

It was easier, now, to achieve resignation. Marie was becoming more of a companion as she reached her teens; and Ailesbury was absorbed — not always unpleasantly — in a struggle with the new Governor, the Marquis de Prié, whose rule so infuriated the Bruxellois that they threatened to revolt, and eventually did so. In theory, Ailesbury and de Prié were friends; but the Englishman's blunt condemnation of certain measures — 'you must expect nothing but fire and blood' — annoyed the Governor, while he irritated Ailesbury by his fussiness and conceit. When he refused to interrupt one of their games of piquet to give audience to a group of petitioners, Ailesbury started up and threw all the cards in the fire, 'rather than that those poor creatures should say I was the cause he came not.' In 1718 the atmosphere became so unpleasant that he left for Paris, taking Marie with him and warning de Prié that if he did not change his methods, 'he would see the town in fire and plunder.'

Soon after his arrival Ailesbury went to wait on the eight-year-old Louis XV at the Tuileries. There, among other old acquaintances, he found Cardinal de Fleury, Louis's preceptor, and was present when His Eminence told his pupil that, having refused the Archbishopric of Rheims, he would be unable to crown him. 'I *will* be crowned by you!' exclaimed the child, but de Fleury was firm. Ailesbury then renewed his friendship with the English ambassador, while Marie, chaperoned by the ambassadress, visited Marly and Versailles. Lady Jersey (Chiffinch's daughter) gave a dinner for him, his doctor's report was excellent and so he stayed on, returning to find that the Bruxellois had refused to plunder his house during the riots he had foretold.

For Ailesbury had now become one of the celebrities of the city; his daily walk in the Place du Sablon was a progress; and when he did consider returning to England, he realized that his religion would be one difficulty and Marie's marriage another, for he would never find a suitable match for her in a Protestant country. In 1721 his old friend's son, the Prince de Hornes, proposed for her – this caused some jealousy, for he was a prince of the Austrian Empire – and the marriage was celebrated in June of the following year. James Bruce, who came over at about this time, was a little disappointed in the bride's looks ('I expected to find her handsomer') but reported her as lively and charming, and the Prince 'a mighty-good-humoured, plain sort of man, without pride or ostentation'.

Having settled Marie, Ailesbury had more time for his favourite hobby, gardening. But his quinces were a worry. ('They will not thrive with me.') He now preferred the opera to balls, but disliked the noisy audiences, who made the opera-house 'a fiddle-faddle place, crammed with people of quality, envious and babbling'. Driving to visit his circle in a berline drawn by six horses and accompanied by four postillions, he was pointed out to visitors as an historical figure. Not only had he been the friend and confidant of the last two Stuart Kings, but he could remember – and his memory was amazing – the celebrations for the Restoration of Charles II, being then in his fifth year. And his collections – he owned several Raphaels, a Poussin and a quantity of the curious japanned furniture which became fashionable in the 1680s – were much admired. He was strict, of course: and a little testy sometimes: but in all else a high fine gentleman of the old school – that school which has never been young. 'My father used to say', he would tell his guests, 'that Charles II's Court was not proper for a sober man,' adding that he himself had found it delightful. 'I remember as if it had happened but yesterday –' he would say, and so the reminiscences began.

England and Spain were at war when George II succeeded in 1727, and James Bruce approached the new King with some misgiving: did this mean that his brother, now in his seventy-second year, might have to leave Brussels? 'Mr Bruce,' replied His

Majesty, 'your brother's conduct hath always been so pleasing to me that I should be very sorry to ask anything of him that should either be disagreeable to his health, or to his satisfaction.' When Ailesbury wrote in grateful acknowledgment, he was told that Queen Caroline, although she had never met him, was anxious to do him any favour he could name. But he had abandoned all thought of return. Houghton was sold; his English contemporaries were dead; and he could not contemplate parting from his youngest grandchild (he had never seen his nine English descendants), the two-year-old Marie. He saw her nearly every day, either at his house or at the de Hornes's château of Yssche. Naturally, 'this dear little one' was quite remarkable. 'If there be twenty people in the room, she distinguishes my voice from them all,' he proudly reported. And she was exactly like her grandmother, 'which ... pleases me not a little.' So his old age promised to be a happy time; and then once more, disaster struck at him — from England.

Unknown to his brothers, James Bruce, that respected Comptroller and Member of the Commons, had been gambling and speculating for many years; as he now owed some £12,000 and had no means of payment, he was in danger of imprisonment in the Fleet. To a man of Ailesbury's calibre this meant utter disgrace, not only for James, but for himself, as head of the family; and for him to provide the whole sum was out of the question. Robert Bruce then interviewed the creditors, and pacified them by arranging for part payment from various members of the family. James's solution was simpler. He proposed to marry a wealthy spinster, described by himself and his brothers as 'worthy, discreet and sober'. He then left England and came to stay with Thomas in Brussels.

Ailesbury, who had been horrified by James's recklessness ('I never was so mistaken in a man's character in all my life') was very kind, supplying him with 'a good but plain suit', linen and a periwig, and introducing him to his circle. James found it difficult to discuss his financial position with the rather formidable brother he had not seen for so many years, and for several weeks they went about together as if nothing had gone wrong. When James nerved himself to begin, he was unable to proceed. No sooner did he mention the name of some creditor, than Thomas would recount an anecdote about him or one of his family, and so continue till the time for confession was long past. James described this reaction to Robert as 'an infirmity of old age', adding that, apart from a slight deafness, this was 'the only one I see in him—he cannot help going on.' He determined to persist when they were alone, after supper. In a tone of benevolent authority Ailesbury replied, 'Well, we will talk of it after dinner tomorrow—for my father never used to talk of business at night.' Next day, and the day after that, and for many days to come, the same thing happened. Ailesbury would 'run away with a discourse of somebody ... which puts him in mind of something else ... and there is no stopping him.'

What James thought was 'a decay' seems to have been a form of self-protection. Ailesbury knew the facts; he did not wish to hear the details, since he had already done what he could for his brother, and may have felt that it was not enough. Also, having become a little garrulous and disliking interruption, he now took advantage of a submissive listener. When Robert wrote asking why James's difficulties had not been mentioned, he blandly replied that the defaulter 'had not opened his lips' on the subject. But the inquiry had effect, and at last Ailesbury himself raised the question in a sympathetic and sensible manner. When James left Brussels (he failed to collect his heiress but escaped bankruptcy) Thomas wrote to Charles Bruce, 'I pity him and love him ... else, I confess, he hath lost my good opinion.'

With the departure of James, he became more active than for many years, accepting invitations to balls, banquets and assemblies, and asking 'handsome ladies' to meet his English guests. He still preferred the opera to all other entertainments, and particularly admired an English soprano, whose rather unfortunate stage name was La Dotti. 'She takes mightily,' he told Robert, adding that whether singing or speaking, she always smiled. This pleased Ailesbury very much, especially when La Dotti appeared in an opera about Queen Elizabeth and the Earl of Essex, in which he found her so charming that he broke his rule of going to bed early in order to enjoy her smiles at a reception. He was more than ever in demand and much frequented. On two points he remained firm: he would not countenance Jacobite spies, or the would-be betrayers of the exiled King—and he would not dress gaudily. He showed two 'rascals' the door when they tried to involve him in their schemes, and appeared at all gatherings in a plain dark suit and the gold waistcoat which was his sole concession to the mode, 'and well accepted of, because it is known I never wear any other.'

With the years, his wealth of fascinating reminiscence and his reputation as a raconteur increased; and then Charles Bruce, fearful that these unique experiences might perish with him, urged him to write his memoirs. Ailesbury demurred; he was neither an author nor an historian. Charles persisted and, touched by his enthusiasm, his father complied, setting about the business in his usual methodical way. In just over a year he had written a quarter of a million words in his firm, slanting hand. He wrote as he spoke, rapidly, correcting himself every now and then by running a line through a sentence, and without regard for chronology. His pleasure in the work is manifest, his awareness of his limitations dignified and engaging. Without reading over the manuscript (what use to labour further?) he had it bound and sent to England and dismissed it from his mind. It was, he knew, only 'a discourse by the fireside', and of no literary merit whatever. That it might be published never occurred to him; he had written to please himself and his dear son.

Ailesbury was in his seventy-eighth year when the Prince of Orange came to Brussels and was entertained by the Viceroy and the city magnates. He set out to enjoy himself—and then withdrew, disgusted by all the fuss and flattery. 'It is fulsome,' he told Charles, 'that all must be dressed in orange from top to toe ... and ridiculous.' How differently Queen Mary or her sister would have been treated! There was no dignity, and far too much 'giggling' about His Highness, who was, poor fellow, very ugly. 'As to his shape,' Ailesbury observed, 'it is the will of God, and we ought all to praise Him we are not so.' (He himself was still a magnificent spectacle, as he may have known.) He preferred to refuse the vice-regal invitations and to entertain, in his own house, old friends and those who came with letters of introduction, one being 'a very pretty gentleman, and well bred—I knew his father, a worthy man.' It might be Mr Woodhouse speaking.

The citizens of Brussels were very proud of the grand old milord who had lived among them for thirty years, supported them against tyranny, helped them in their need and—perhaps this impressed them most—sustained a standard of behaviour with which they could find no fault. They decided to show their gratitude by absolving him from the tax on wine, beer, flour and meat. In return, Ailesbury resolved to present the city with a memorial.

Having made inquiries, he was assured that his plan for a fountain would be acceptable, and he set aside 5,000 crowns for the work, which was completed ten years after his death. His other arrangements were characteristically businesslike and correct. He was to be buried beside Charlotte in the Church of the Brigittines, 'en simple bourgeois, et en toute obscurité'; their hearts were to be taken back to England and placed in the family mausoleum beside the coffin of his first wife.

So everything was settled. There were no more domestic troubles, no political disturbances. Callers, old and young, enjoyed his stories; the Prince and Princesse de Hornes were dutiful and loving; the worthy Bruxellois honoured and respected him; his little Marie and Élisabeth, the 'chères petites filles' mentioned in his will, came to stay. Thirty years later Élisabeth's daughter, Louise of Stolberg, married — disastrously — Charles II's great-nephew, Prince Charles Edward, the drunken, ageing Chevalier.

At last Ailesbury entered the calm waters he had so long desired; and floating on the surface, revolving in their depths, were his dearest and most indestructible possessions: faces, scenes, voices from the past. James II at his brother's dying bed with a slipper on one foot and a shoe on the other: the woods at Houghton: Elizabeth's last embrace: his father's talk of the Civil War and the Martyr King: Shaftesbury's cold smile: Lauderdale's 'Saracen, fiery face'; Henrietta Wentworth whispering her thanks for his protection of her lover: Monmouth in a countryman's dress: Bishop Ken's sweet voice: James's catch-phrase, 'What I have done I will stand by'; Oates drawling out his venom in Westminster Hall: 'Lillibullero' and the shrieking mob: the Thames on a clear day, thronged with hoys and barges: the open jaws of Traitors' Gate: a wooden shoe in the Speaker's chair: Sarah Churchill exclaiming, 'Lord! they keep such a noise at our wealth, I do assure you it doth not exceed £70,000'; blue-and-white Dutch sentinels in St James's Palace: his tipsy coachman shouting, 'God damn Father Petre!'; King William's dry cough; the Matted Gallery; Hampton Court; Windsor, with its battlements and flags and towers ... And always, above all the rest, best loved, most treasured, that tall, striding figure, sombre, elegant, gracious and noble — and yet, somehow, baffling: strange. 'My lord, give your cards to another, I must speak with you ... I see you love me dying as well as living ... I will instruct you for my service ... A King that is not slave to five hundred kings is great enough ... '

Yes! great enough, indeed; greater than all those of whom he had written, 'I have so fresh an idea of them, as, if I were a painter, I could draw their pictures.'

And so he has. That crowded, untidy picture-book is unique. On December 16th, 1741, its creator died in his house in the Place du Sablon, at the age of eighty-five. The Hôtel Ailesbury has long since disappeared. The marble fountain, with its robustly exuberant statues and grave Latin inscription, still stands, its springing waters endlessly renewed.

PRINCIPAL SOURCES OF INFORMATION

with dates of the most recent editions

Ailesbury MSS
Ailesbury, Thomas, Earl of,   *Memoirs*, ed. W. E. Buckley (London, 1890)
Cardigan, Earl of,   *The Life and Loyalties of Thomas Bruce* (London, 1951)
Chapman, H.W.,   *Mary II, Queen of England* (London, 1953)
Clarke, J.S.,   *Life of James II* (London, 1816)
Domestic State Papers, 1677–98
Historical Manuscripts Commission,   *Hastings MSS*
Macaulay, T.B.,   *History of England* (London, 1953)
Ogg, D.,   *England in the Reign of Charles II* (London, 1955)
   England in the Reigns of James II and William III (London, 1955)
Turner, F. C.,   *Life of James II* (London, 1948)

EPILOGUE

As in a country dance, when the participants come into brief contact with those separated from them and then recede, so, during the years which cover these four lives, a pattern seems to emerge. The English aristocrat is momentarily linked with the German Princess, the Princess and her husband with the Italian Duchess, the Duchess with the French King's successor, and that King with the Duchess's uncle. The microcosm in which these persons moved was overshadowed and reshaped by those who saw beyond it — Cardinal Richelieu, Louis XIV, William III: makers of history, creators. While the impact of such beings on their dependants varied, it might now be seen as part of a subsidiary design, underlying the destinies of the dominated and the dominators, drawing them together and thus clarifying the outlines of the conflicts in which they were engaged. That the result of those conflicts survives is obvious: France is still paying for Louis XIV, England remains in debt to William III. Yet to study Louis XIII rather than his elder son, or the contemporaries of William rather than himself, may produce a curiously intimate atmosphere; for looking through the keyhole while the bills are being run up can sometimes be more enjoyable than observing the consequences when the doors are flung open on pay-day. So it follows that although the share of these lesser characters in great historic events was inconspicuous, their feelings, whether transient or profound, reflect values which facilitate a partial comprehension of the past.

INDEX

INDEX

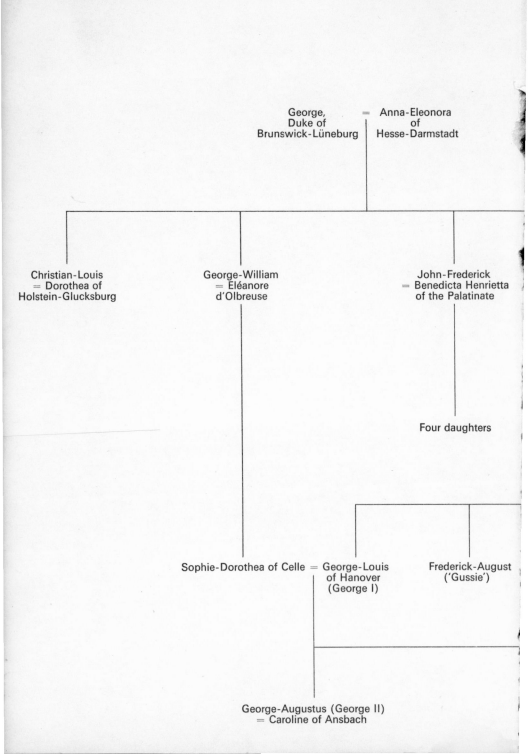

George,
Duke of
Brunswick-Lüneburg = Anna-Eleonora
of
Hesse-Darmstadt

Christian-Louis
= Dorothea of
Holstein-Glucksburg

George-William
= Eléanore
d'Olbreuse

John-Frederick
= Benedicta Henrietta
of the Palatinate

Four daughters

Sophie-Dorothea of Celle = George-Louis
of Hanover
(George I)

Frederick-August
('Gussie')

George-Augustus (George II)
= Caroline of Ansbach